Praise for *What to Read and Why*

"Prose's writing sharpens, focuses, and . . . even thrills when she writes of the authors who move her most deeply. These essays on their own make the book worth reading and buying; they made me buy a couple of the books she most passionately endorses."

—*Wall Street Journal*

"With characteristic elegance, literary critic and novelist Prose (*Mister Monkey*) passionately pushes great books and good writing in a wide-ranging assemblage of previously published and new essays. . . . Prose's stimulating collection of essays will move readers to pick up, for the first or the fifteenth time, the books she so enthusiastically recommends."

—*Publishers Weekly*

"A prolific and provocative writer and longtime teacher, Prose remains enthralled by books, especially fiction, fascinated by both technique and the 'humanizing' power of story. A fluent and exacting critic, Prose conducts incisive, stirring readings of works spanning centuries, from George Eliot's *Middlemarch* to Jennifer Egan's *Manhattan Beach* . . . all the while urging readers to enter their own book bubbles and nurture body and soul."

—*Booklist*

"An unabashed fan of reading recommends some of her favorite books . . . with an eclectic collection of previously published pieces that continue her clarion call for how books can 'transport and entertain and teach us.'"

—*Kirkus Reviews*

"Written with warmth, wit, and a keen intellect."

—*Library Journal* (starred review)

WHAT
TO READ
AND WHY

WHAT
TO READ
AND WHY

FRANCINE
PROSE

HARPER ⬤ PERENNIAL

NEW YORK • LONDON • TORONTO • SYDNEY • NEW DELHI • AUCKLAND

HARPER ● PERENNIAL

A hardcover edition of this book was published in 2018 by
HarperCollins Publishers.

WHAT TO READ AND WHY. Copyright © 2018 by Francine Prose.
All rights reserved. Printed in the United States of America.
No part of this book may be used or reproduced in any manner
whatsoever without written permission except in the case of
brief quotations embodied in critical articles and reviews. For
information, address HarperCollins Publishers, 195 Broadway,
New York, NY 10007.

HarperCollins books may be purchased for educational,
business, or sales promotional use. For information, please
e-mail the Special Markets Department at
SPsales@harpercollins.com.

FIRST HARPER PERENNIAL PAPERBACK EDITION PUBLISHED 2019.

Designed by Fritz Metsch

Library of Congress Cataloging-in-Publication Data has been
applied for.

ISBN 978-0-06-239787-4 (pbk.)

19 20 21 22 23 LSC 10 9 8 7 6 5 4 3 2 1

For Howie

CONTENTS

AUTHOR'S NOTE

SOME OF THE ARTICLES IN THIS COLLECTION FIRST APPEARED in the following publications, sometimes in slightly different form:

American Scholar: "Ten Things That Art Can Do"

Introduction to *Frankenstein* by Mary Shelley (Restless Books, 2016)

Introduction to *Great Expectations* by Charles Dickens (Penguin Classics, 2002)

Introduction to *Cousin Bette* by Honoré de Balzac (Modern Library Classics, 2002)

Introduction to *Middlemarch* by George Eliot (Harper Perennial, 2015)

Introduction to *New Grub Street* by George Gissing (Modern Library Classics, 2002)

Harper's Magazine: "More is More" (on Roberto Bolaño, *2666*)

Michigan Quarterly Review: "Complimentary Toilet Paper: Some Thoughts on Character and Language" (on Michael Jeffrey Lee, George Saunders, John Cheever, Denis Johnson)

New York Times Book Review: "Wit's End" (on Edward St. Aubyn, *Never Mind*; *Bad News*; *Some Hope*; *Mother's Milk*)

Harper's Magazine: "The Coldest Eye" (on Paul Bowles, *The Spider's House*)

New York Review of Books: "Giddy and Malevolent" (on Patrick Hamilton,

Twenty Thousand Streets Under the Sky: A London Trilogy, The Slaves of Solitude; Hangover Square: A Story of Darkest Earl's Court)

Harper's Magazine: "The Bones of Muzhiks" (on Isaac Babel, *The Complete Works of Isaac Babel*)

Lapham's Quarterly: "Eros Between the Covers" (on Vladimir Nabokov, *Lolita*)

New Yorker: "Dark Passage" (on Gitta Sereny, *Cries Unheard*)

New York Review of Books: "The Shy Clumsy Lover" (on Andrea Canobbio, *Three Light-Years*)

Harper's Magazine: "Revisiting the Icons" (on Diane Arbus, *Revelations*)

Introduction to *Crosstown* by Helen Levitt (Powerhouse Books, 2001)

Preface to *Mr. and Mrs. Baby and Other Stories* by Mark Strand (Ecco, 2015)

Harper's Magazine: "Master of the Mundane" (on Karl Ove Knausgaard, *My Struggle: Book Three*)

Sunday Times (London): Elizabeth Taylor, *Complete Short Stories*

O Magazine: "In Praise of *Little Women*" (on Louisa May Alcott, *Little Women*)

American Benefactor: "On Jane Austen"

New York Times Book Review: "Midwestern Civ" (on Charles Baxter, *Believers*)

New York Times Book Review: "Naked Came the Stranger" (on Deborah Levy, *Swimming Home*)

Real Simple: "Friend of Our Youth" (on Alice Munro, *Lives of Girls and Women*)

New York Review of Books: "On the Wilder Shores of Brooklyn" (on Jennifer Egan, *Manhattan Beach*)

New York Review of Books: "Courts Without Reporters" (on Rebecca West, *In Greenhouse with Cyclamens, I*)

Harper's Magazine: "Door to Door" (on Mohsin Hamid, *Exit West*)

New York Review of Books: "The Cult of Saint Franz" (on Reiner Stach, *Is That Kafka? 99 Finds*)

"What Makes a Short Story?" (contribution to *On Writing Short Stories*, edited by Tom Bailey, Oxford University Press, 2010)

Sewanee Review: "On Stanley Elkin"

INTRODUCTION

READING IS AMONG THE MOST PRIVATE, THE MOST SOLITARY things that we can do. A book is a kind of refuge to which we can go for the assurance that, as long as we are reading, we can leave the worries and cares of our everyday lives behind us and enter, however briefly, another reality, populated by other lives, a world distant in time and place from our own, or else reflective of the present moment in ways that may help us see that moment more clearly. Anyone who reads can choose to enter (or not enter) the portal that admits us to the invented or observed world that the author has created.

I've often thought that one reason I became such an early and passionate reader was that, when I was a child, reading was a way of creating a bubble I could inhabit, a dreamworld at once separate from, and part of, the real one. I was fortunate enough to grow up in a kind, loving family. But like most children, I think, I wanted to maintain a certain distance from my parents: a buffer zone between myself and the adults. It was helpful that my parents liked the fact that I was a reader, that they approved of and encouraged my secret means of transportation out of the daily reality in which I lived together with them—and into the parallel reality that books offered. I was only pretending to be a little girl growing up in Brooklyn, when in fact I was a privileged child in London, guided by Mary Poppins through a series of marvelous adventures. I could manage a convincing impersonation of an ordinary fourth-grader, but actually I was a pirate girl in Norway, best friends with Pippi Longstocking, well acquainted with her playful pet monkey and her obedient horse.

I loved books of Greek myths, of Hans Christian Andersen fairy tales, and novels (many of them British) for children featuring some element of magic and the fantastic. When I was in the eighth grade, I spent most of a family cross-country trip reading and re-reading a dog-eared paperback copy of *Seven Gothic Tales*, by Isak Dinesen, a writer who interests me now mostly because I can so clearly see what fascinated me about her work *then*. With a clarity and transparency that few things provide, least of all photographs and childhood diaries, her fanciful stories enable me to see what I was like—how I thought—as a girl. I can still recall my favorite passage, which I had nearly memorized, because I believed it to contain the most profoundly romantic, the most noble and poetic, the most stirring view of the relations between men and women—a subject about which I knew nothing, or less than nothing, at the time.

The passage comes from a story entitled "The Roads Round Pisa." Augustus, a Danish count, is traveling in Italy, where he meets a young woman disguised as a boy. He admires her confidence and forthrightness, and he realizes that he has, all his life, been looking for such a woman. Their flirtation culminates in the following conversation, heavy with suggestion as it delicately euphemizes and maneuvers its way around its real subject, which is sex:

> *"Now God," she said, "when he created Adam and Eve . . . arranged it so that man takes, in these matters, the part of a guest,*

and woman that of a hostess. Therefore man takes love lightly, for the honor and dignity of his house is not involved therein. And you can also, surely, be a guest to many people to whom you would never want to be a host. Now, tell me, Count, what does a guest want?"

"I believe," said Augustus . . . , "that if we do, as I think we ought to here, leave out the crude guest, who comes to be regaled, takes what he can get and goes away, a guest wants first of all to be diverted, to get out of his daily monotony or worry. Secondly the decent guest wants to shine, to expand himself and impress his own personality upon his surroundings. And thirdly, perhaps, he wants to find some justification for his existence altogether. But since you put it so charmingly, Signora, please tell me now: What does the hostess want?"

"The hostess," said the young lady, "wants to be thanked."

The hostess wants to be thanked? What does that even mean? Is *that*—to answer Freud's question—what women want? A polite expression of gratitude? What about pleasure, kindness, loyalty, respect . . . ?

And yet, decades later, I can see how this poetic discussion of the erotic, with only the most vague and delicate suggestion of the mechanics of sex, would have appealed to me at thirteen. How I longed to meet a man someday who would court me with language only a few steps removed from that of the medieval troubadours; how divine it would be to experience a seduction that would verge so closely on poetry. And how I wanted to be the sort of young woman who could travel on her own, charm a man with my courage and independence, and come up with the perfect punch line to answer his mannerly disquisition on what the sexes desire from each other.

I can still see the charm in the passage, even though it seems quaint, artificial, hopelessly old-fashioned. What's more important is that reading it functions, for me, like a kind of time machine, transporting me to the back seat of our family car, crossing the Arizona desert, being urged to *just look* at the Grand Canyon while I was somewhere else: near Pisa, in 1823, listening to a man and woman have the type of conversation that I hoped to have someday with a handsome (and preferably aristocratic) stranger.

All of which seems to suggest: reading is not *exactly* like being alone. We are alone with the book we are reading, but we are also in the more ethereal company of the author and the characters that author has created. There I was in the car, with my parents in the front seat, my younger brother beside me, and Isak Dinesen, Count Augustus, and the brave little cross-dresser all floating around in my consciousness.

We may find ourselves surrounded by dozens, even hundreds, of imaginary people, or deep inside the mind of the man or woman whom the narrator has designated to stand at the center of the action. We can close the book and carry these characters around with us, much the way a child can transport any number of imaginary friends from place to place. And because they are imaginary, we can always stop reading without hurting their feelings, a transaction far less complicated than most of our dealings with flesh-and-blood human beings.

Lately it's been noted that this privacy has been at least partly compromised when we read on electronic devices that are able to monitor how much of a book we read, where we stop, and what we reread. It's disconcerting to think about, and yet (especially if we are as engrossed in a book as we wish to be) it's possible to forget about these invisible watchers, who at least aren't talking on—or checking—their phones. And of course we can always read a "physical book," which will never disclose the secrets of our reading habits.

Reading and writing are solitary activities, and yet there is a social component that comes into play when we tell someone else about what we have read. An additional pleasure of reading is that you can urge and sometimes even persuade people you know and care about, and even people you don't know, to read the book you've just finished and admired—and that you think they would like, too. We can talk about books to our friends, our colleagues, our students. We can form and enjoy communities that we wouldn't have otherwise had. Read Proust and you have something in common with other readers of Proust: not only the thrill of experiencing a marvelous and complex work of art, but the fact that you and those others now have, as your mutual acquaintances, his enormous cast of characters. You can gossip about people you know in common. *Can you* believe *what happens to the Baron de Charlus by the end of the novel?*

Almost twenty years ago, the novelists Ron Hansen and Jim Shepard put together an anthology entitled *You've Got to Read This*, to which a group of writers contributed an introduction to a favorite short story of their own choosing. (I wrote about Isaac Babel's "Guy de Maupassant.") I've always thought that every book about reading and about books should be called *You've Got to Read This*. In fact, I might have called this book that had the wonderful Hansen-Shepard anthology not already been sitting on a bookshelf in the study in which I am writing this. I've also thought that "You've got to read this" should be the first line of every positive book review. The essay about Roberto Bolaño's great novel *2666*, first printed in *Harper's* magazine and included here, begins with a description of that impulse, of the desire to say just that, to direct magazine readers toward a great novel.

I've always been delighted when an editor asked me to write an introduction to a classic that is being reissued in a spiffy new edition with a stylish, handsome new cover. Because what I am doing, basically, is saying: *You've got to read this—and here's why.* I feel the same way about certain book reviews that, to me, are a way of telling people—strangers—about something terrific I think they should read. Drop everything. Start reading. Now.

Some of the essays collected here are introductions to republished classics. Others are reviews of books that I particularly admired and enjoyed. Mixed in are a few essays that attempt to grapple with the social and political conditions that inform our reading habits and the judgments we make about books. Others ("On Clarity") address problems that beginning writers may find themselves facing. Still others are less about reading in specific than about art in general, but have so much to do with what I think about literature that I have chosen to include them. It's why I decided to put "Ten Things That Art Can Do" at the beginning of the book; in my view, the ideas, thoughts, and observations in that essay inform everything else.

The essays gathered in this volume contain reading suggestions and imprecations, records of enthusiasms, pieces that start with particular books and move toward the larger subject of how and what and why we read: why books can transport and entertain and teach us, why books can give us pleasure and make us think. Ultimately, what I am writing about here are the reasons why we continue to read great books, and why we continue to care.

WHAT
TO READ
AND WHY

Ten Things That Art Can Do

One: Art can be beautiful.

That is all it has to do. That is the only thing we require of it. But what do we mean by beauty? Did the cave dwellers think, *Hey, that's really beautiful* when someone drew the first bison on the wall? Did anyone think, *That's beautiful* when the Serbian performance artist Marina Abramovic invited the gallery audience to cut her with razor blades—or shoot her?

Critics and philosophers have devoted their entire lives to defining beauty, while artists have pursued it from another part of the brain. Is there a meaning of *beauty* on which we can agree? Is a Netherlandish portrait beautiful? What about Vermeer's *The Love Letter*? Cézanne's apples? Perhaps it would be possible to know nothing about art, to have never seen a painting, and to look at any one of those works and think, *Well, that is really gorgeous.*

But what about those early viewers who saw Cézanne's apples as the smudgy scrawlings of an untalented child? What about Jackson Pollock? It took me years to see the beauty in his paintings. When I say that there is nothing so beautiful as a certain phrase in Bach's *St. Matthew Passion*, or Mozart's *Così Fan Tutte*, or Miles Davis's "Flamenco Sketches," or Mary Wells's version of "You Beat Me to the Punch," what am I saying, exactly?

Unraveling the word *beauty* can get us so ensnarled that it's no wonder that for a time, critics and academics and even some artists agreed that it was probably better not to use it at all. For all I know—I haven't kept up—this taboo still exists. And, really, who can blame anyone for not wanting to sling around this vague, loaded, indefinable, and antiquated term in the learned journals? Though it does seem a little strange to ban the word from the conversations of people for whom it is a matter of life and death.

The Greeks, at least, had some ideas: order, harmony, structure. But all of that had gotten a radical shaking up even by the time of, let's say, Hieronymus Bosch. If we think the *Apollo Belvedere* is beautiful, what do we say about the naked bottom and legs of a man emerging from a strawberry and scurrying around Bosch's *Garden of Earthly Delights*?

Obviously, content is only a fraction of what matters. There's beauty of conception and beauty of execution, which is, to oversimplify, part of what makes Cézanne's apples different from the apples we doodle on our notepad or the scribblings of a child. Conception and execution are major factors in the narratives on the page and screen that I tend to remember as beautiful. For example, I find great beauty in the scene in Mavis Gallant's story "The Ice Wagon Going down the Street," in which the self-deluded and heartbreakingly sad office worker at the League of Nations in post–World War II Geneva is asked to take home a mousy co-worker who has gotten drunk at a costume party. What happens (nothing happens) may well be the most important event in their lives. Yet one of them thinks that the nothing that happened was about the two of them not having sex, while the other thinks that "nothing happened" meant that she didn't commit suicide, as she seems to have considered doing.

There is a startling and deeply melancholy scene in the great Hungarian writer Dezso Kosztolanyi's novel *Skylark*. An elderly couple's beloved, burdensome, unmarried thirty-five-year-old daughter has gone away on vacation, freeing them for a week of unaccustomed pleasures and shattering realizations about their domestic life. On her return, they go to greet her at the station. Dressed in an unflattering rain cape and a silly hat, and carrying a scruffy pigeon, her new pet, in a cage, she is even homelier than they remember, just as she is even more intensely the love of their life and their jailer. Suddenly they notice that autumn has arrived. "A desolate boredom settled over everything. The warm days are over." Why should that seem beautiful?

And why should I be so taken with the moment in Mike Leigh's film *Life Is Sweet* when Timothy Spall, as the sublimely geeky Aubrey, opens a restaurant, a bistro called the Regret Rien, fashioned on an Edith Piaf theme. "Très exclusive." On opening night, no customers come, and Aubrey, who has been drinking wine as he waits for the nonexistent onslaught of diners, trashes the place and winds up passed out on the floor, stripped down to a pair of unnervingly creepy Speedos. Why do I love the marvelous scene in Francis Ford Coppola's *The Godfather* in which Sonny speaks out of turn and the Tattaglia family knows that the Corleones are vulnerable and can be attacked? And why do I think there is beauty in every moment of Michael K. Williams's portrayal of Omar Little in David Simon's TV series *The Wire*?

There is little that could be considered conventionally pretty about watching Gallant's filing clerk, dressed as a hobo, nearly fall down in a Geneva street, or Kosztolanyi's woman arrive, with her pigeon, at a rural Hungarian train station, or Leigh's chef—a man with heartbreakingly hilarious pretensions to coolness and sophistication—charging around his empty bistro, overturning elaborately set tables, or a Mafia don's meeting with his enemies and his unruly son, or a scar-faced Baltimore hit man sticking up a drug dealer. But how, I wonder, can we not feel the beauty of these scenes?

Each of us has heard—and probably, in a charitable moment, thought—that beauty is in the eye of the beholder, but each of us secretly believes that we are the one with the eye for beauty. Why *do* I see these melancholy scenes, these dark moments, as beautiful? It's a question to which there is no real answer, except to mention truth, another difficult and complicated thing, and to add that we *do* feel we know beauty when we see it. We could quote Emily Dickinson's famous definition of poetry as applying also to beauty:

"If I read a book and it makes me so cold no fire can ever warm me I know *that* is poetry. If I feel physically as if the top of my head were taken off, I know *that* is poetry. These are the only way I know it. Is there any other way." Or, less gloriously, we have Supreme Court Justice Potter Stewart's ruling that hard-core pornography is difficult to define, but "I know it when I see it."

Two: Art can shock us.

I don't mean *shock* as in bad news or brutal murder or horrific catastrophe or embarrassing scandal. I don't mean *shock* as they did on a reality show that ran some years ago, a series entitled *Work of Art: The Next Great Artist*, modeled after *Top Chef*. In one episode, the contestants competed to make "shocking art." Among the judges was the photographer Andres Serrano, once considered shocking by, among others, the late Senator Jesse Helms, who was shocked that a government arts grant should go to a person who had photographed a crucifix submerged in a vial of urine. (Did Andres Serrano think, *Beautiful!* when those contact sheets came back?) On the show, Serrano spoke about the difficulty of making art that shocks at this particular political and historical moment. And in fact I wasn't shocked enough to remember which artist contestant won.

In any case, I mean something less aesthetic and moral and more neurological: the shock that travels along our nerves and leaps across our synapses when we look at a Titian portrait or read a Dickinson poem. We understand it, and we don't. It's irreducible; it can't be summarized or described; we feel something we can't describe. I often think of that feeling as resembling those moments in dreams when we fall off a cliff and then discover we can fly. Dropping, then soaring. We can no more explain or paraphrase or categorize our response than we can explain why a Chinese scroll can transport us out of a gallery or museum and return us, moments later, jet-lagged, giddy with the aftereffects of travel through time and space. The effect of those tiny art shocks is cumulative and enduring. Enough of them can change our consciousness, perhaps even our metabolism. Dieters, take notice.

I've always hoped that someone would fund a research project to measure the changes that occur in our brain waves when we lose ourselves in a book. What if it turned out that these changes have a beneficial effect on our health, not unlike the benefits we have been told can be obtained from exercise and a daily glass of red wine? What if reading were proved to be even healthier than exercise? Imagine the sudden spike in reading everywhere as the health and longevity conscious allowed their gym memberships to lapse and headed to the library and the bookstore?

Three: Can art make you a better person?

Not long ago, I read a Facebook post that suggested that Shakespeare was a sadist for subjecting us to something as gloomy as *King Lear*. And I thought of how a doctor's assistant once told me that the only books and films she likes are those that are cheerful and uplifting, because there's enough doom and gloom in the world without looking for more. She said she hardly ever reads fiction, because it's so depressing. She prefers books on philosophy. "What kind of philosophy?" I asked. She said, "Well, actually, I like books that tell you how to be a better person."

Art will not necessarily make you a better person. When I was a child, my favorite aunt was a great fan of Wagner, and though my mother and father teased her for going to see fat women in braids and Viking helmets sing for five hours at a time, she secretly indoctrinated me into her cult of Wagner. I can still picture the cover of her record of *Tristan und Isolde*. Later, of course, I discovered that Wagner was extremely anti-Semitic and a favorite of the Nazis and so forth, facts that had little bearing on my falling out of love with Wagner as an adult. Recently I learned from a documentary something that everyone else has probably known about forever: the manic intensity of Hitler's passion for Wagnerian opera, how he felt his whole life had changed after seeing a performance of *Rienzi*, whose hero, a medieval Roman tribune, leads his people to rise up against their oppressive rulers. Hitler would say of that performance, "It was in that hour that it all began," and claim that Nazism could not be understood without understanding Wagner.

Hitler had notoriously terrible taste in visual art, a predilection for the cream-puff nudes of kitschy French painters like Bouguereau. There is a famous story about Hitler's visit to Berlin's National Gallery in the 1920s. Enraged to discover that Germany did not possess any work by Michelangelo, his favorite artist, Hitler was mildly consoled to find a painting by Caravaggio—Michelangelo Merisi da Caravaggio—whom Hitler thought was the same person as Michelangelo Buonarroti. Next, he became enchanted by Correggio's highly erotic depiction of *Leda and the Swan*, though, when his guide discovered him, transfixed before the painting, Hitler insisted that he was only admiring the subtle play of light and shadow. Finally, and most revealingly, he sought out Rembrandt's *Man with the Golden Helmet*, an image that, Hitler claimed, proved Rembrandt was a true Aryan who, despite the many works he'd done in the Jewish Quarter, had no real interest in the Jews after all. Hitler's henchmen had better taste—refined enough to know what they wanted when they looted the museums and private collections of Europe and carried off countless masterpieces. But Hitler had originally wanted to be an artist, and during his final days in the bunker, he puttered over an architectural model showing his plan for remaking the Austrian city of Linz.

It's true, or I want to believe it's true, that there is something humanizing about the intimacy a book creates between the author and the reader, between the reader and the character, something humanizing about experiencing the vision and work of another human being. We are so accustomed to speaking about "the humanities" that we no longer think about why these fields of inquiry and study are called that. One of the things that most disturbs me about the way in which children may come to prefer electronic devices and video games to books is that they no longer know or intuit that an individual person has created the thing that is the source of their pleasure. Rather, they come to understand, consciously or subconsciously, that a corporation has provided them with entertainment and happiness. Thank you, Google. Thank you, Apple.

Years ago, I used to comfort myself with the thought that reading a novel by an author from any of the countries in what George W. Bush termed the Axis of Evil could persuade us that the men and women and children who inhabit these so-called evil lands are— beneath the surface created by custom and culture—very much like us and our friends and loved ones. That is, no more or less good, no more or less evil. But how much will that realization influence our actions?

While writing a book about *The Diary of Anne Frank*, I met a group of inspiring young people who worked for the Anne Frank Foundation and were convinced that Anne's diary could turn other young people away from the path of prejudice and violence. In their company, I, too, was convinced. I wanted to be convinced. But some crabby, skeptical inner voice couldn't help playing devil's advocate—asking who, high on the chemical rush of violence, on the brink of committing a hate crime or perpetrating a genocidal massacre, would be stopped by the memory of a young girl's diary?

In any case, it is neither the responsibility nor the purpose of art to make us better human beings. And it's no wonder that art that takes on this solemn task so often winds up being didactic, preachy, cloying, and less effective than art with a less exalted notion of its purpose. Careers and talents have been ruined when an artist was intoxicated and ultimately silenced by an exaggerated sense of importance. Among the more famous and tragic examples of this was Nikolai Gogol; the misery he experienced in trying to write a sequel to *Dead Souls* was intensified by his belief that the second volume of his masterpiece was destined to save Russia.

In one of his letters, Chekhov said:

You scold me for objectivity, calling it indifference to good and evil, lack of ideals and ideas, and so forth. When I am writing about horse thieves, you want me to say that it is evil to steal horses. However, everyone knows this already without my having to say so. Let the members of the jury pass their judgment. My job is merely to show what sort of people these horse thieves are. Here is what I write: we are dealing with horse thieves here, so bear in mind that they are not beggars but well-fed men, that they are members of a cult, and that for them stealing horses is not just thieving but a passion. Certainly, it might be nice to combine art with preaching, but for me personally this is exceptionally difficult and technically next to impossible. After all, if I want to describe horse thieves in seven hundred lines, I have to talk and think and feel as they talk and think and feel; otherwise, if I let myself get subjective, my characters will fall apart and the story will not be as concise as all very short stories need to be. When

I am writing, I rely on my readers, and I trust them to fill in any subjective elements that might be missing.

Four: Though art cannot teach us how to be better human beings, it can help us understand what it means to be human beings.

If you were to read every novel and story ever written, you would have a pretty good—if not entirely complete—sense of the range of qualities and ideas and emotions that characterize our species. Stare at a Rembrandt or a Rodin or a Helen Levitt photograph long enough and afterward people look different: lovelier and more complex, if not necessarily more explicable to themselves or us.

Art—and here I am speaking not of music or abstract painting but of the narrative and figurative, of literature and portraiture—can describe certain experiences that seem to be common to human beings: birth, death, procreation, falling in and out of love. It can show us that we share these experiences with other human beings. In depicting the emotions and longings and acts that we might not choose to discuss with our families or our neighbors, art can diminish our loneliness and solitude. Books in which the characters express negative emotions—or even commit crimes—can console those who have experienced similar emotions or have committed—or merely considered committing—a crime.

Five: Art can move us.

Surely it must be possible to walk into the cathedral of Chartres or Borromini's Chapel of Saint Ivo, or to stand in front of Caravaggio's *Crucifixion of Saint Peter*, and feel nothing. But it might require some effort. To say that we try to avoid art that is depressing or disturbing is a backhanded compliment to its power to affect us.

Perhaps, at some point, each one of us experiences his or her own version of the Stendhal syndrome, the psychosomatic response (which can involve fainting, a rapid heartbeat, vertigo, and hallucinations) to the power of art, a disease first identified with and endemic to Florence, where even today a few cases are diagnosed every year.

For years, I suffered from an inability to hear Mozart performed in public without bursting into tears. The quality of the performance made no difference at all, as I discovered when hearing a middle school string orchestra play a simplified excerpt from the "Jupiter" Symphony. Once, after a crowd of youths had nearly rioted and almost broken down the heavy wooden doors before they were admitted to the Basilica di Santa Maria in Aracoeli, where a crowd of exquisitely dressed Romans had assembled to hear Mozart's Requiem, I started sobbing out loud. At moments, I've wondered whether these feelings would have been less intense if Mozart had been rich, successful, and sure of himself, like Handel, whose work I also love.

Six: Can art make us smarter?

My sons were in school when a study was published proving that students at Stanford scored better on standardized tests after listening to Mozart than did the control group, which hadn't listened to Mozart. I prided myself on not being the kind of parent who made her kids play *Don Giovanni* on the way to take their SATs, though—confession—I did suggest that one of my sons put some Mozart on his Walkman (the forerunner of the iPod). Having taken so little advantage of the available information about the relationship between classical music and test taking, I was relieved when a more recent study questioned the results of the earlier research, though I'd liked the idea of Mozart, dead in his pauper's grave, revived to help American students score on standardized testing.

Clearly, more research is needed. Is a Wallace Stevens poem an exercise for the brain? Will a half hour spent in front of a Velázquez help you ace the math exam? Will reading Henry James's *The Turn of the Screw* make you realize—as any reader or judge or prospective juror or citizen of a democracy or any form of government should know—that two different conclusions can be drawn from the same set of facts? Will James's novella make it easier for its readers to tolerate ambiguity?

Art can be informative, though it is always a mistake to equate intelligence with the amount of information one possesses. Read *War and Peace* and you learn something about the Napoleonic Wars. Look at a portrait by Bronzino and you find out how a certain class of people dressed in the sixteenth century. Read Philip Roth's *American Pastoral* for an education in, among other things, the workings of a glove-making factory. Read Gabriel García Márquez to discover an earlier meaning of "banana republic," and Roberto Bolaño's *2666* to learn about the murders of hundreds (or perhaps thousands) of women that have been taking place for decades along the U.S.–Mexico border. A film such as Jean Renoir's *The Rules of the Game* or Michael Haneke's *Caché* or Florian Henckel von Donnersmarck's *The Lives of Others* can help us understand why people, at certain historical moments, make certain moral choices. And Otis Redding's version of "Try a Little Tenderness" can step in to answer Freud's question about what women want, or at least one of the things they want—in addition to equal rights and equal pay.

Art can make you smarter, if by *smart* we mean more aware, responsive, cognizant, quicker, and so forth. Art can make you more aware of the ways in which history, social class, race, gender, and good and bad luck affect us. Art is the cerebral, spiritual, and emotional equivalent of the toners we splash on our faces to improve our complexions. Art opens our heart and brain cells. Put

Mozart on your iPod and you will do better on the exam, especially if you've studied.

Seven: Art is a time travel machine.

There is no better way, including the Ouija board and the séance, to get in touch with people who have been dead for hundreds of years. If you want to know how a seventeenth-century Dutchman saw light, look at a Vermeer. If you want to know how it felt to be a bored housewife in a nineteenth-century French town, read *Madame Bovary*. If you want a preview of an alternate or possible future, read Philip K. Dick. If you want to see how this country looked fifty years ago, study Robert Frank's photos, or to see what Rome was like for a certain group of people in the 1960s, watch *La Dolce Vita*. If you want to know how it felt to live in a slaveholding society—that is to say, this country before the Civil War—*Huckleberry Finn* can tell you more than the most incisive, comprehensive, and meticulously researched history book ever written.

Eight: Art can not only transport us through time.

It can transcend and erase time as we discover that those characters squabbling over the inheritance in a Balzac novel are upsettingly like our relatives. Or that Billie Holiday knew how to sing a phrase in the way that would most affect you and only you, knew how to bend and hold a note until you couldn't help but notice.

One marvelous thing about Proust is how his consideration of the relationship between art and life extends outside of his masterpiece to make you consider the relationship between its art and your life. Reading the opening section of *Swann's Way*, in which the child insomniac is waiting for the sounds that indicate his mother is coming to kiss him good night, we are restored to that moment in childhood when we lay awake in the dark listening for a longed-for or dreaded noise. Thus we *begin* the book by achieving the hoped-for result of the project that the narrator attempts in volume after volume: recovering lost time, a project in which he eventually succeeds, thanks to the linden tea and the madeleine, whereas we readers have already succeeded, at least partly, by reading the opening section.

Nine: Can art protect us? Art can protect us.

If it can't, why have so many people, probably starting with the first person who drew that bison on the wall, assumed it could? The conversation about whether tribal or indigenous art is actually art is, to my mind, as arid and pointless as the conversation about whether it should be forbidden to mention the word *beauty*. Consider those towering wooden figures made by the Asmat people, those nail-studded totems from Benin, the icons and reliquaries in the treasure vaults of cathedrals, or a Fra Angelico fresco on the wall of his brother monk's cell, and convince me that art doesn't have magic power.

Idolatry is only the most extreme form of art appreciation. According to the painter Alexander Melamid, the way we know that artists are the priests of art is that they all wear black. Regardless of whether we believe that our novel can make the rains come and help our crops to grow, art is the driftwood humans cling to when they worry, as they always have, that our species is drowning.

Ten: Art can give us pleasure.

Now we have come full circle, for to define aesthetic pleasure is as freighted, as complex, as arguable, and as impossible as defining beauty. Emily Dickinson likened poetry to freezing and partial decapitation. There is pleasure in watching the films of Chabrol and Kurosawa, and a related, if different, pleasure in admiring the skill with which Chardin paints a bubble or a dead rabbit. There is pleasure in observing the small but precise incisions with which George Eliot lays bare a soul, or the inventive turns of phrase with which Dickens sketches a vast, interconnected population, or the plot twists and bold declarations with which Kafka and Kleist persuade us to accept and believe the most improbable premises.

As my doctor's assistant said, there's enough gloom and doom in the world. How fortunate, then, that we have art to amuse us, move us, inform us, comfort us, protect us, and console us for what we already know: that life is strange and hard and often dark, and we should be grateful—more than grateful—for those pinpoints of radiance, the cord of runway lights that guides us back through time and death to the hand that first drew that bison on the wall.

2

Mary Shelley, *Frankenstein*

IN THE INTRODUCTION TO THE 1831 EDITION OF *FRANKENSTEIN*, which was originally published anonymously in 1818 and which over the intervening years (thanks partly to a series of low-comedy theatrical adaptations) had become a bestseller, Mary Shelley offered a persuasive and romantic explanation of how her book came to be written. The account of where and how Mary Shelley's novel originated may be among the most famous creation stories in literature; we know, or we think we know, the circumstances and the pressures under which a very young woman turned a sort of parlor game into a book that would long outlive her.

It was the summer of 1816. Mary Shelley was eighteen years old. Two years before, she had fallen in love with the poet Percy Bysshe Shelley, a frequent visitor to the home of her father, William Godwin, the political radical, freethinker, novelist, and, most famously, author of *Enquiry Concerning Political Justice*. Mary's mother, the equally radical and perhaps even more unconventional Mary Wollstonecraft, had written *A Vindication of the Rights of Woman*, a protofeminist work that argues for the importance of educating females.

Before conquering her disapproval of the institution of marriage in order to marry Godwin, who shared her opinion of state-sanctioned wedlock, Mary Wollstonecraft had endured an unhappy love affair with the painter Henry Fuseli. And she had borne an illegitimate daughter, Fanny, to an American entrepreneur and cad named Gilbert Imlay, whom she had met in Paris, where she had gone to observe, firsthand, the aftermath of the French Revolution. Mary Wollstonecraft died of an infection within days of giving birth to her second daughter, Mary.

Having reversed his position on marriage, William Godwin wed again. Mary Godwin despised her new stepmother, who brought to the household her own son, Charles, and her daughter, Jane, a high-strung, impulsive girl two years younger than Mary. Jane, who would later rechristen herself Claire, was, for much of Mary Shelley's early married life, the bane of her existence. Claire flirted intensely with Shelley, then threw herself at—and had a daughter with—Lord Byron.

When he began visiting Godwin, Shelley was married and the father of a child. Nonetheless, he and Mary fell passionately in love. They eloped and—together with fifteen-year-old Jane—left London for the Continent. What followed was a difficult period, its sufferings mediated only by the deepening of the young couple's love. The emotionally volatile threesome traveled semi-constantly, under adverse conditions and nearly always on the verge of destitution. Mary gave birth to a baby daughter, who was born prematurely and who died after a few days.

Eventually Mary, Percy, and Jane (now Claire) came to rest at a cottage on the shores of Lac Léman, in Switzerland, not far from where Lord Byron, who had become Claire's lover, was staying at the Villa Diodati. The group—Percy and Mary, Byron and Claire, and Byron's physician, John William Polidori—had planned on spending the summer enjoying the beauties of the landscape and the lake. But when the weather became cold and rainy—a volcanic eruption had turned the summer into one of the most inclement in European history—they sought another way to amuse themselves.

Perhaps in search of a respite from the long hours of intense and fevered conversation, the friends, who had been reading ghost stories translated from the German, agreed (at Byron's suggestion) to each write a tale of the supernatural.

The preface that Percy Shelley wrote to the original 1818 edition of *Frankenstein*—an introduction that caused many to conclude that the book had been written by the poet himself—contains a somewhat simpler, less personal, and more truncated version of the events leading up to the novel's composition than his wife would offer thirteen years later: "The season was cold and rainy," wrote Shelley, "and in the evenings we crowded around a blazing wood fire, and occasionally amused ourselves with some German stories of ghosts, which happened to fall into our hands. These tales excited in us a playful desire of imitation. Two other friends . . . and myself agreed to write each a story founded on some supernatural occurrence."

Shelley wrote, and never finished, a story set in childhood. A fragmentary work about a vampire was attributed to Byron and later published by Polidori, who was in fact its author. Less facile and more reticent than her lover and his friends, Mary claimed to have had a harder time with the assignment. Perhaps part of her difficulties stemmed from the tensions among the storytellers. Byron had little respect for Mary and, it seems, even less for Claire, who was pregnant with his child. Polidori seems to have been in love with Mary, and Shelley was torn between his admiration for Byron and his desire to protect Mary and keep peace within the group.

These fraught interpersonal relationships were clearly a distraction. But what must have posed even more of a challenge for

Mary was creating the effect that she sought: a story "which would speak to the mysterious fears of our nature, and awaken thrilling horror—one to make the reader dread to look round, to curdle the blood, and quicken the beatings of the heart. . . . I felt that blank incapability of invention which is the greatest misery of author-ship, when dull Nothing replies to our anxious invocations. *Have you thought of a story?* I was asked each morning, and each morning I was forced to reply with a mortifying negative."

One can hardly think of worse circumstances under which to create fiction than this ur–writers' colony from hell, but Mary Shel-ley persevered. She mostly listened to the conversations between her husband and Lord Byron, discussions about philosophy, about the possibility that "the principle of life" would ever be "discov-ered and communicated." They spoke about attempts to reanimate corpses of the newly deceased by the application of galvanic shocks, and about Dr. Erasmus Darwin, who was said to have preserved bits of vermicelli under glass until they began to move of their own volition. "Perhaps," she wrote, "the component parts of a creature might be manufactured, brought together, and endowed with vital warmth."

During this time, Mary appears to have been thinking of a trip that she and Shelley took, not long after their initial departure from London, along the Rhine. There, they visited Frankenstein Castle. According to local legend, a young man named Johann Kon-rad Dippel was accused of robbing graveyards for corpses that he believed could be reanimated by injecting them with a mixture of blood and bone.

One night, still puzzling over Byron's assignment and trying to sleep, Mary had a vision in which she saw "the pale student of unhallowed arts kneeling beside the thing he had put together. I saw the hideous phantasm of a man stretched out, and then, on the working of some powerful engine, show signs of life, and stir with an uneasy, half-vital motion." She lay awake, trying to imagine a story that would frighten the reader as much as she had been frightened, then realized that she had found it. "'What terrified me will terrify others; and I need only describe the spectre which had haunted my midnight pillow.' On the morrow I announced that I had *thought of a story*" and set herself to making "a transcript of the grim terrors of my waking dream." Shelley suggested that the narrative might be longer than what Mary originally had in mind.

The book was completed almost a year later, in June 1817. In the interim, Mary and Percy had returned to England. Mary's half sister Fanny Imlay committed suicide in October. And at the end of 1816, the Shelleys were married in London, their union having been facilitated by the fact that Shelley's first wife, Harriet, had drowned herself. Mary was pregnant with Shelley's child, doubtless a source of anxiety, since her first child, Clara, had died soon after birth and Mary's own mother had died in childbirth. Little wonder, then, that the story Mary wrote would be so thoroughly steeped in violence, in grief, in loneliness and fear, in remorse and guilt.

IN a survey of texts taught in schools, conducted by the Open Syllabus Project, *Frankenstein* is the fifth most commonly taught book, and *the* most commonly taught literary text. And according to the preface to Miranda Seymour's marvelously lucid and comprehensive biography, *Mary Shelley* (2000), "A recent survey among American children showed [Frankenstein's] name to be more familiar than that of the President." Seymour fails to note whether the interlocutor asked the American children to distinguish between Frankenstein the scientist in Mary Shelley's novel and Frankenstein the monster (played by Boris Karloff) in the 1931 film. My four-year-old granddaughter is very fond of a picture book entitled *Frankenstein Makes a Sandwich*, in which the sandwich maker appears, with the cinematic monster's unsightly facial stitches and elongated head, and with his complexion inexplicably turned bright green.

The fact that the novel is so widely taught is more perplex-ing. It's understandable that, as a novel of ideas, it should serve as a convenient prompt to inspire class discussions on a range of important questions: What is a human being? Is it dangerous to play God? What are the ethical implications and limits of scientific research? What is the effect of isolation and alienation? But what makes it a slightly less obvious choice is the fact that it is a very difficult book—not so much because the language is old-fashioned but because the structure is exceedingly complex, containing sto-ries within stories, letters within narratives, and multiple narrators. Each segment of the novel informs and reflects upon the tone and content of the others.

THE form of *Frankenstein*, the nest of stories within stories, each told by a different narrator, has mostly fallen out of fashion. But the "frame story" was very much in vogue during the heyday of the Gothic novel, a genre popular during the late eighteenth and early nineteenth centuries. *Frankenstein* is perhaps the most famous and enduring example, though Muriel Spark, in *Mary Shelley: A Biogra-phy* (1951), argues persuasively that Frankenstein "was the first of a new and hybrid fictional species."

Shelley's novel, Spark suggests, combines elements of the Gothic (the supernatural, the grotesque, the theme of pursuit, the frisson of terror) with a more modern portrayal of the relationship between Frankenstein and his monster. *Caleb Williams*, the novel that Mary's father, William Godwin, published in 1794, is also a frame narrative and also locks its two main characters in a murderous game of flight and pursuit. Emily Brontë employed a similar strategy in *Wuthering Heights*, which appeared in 1847. In the novel, Lockwood's narrative (and diary entries) give way to, and are interspersed with, the house-keeper Nelly Dean's account of the dramatic events at Wuthering Heights and Thrushcross Grange.

Gothic novels abound with manuscripts found in dusty trunks, with letters and pages ripped from journals, with narrators who happen to meet other narrators whose stories advance and explain their own. Such structures serve several purposes: they allow the writer to vary the pace and tone; they facilitate the introduction of information to which only one of the (multiple) narrators could have been privy; they provide the old-fashioned pleasures of eavesdropping on a storyteller telling a story; and they add an element of authority and credibility to a plot that contains fantastic and supernatural elements, and which might otherwise seem more unlikely than it does when we know that a presumably sane and reliable character is testifying to the truth of the wild events being described.

The advantages of this method were not lost on Henry James. *The Turn of the Screw* is framed as a story told by a man who knew the ghost-plagued governess when he was younger, and who is in possession of a manuscript, written in her hand, that is "beyond everything. . . . For general uncanny ugliness and horror and pain."

Something similar could be said about the ugliness and horror of the events in *Frankenstein*. The outside frame of the narrative comes to us from a presumably reliable source: Captain Robert Walton, who is writing to his sister, Margaret. Having given up hope of succeeding as a poet, Walton is traveling to the North Pole to conduct scientific research. His desire to discover the secret of magnetism ("the wondrous power which attracts the needle") makes him the ideal listener for Frankenstein's tale of scientific experimentation gone disastrously wrong.

Everything about Walton's voice suggests rationality and plausibility, even as he describes what may be the most bizarre and disturbing (and possibly the most memorable) image in the novel, a "being which had the shape of a man, but apparently of gigantic stature," driving a dogsled across the icy wasteland. The next day, Walton's shipmates rescue yet another traveler, this one "not

a savage inhabitant of some undiscovered island, but a European"
(albeit with a foreign accent), who is half-frozen, half-dead, emaci-
ated, and stranded on an ice floe, also with a dogsled, though only
one of his dogs survives. As we learn, this unfortunate traveler has
been pursuing the giant whom Walton and his crewmates saw the
day before.

This hapless voyager is Dr. Victor Frankenstein, who takes over
the role of narrator as he tells his harrowing tale to the captain. He
describes his youth, his upbringing, his family, his early interest in
science, and the way in which that interest lured him down a dangerous path of inquiry. Fascinated by the work of Paracelsus and
Albertus Magnus, encouraged by his professors, he'd immersed
himself in chemistry and anatomy. He had begun to wonder if the
dead could be reanimated, if new life could be created from what
remains after the soul has left the body. After spending "days and
nights in vaults and charnel houses," observing "how the worm inherited the wonders of the eye and brain" and "the change from life
to death, and death to life," Frankenstein achieved a breakthrough:
"After days and nights of incredible labour and fatigue, I succeeded
in discovering the cause of generation and life; nay, more, I became
myself capable of bestowing animation upon lifeless matter."

To follow Frankenstein from his graveyard researches to the
point at which he is able to restore the dead to life places a certain strain on the reader's credibility—even those readers steeped
in the conventions of the Gothic. Ghosts? Certainly. Resurrection
by science? Not so much. Wisely, Shelley has Frankenstein inform
Captain Walton that he is withholding the secret of his scientific
success for the captain's protection, for his (and our) own good:

> I see by your eagerness, and the wonder and hope which your
> eyes express, my friend, that you expect to be informed of the se-
> cret with which I am acquainted: that cannot be; listen patiently
> until the end of my story, and you will easily perceive why I am

reserved upon that subject. I will not lead you on unguarded and
ardent as I then was, to your destruction and infallible misery.
Learn from me, if not by my precepts, at least by my example,
how dangerous is the acquirement of knowledge.

Thus Mary Shelley finesses what we might now term "a plot
hole." Not only does the author advise us (in the interest of our
own safety) to stop wondering about how, precisely, Frankenstein
achieved his unholy effects, but she offers us yet another reason to
keep reading, in case the mystery of the icy dogsled chase hasn't
sufficiently intrigued us. Read on, we are told, and you will find out
why you would rather *not* be able to duplicate Victor's experimen-
tal methods, "the horrors of my secret toil, as I dabbled among the
unhallowed damps of the grave, or tortured the living animal to
animate the lifeless clay."

The thrill of victory and discovery is transient. Almost as soon
as he succeeds in bringing his creation to life, Frankenstein comes
face-to-face with a being whose hideousness seems to augur the
presence of an equally unappealing nature. One can't help noting
how often in the novel physical beauty is assumed to be an indication of good character, while ugliness is the manifestation of some
moral flaw. This seemingly superficial but sadly accurate observation of how humans make judgments will become all the more
important as the book progresses and as the monster—whose ugliness, size, and obvious abnormality are ultimately what make him
a pariah—takes over the narrative and tells his own sad tale.

Frankenstein flees the monster and spends a restless night wandering the streets, where, by lucky accident, he runs into his friend
Henry Clerval, who has just at that moment arrived from Switzerland. (The coincidence averse may have reason to wonder at many
such points in the book.)

Clerval remarks on the fact that his friend seems to be unwell—
a bit of an understatement, considering what the reader knows of

Victor's recent travails. Feeling that he has no choice but to bring Clerval back to his rooms, while at the same time fearing that the monster will still be there, Frankenstein returns home, in one of the novel's most successful moments—successful in the sense that we feel Shelley truly inhabiting her hero; she is making us feel what he feels.

> *My hand was already on the lock of the door before I recollected myself. I then paused; and a cold shivering came over me. I threw the door forcibly open, as children are accustomed to do when they expect a spectre to stand in waiting for them on the other side; but nothing appeared. I stepped fearfully in: the apartment was empty; and my bedroom was also freed from its hideous guest.*

What Victor first experiences as relief and joy is in fact a recurrence of exhaustion, fear, and horror; the monster has escaped. Victor falls ill and is nursed back to health by the loyal Clerval. Meanwhile, the narrative switches back to the epistolary form, in this case a letter from Victor's beloved fiancée, Elizabeth. The letter serves to introduce a character—the noble and loyal servant (though, as we are informed, "a servant in Geneva does not mean the same thing as a servant in France and England") Justine, who has nursed Elizabeth's difficult aunt through her final illness, has gone home to witness her own unstable and unkind mother's death, and has returned to be a help to the household. All in all, there is only good news, and Victor's little brother William is reported to be thriving.

What seems like domestic gossip is in fact a clever setup for what is to follow: After a brief remission, during which Victor's health rallies and he pays a polite, if not entirely honest, visit to his former teachers, another letter comes. This one is from Victor's father, and it is in effect an announcement that the nightmare has begun in earnest. Little William has been murdered.

It has often been remarked: the strangeness of Mary Shelley calling the dead child William, which was the name of her own beloved son, born in January 1816. But it has just as frequently been observed that it is common for writers, especially young ones, to spur themselves on with some version of their fantasies of the worst that could happen.

The unfortunate Justine, whom we have heard so much about in Elizabeth's letter, has been accused of William's murder. Like Victor, who knows that his monster is guilty of the crime but is certain that no one will believe him if he tells the truth, the reader can only watch as Justine is convicted of, and executed for, killing the child.

One hesitates to spoil the rest of Mary Shelley's wild, inventive, twisting, but admirably coherent plot—coherent, that is, by the standards of the Gothic novel, in which one often feels as if the author is piling event upon event to maintain a slightly frantic pace and an unbroken sequence of dramatic events. And yet one can't help noting a striking section that not only changes the way we read the novel but also alters our understanding of its author's sympathies.

Racked by guilt, wandering in a sort of desperately penitential way through the mountains, Victor again meets his monster, who now tells his own story: how he discovered a hut occupied by a blind man and his family; how he learned, from observing this family, about human behavior and the ideal sweetness that suffuses a household governed by love; how he was able to master the rudiments of language; how he taught himself to read by studying discarded books; how he first saw his reflection and understood how "deformed and horrible" he was; how he hoped that he could be accepted and welcomed by the old man's family despite his frightening appearance; and how cruelly that hope was dashed. Now his only wish is that Victor will create another artificial being, a mate for the monster, so that he will have a companion and not be doomed to go through the world alone.

In the process of telling his unhappy story, the monster shows himself capable of a complexity of moral and philosophical reflection that the other characters—spurred by near-diabolic ambition or overwhelmed by tragedy—cannot or will not allow themselves. Hidden outside the blind man's hut, listening to one of its residents read aloud from a book entitled *Ruins of Empires*, the monster reflects on the human condition:

> *"These wonderful narrations inspired me with strange feelings. Was man, indeed, at once so powerful, so virtuous, and magnificent, yet so vicious and base? He appeared at one time a mere scion of the evil principle, and at another, as all that can be conceived of noble and godlike. To be a great and virtuous man appeared the highest honour that can befall a sensitive being; to be base and vicious, as many on record have been, appeared the lowest degradation, a condition more abject than that of the blind mole or harmless worm. For a long time I could not conceive how one man could go forth to murder his fellow, or even why there were laws and governments; but when I heard details of vice and bloodshed, my wonder ceased, and I turned away with disgust and loathing."*

How brilliant of Mary Shelley to have put these thoughts and these speculations into the brain and the mouth of a monster, and how savvy of her to realize that the questions he poses have never and will never be answered. Nor will we tire of asking these inquiries into the limits of science and the essence of a human being. Her novel functions as an intellectual challenge, inviting us to ponder the profound issues raised by the monster and by the very fact of his existence.

At the same time, *Frankenstein* exerts an emotional pull as powerful as the one for which Mary Shelley claimed, in her preface, to have strived: "One which would speak to the mysterious fears of our nature, and awaken thrilling horror." To this day, her book remains terrifying, not only because it traffics in graveyard horrors, in child murder and reanimated corpses, but also because it speaks to the anxieties to which all of us are prone. Which of us is immune to the fear that we, like Victor Frankenstein, may discover that our own work, our proudest creations, the offspring of whom we are so proud may turn against us—and that, with all the best intentions, we may wreak mayhem and havoc on those we love most, and least wish to hurt?

Charles Dickens,
Great Expectations

ANYONE WHO DOUBTS (AS MOST WRITERS DO NOT) THAT some books have wills of their own, ideas about their shape and destiny and about the paths they mean to take, routes along which an author may feel less like the navigator than like a compliant traveling companion—anyone who has reservations about this may consider how many masterpieces have welled up from the gap between a writer's intentions and the book that resulted. Working on *Anna Karenina*, Tolstoy imagined recording the deserved punishment that was visited upon a sinful woman—and gave us one of literature's most deeply sympathetic heroines. Melville conceived of *Moby-Dick* as one of the ripping travel adventure yarns he'd told so successfully before, until his friend Nathaniel Hawthorne suggested he might want to steer his literary voyage toward the deeper waters of metaphysics.

In October 1860, when Charles Dickens was writing the first chapters of *Great Expectations*, he described his plans in a letter to his friend and future biographer John Forster:

The book will be written in the first person throughout, and . . .
you will find the hero to be a boy-child, like David. Then he will
be an apprentice. You will not have to complain of the want of
humour as in The Tale of Two Cities. *I have made the open-*
ing, I hope, in its general effect exceedingly droll. I have put a
child and a good-natured foolish man in relations that seem to me
very funny. Of course I have got in the pivot on which the story
will turn too—and which indeed, as you remember, was the gro-
tesque tragicomic conception that first encouraged me.

As commonly happened in his career, Dickens's aesthetic goals
were being heavily influenced by practical considerations. The
weekly journal *All the Year Round*, which Dickens had founded in
1859, and which he co-edited and had made popular with serial-
izations of his own novel *A Tale of Two Cities* and of Wilkie Collins's *The Woman in White*, had recently suffered a precipitous and
worrisome drop in circulation. This decline was attributed to the
public's steadily waning interest in the novel that the magazine was
currently serializing, *A Day's Ride: A Life's Romance*, by Charles Le-
ver, a once-esteemed novelist who has had the misfortune to be
remembered as the man whose failure inspired Dickens to step in
and speed up the writing and publication of *Great Expectations*.

In Dickens's view, the suspenseful, funny, audience-pleasing
story he meant to write, and which would be kicked off by the
grotesque confrontation between a plucky, frightened boy and an
escaped convict, could function as a sort of literary life preserver,
thrown out to rescue *All the Year Round* from going under and
drowning.

In an earlier exchange of letters, Forster had expressed some
reservations about the pressure that it would exert on his friend to
write another big novel in segments to be published weekly, and
about the effects that this pressure might have on the work itself.

Dickens, who had already decided upon his novel's title, explained how much depended on his decision—nothing less than the survival of the magazine in which he had a great emotional and financial stake.

> *The sacrifice of* Great Expectations *is really and truly made for myself. The property of* All the Year Round *is far too valuable, in every way, to be much endangered. Our fall is not large, but we have a considerable advance in hand of the story we are now publishing, and there is no vitality in it, and no chance whatever of stopping the fall, which on the contrary would be certain to increase. . . . By dashing in now, I come in when most wanted.*

At the start of his lecture on *Bleak House*, Vladimir Nabokov wrote:

> *If it were possible I would like to devote the fifty minutes of every class meeting to mute meditation, concentration, and admiration of Dickens. However, my job is to direct and rationalize those meditations, that admiration. All we have to do when reading* Bleak House *is to relax and let our spines take over. Although we read with our minds, the seat of artistic delight is between the shoulder blades. That little shiver behind is quite certainly the highest form of emotion that humanity has attained when evolving pure art and pure science. Let us worship the spine and its tingle.*

Many things amaze us about the life and work of Charles Dickens: his energy and productivity, the depth and range of his vision, the beauty of his sentences and the freshness of his wit, his ability to combine a prodigious literary career with parallel lives in the theater and as an editor, publisher, and traveler, to keep up a voluminous correspondence, to make his own business arrangements, to undertake charitable projects, and to head a household

that included ten children. Also unusual and admirable is the con-
sistency of his ability to inspire, with such deceptive effortlessness,
that tingle between the shoulder blades. But what most impresses
many of his readers, and surely what most astonishes writers, is
that he wrote and published his long, complicated, densely populated, elaborately plotted, and thematically ambitious novels in
weekly or monthly serial installments.

Accustomed to the luxury of time and leisure, the freedom to
do major and minor revisions, to produce multiple drafts, to have
months or years in which to add or delete a single comma, we can
barely comprehend the imagination and the technical skill required
to compose an eight-hundred-page masterwork in regular installments of a length determined not by the needs of the artist but for the
convenience of the printer. Though Dickens wrote notes for some
of his novels and sketched out the conclusion of *Great Expectations*
in advance, this working method demanded a prodigious ability to
keep a large cast of characters and an elaborate narrative constantly
in mind. The astonishment we feel when we contemplate this stren-
uous mode of composition has, in my opinion, been best expressed
in the question posed about Dickens, in an introduction to *David
Copperfield*, by the novelist David Gates. "Was he a Martian?"

As Dickens plotted another novel about the social and moral
development of a boy into a man, he reread *David Copperfield* and
told Forster that he "was affected by it to a degree you would hardly
believe." His reason for going back to the earlier book, written a decade before, was "to be quite sure I had fallen into no unconscious
repetitions."

Perhaps he shouldn't have worried so. Because in those intervening ten years, Dickens's life and mood—and the man himself—had
been greatly changed. He had separated from his wife, Catherine,
an acrimonious rupture in the course of which he had forced his
children to side with him against their mother. He had weathered
a public scandal involving rumors that his sister-in-law Georgina

was the mother of his sons and daughters, as well as gossip (the truth of which has been alternately established and challenged) that he had taken as his mistress the eighteen-year-old actress Ellen Ternan. His daughter Kate had married a man she didn't love, in order, Dickens believed, to escape her father's troubled household. He had begun to suffer from attacks of painful rheumatism and facial neuralgia. His brother Alfred died of tuberculosis at thirty-eight, and Dickens's sons were beginning to show signs of having inherited the flaws that had landed their paternal grandfather in debtors' prison.

Later, Dickens would tell Forster that the "never-to-be-forgotten misery" of these years (the late 1850s) had revived in him the "certain shrinking sensitiveness" that he'd experienced during the now famous humiliation of his early life, when, at the age of twelve, the fragile boy had been forced to work ten hours a day, six days a week, pasting labels on bottles of boot and stove polish, in full view of the public, in the window of a London blacking factory.

Though it addresses many of the same concerns—class mobility, urban life, the ways in which children are nurtured or (more often) mistreated, the effort required to solve the riddle of one's own nature and identity—*Great Expectations* is in every way a darker book than *David Copperfield*. Despite Dickens's stated intention—to write something funny and "exceedingly droll" that would reinvigorate the readership of *All the Year Round* with its grotesquerie and humor—*Great Expectations* is among the most melancholy of his novels, and the one in which we may find confirmation of our most troubling doubts (so contrary to the aspirational spirit of the Victorian age) about the possibility and limits of self-improvement.

GREAT *Expectations* is rich in set pieces, in scenes so vivid and fully imagined, so nearly complete in themselves, that we can shut the book and be sure that, whether we like it or not, an image or sequence has been branded forever on our psyches. Perhaps the most indelible of these is the picture of Miss Havisham's room, where the clocks have been stopped and the light forbidden to enter, a domestic interior permanently frozen in some quasi-psychotic attempt to turn back time to the moment when the bride-to-be's heart was broken by the suitor who disappeared on her wedding day. No matter how familiar we are with the brushstrokes with which Dickens paints this deliriously creepy setting, no matter how many times we have read the novel and how well we think we know it, it's thrilling to be guided once more along the banquet table and past the disgusting remains of the wedding cake:

> A fire had been lately kindled in the damp old-fashioned grate, and it was more disposed to go out than to burn up, and the reluctant smoke which hung in the room seemed colder than the clearer air—like our own marsh mist. Certain wintry branches of candles on the high chimney-piece faintly lighted the chamber: or, it would be more expressive to say, faintly troubled its darkness. It was spacious, and I dare say had once been handsome, but every discernible thing in it was covered with dust and mould, and dropping to pieces. The most prominent object was a long table with a tablecloth spread on it, as if a feast had been in preparation when the house and the clocks all stopped together. An epergne or centre-piece of some kind was in the middle of this cloth; it was so heavily overhung with cobwebs that its form was quite indistinguishable; and, as I looked along the yellow expanse out of which I remember it seemed to grow, like a black fungus, I saw speckle-legged spiders with blotchy bodies running home to it, and running out from it, as if some circumstance of the greatest public importance had just transpired in the spider community.

There is, of course, no substitute for reading the novel, but I do want to recommend, to lovers of *Great Expectations*, the 2011 BBC miniseries based on the book. The casting of the remarkable Gillian Anderson as Miss Havisham suggests something that, as far as I know, has never been intimated by any of the previous cinematic or theatrical adaptations of the novel: namely, that Miss Havisham was, and—regardless of the ruined state in which Pip meets her—is still a great beauty. Utterly mad and ferociously vengeful, but lovely nonetheless.

Quotable aphorisms and astute psychological observations are liberally sprinkled throughout the novel. Worried that Joe's country manners may arouse the contempt of the despicable boor Bentley Drummle, Pip observes, "So, throughout life, our worst weaknesses and meannesses are usually committed for the sake of the people whom we most despise." Even as the plot speeds us forward, we pause to reflect on the psychological incisiveness of moments such as the one in which Pip's guilt over leaving Joe and Biddy for London makes him resent *them* for their grief about his departure.

There are extraordinary flights of dialogue, thrilling passages such as the one that records the giddy rhetoric of euphemism and avoidance with which the lawyer Jaggers avoids mentioning certain truths of which both the speaker and the listener are uncomfortably aware, and moments when a single word (kindly Herbert Pocket reassures an insecure actor that an abysmal performance of *Hamlet* has gone "capitally") tells us all we need to know about the person who has said it. Though Dickens has been accused of using verbal and physical tics as a means of creating caricatures without having to delve beneath a shallow and quirky surface, the gestures and habits of speech in *Great Expectations* are particular and telling. The way in which Pip catches the convict at the Three Jolly Bargemen stirring his rum-and-water with a file—a bold and secret reference to the stolen tool with which Pip helped free Magwitch—is among the most inspired examples of a small but meaningful physical gesture anywhere in fiction.

Landscape and weather are described in a seemingly effortless shorthand that makes it seem as if it were the easiest thing in the world to get nature and climate down on the page without resorting to cliché. We are introduced to characters in homes and places of business furnished with Dickens's astute and unfailing awareness of how decor reflects the deepest reaches of our souls. We are invited to compare the playhouse-cottage that Wemmick has created for himself and his aged father with the self-serious crepuscular gloom of his employer's office.

There are scenes of action and high suspense. Magwitch's botched escape, near drowning, and rescue from the Thames can be studied as a model for the clarity and order that allow us to follow a scene of roiling, fast-paced, densely populated, and potentially confusing action. There are touching events, such as the death of Pip's sister, a formerly brutal woman brought low by an assault that alters the plot and determines one of its many dramatic turns. And there are satisfying parallels, among them the likeness between Pip's sister's deathbed apology and the repentance of the novel's cruel queen bee, Miss Havisham.

Though the tightly constructed plot and massive cast of characters are appealing enough in themselves, the general reader, the writer, and the literary critic can find further entertainment in tracking an elaborate web of patterns and themes through the novel. Fathers and sons, names and naming, generosity and selfishness, lying and sincerity, crime and punishment, love and sacrifice, sex and class, imprisonment and freedom, cowardice and courage, and forgiveness and revenge are just a few of the many threads with which Dickens stitches together his grand design. Though the book is full of mysteries and questions, discovering their solutions doesn't mean that we enjoy it less on rereading, after we know where the plot is going and what secrets will be revealed. That knowledge only increases our admiration for how cleverly Dickens succeeds at keeping his readers in the dark until the light of truth illuminates the book's many shadowy corners. For example, we repeatedly marvel at the skill with which Dickens piles on evidence to persuade us that Pip is correct in what he believes—what he wants to believe—about the identity of his benefactor.

You can open the book at random and find that the scene you are reading is thematically and structurally related to every other scene in the book, and functions like a column or beam to support the whole. Take, for example, Pip's visit, in chapter nineteen, to Uncle Pumblechook, the self-important dealer in corn and seeds who so often takes false credit for Pip's good fortune that, by the end, he seems convinced that he *is* actually responsible. Earlier, Pumblechook's treatment of Pip has ranged from dismissive to mocking to abusive, reminding us how much of the novel (how much of Dickens's fiction) deals with the mistreatment and powerlessness of children.

During the Christmas dinner, interrupted by the arrival of the soldiers hunting for Magwitch, Pumblechook regales the company by speculating on what would have happened if Pip had been born a pig: "Dunstable the butcher would have come up to you as you lay in your straw, and he would have whipped you under his left arm, and with his right he would have tucked up his frock to get a penknife out of his waistcoat-pocket, and he would have shed your blood and had your life." Like almost everyone at the start of the book, Pumblechook feels free to manhandle the boy; one measure of young Pip's helplessness is how often he is touched against his will and roughed up by the adults. When Pip visits, Pumblechook feeds him crumbs, waters his milk, and compulsively and punitively quizzes him on the multiplication tables so that "his conversation consisted of nothing but arithmetic."

Inevitably, we are reminded of all this by the enormous change that occurs in Pumblechook when Pip, now under the protection of his mysterious benefactor, appears at his door in the finery newly acquired from the tailor and haberdasher. The former adult bully has been transformed into the obsequious peer and "dear friend." Instead of pulling Pip from his chair and crudely rumpling his hair, Pumblechook grasps both of the boy's hands in his; instead of starving him on a diet of crumbs and watered milk, Pumblechook offers him a choice of chicken or tongue, "one or two little things had round from the Boar, that I hope you may not despise." Instead of reminding Pip of how fortunate he is to have enjoyed the harsh child-rearing practices of Mrs. Joe, Pumblechook invites Pip to look down upon the simpletons who have raised him.

So many of the novel's themes—the powerlessness of children, the supreme importance of class, the ways in which our real or perceived social standing affects the ways in which we are treated—are evoked in this scene, which ends with a passage that reveals a great deal about Pip's character: specifically, his dangerous susceptibility to the seductions of flattery and kindness, no matter how false or ill intentioned.

> *Then he asked me tenderly if I remembered our boyish games at sums, and how we had gone together to have me bound apprentice, and, in effect, how he had ever been my favorite fancy and my chosen friend? If I had taken ten times as many glasses of wine as I had, I should have known that he never stood in that relation towards me, and should in my heart of hearts have repudiated the idea. Yet for all that, I remember feeling convinced that I had been much mistaken in him, and that he was a sensible, practical, good-hearted, prime fellow.*

In addition to all this, the scene of Pumblechook's metamorphosis from tormentor to toady is extraordinarily funny. For, as Dickens promised Forster, there is plenty of humor in *Great Expectations*—sly turns of phrase, satirical observations, entertaining disasters such as the dismal performance of *Hamlet* that Pip and Herbert attend.

Often, in his work, Dickens—who hated disorderly households and was obliged to live in one as long as he remained with his understandably harried wife—finds great hilarity in depicting domestic chaos. Here, the joke is at the expense of the family of Matthew Pocket, whose wife is so obsessed with social position that Flopson and Millers, her inattentive servants, have assumed complete command of the home, much to the disadvantage of the neglected and imperiled baby.

> *Mr. Pocket was out lecturing; for he was a most delightful lecturer on domestic economy, and his treatises on the management of children and servants were considered the very best text-books on those themes. But Mrs. Pocket was at home, and was in a little difficulty, on account of the baby's having been accommodated with a needle-case to keep him quiet during the unaccountable absence (with a relative in the Foot Guards) of Millers. And more needles were missing than it could be regarded as quite wholesome for a patient of such tender years either to apply externally or to take as a tonic.*

There is much to be laughed at chez Matthew Pocket, and in a city and countryside populated by genial clowns, blowhards, and poseurs. But for all of its humor, *Great Expectations* is, as I have said, an intensely sad book. Dickens famously changed the ending on the advice of his friend and colleague Edward Bulwer-Lytton, who proposed altering the last meeting between Pip and Estella from an obviously final conversation to a more hopeful scene in which Pip takes Estella's hand and sees "no shadow of another parting from her." Even so, we feel that this ending, unlike that of *David Copperfield* or *Little Dorrit*, is not the sort of conclusion that allows us to cheer a happy couple's ultimate emergence from adversity and darkness into harmony and light.

Despite the changed ending, we feel that Pip has lost Estella, just as he has lost his money, the care and help of Magwitch, and everything he might conceivably desire or value. What makes it all the more heartbreaking is that he had sacrificed all this largely because of his own faults and failings, most of which he is conscious of but powerless to change: cowardice, snobbishness, thoughtlessness, disloyalty, misplaced ambition, and the complete lack of any idea of what it might mean to love someone and be loved in a way that goes beyond the adolescent pangs of unrequited longing.

At the same time, we notice (and it's one of the wonders of the book) that none of this makes him any less understandable and sympathetic. In his dealings with Magwitch, near the end of the novel, he develops and demonstrates a new capacity (or perhaps just shows an untapped one) for sacrifice, gratitude, and compassion. But it's too little, too late. Pip jumps into the Thames to save Magwitch, just as Dickens jumped in, with his novel, to save *All the Year Round*. Dickens did better than his hero: the magazine lasted till the end of his life, and he bequeathed it to his son Charley.

Throughout his career, Dickens worked and reworked the question of class mobility, seen from within and without, a topic with which he was intimately and painfully familiar. One of the most affecting scenes in *Little Dorrit* occurs when its heroine, having recently come into money, is on her way to Italy and struggling to reconcile her present incarnation with her recent past life as the angel of the Marshalsea debtors' prison. Part of the scene's power derives from our sense that Dickens is writing autobiographically, that he knows all too well how confusing and disorienting it is to have been poor—and to become wealthy.

But Little Dorrit is a good poor girl, and later a good rich one, whereas Pip is the creation of a writer who has learned that even the best of us may act from motives that mix decency with selfishness, irresponsibility, shallowness, pettiness, and desperation. For all his great expectations, for all his dreams and hopes and fears, Pip is never going to be anyone but himself—and that's a problem.

Society is another problem, as are class divisions and institutional lying. But Pip's life, we feel, could have turned out more happily, or at least more satisfyingly, if he hadn't so readily bought into the richest desires, the brightest baubles, the least rewarding or worthy behaviors.

The fate that keeps our higher selves bashing against the prison walls of our small, ignoble impulses is a difficult reality for anyone to absorb. And even as the novel draws us in, enthralls and amuses us, it's always a little melancholy to watch Pip compelled to face those aspects of his personality that we know he will have to confront. I've often wondered why *Great Expectations* should have become one of the two Dickens novels (along with *A Tale of Two Cities*) most often assigned to high-school-age students. Perhaps because it's one of his shorter books, among the most tightly plotted.

Actually, kids *should* read it—and keep on rereading it throughout their adulthood. It's fun, it's got an engaging plot, it's smart and beautifully written. We feel we would have been among those nineteenth-century readers who returned, in droves, to buying the weekly issues of *All the Year Round*. In addition, it's a novel that gives us plenty to ponder. It's never too early or too late to meditate on the subject of what Pip discovers about the extent to which his all-too-human nature has affected the odds of his ever getting, or even knowing, what he wants from the world.

4

Honoré de Balzac, *Cousin Bette*

READING THE FIRST CHAPTER OF *COUSIN BETTE* IS LIKE entering a foreign city that seems eerily like our own—and turning a corner and coming upon a brutal mugging in progress. Few novels have more violent beginnings, though the violence is all psychological and, seen from a distance, by a casual observer, may even pass for polite conversation.

The fierceness of Balzac's courage and his reckless determination to portray the human comedy precisely as he saw it become clear when we consider how few contemporary writers would risk beginning a work of fiction with a scene so repulsive, and so brave in its refusal to hint or promise that, by the novel's conclusion, sin will be punished, virtue rewarded, and redemption freely offered to the wicked and the innocent alike.

Eloquently translated by Kathleen Raine, *Cousin Bette* portrays a world in which almost everyone will do anything to anyone if sex and money are at stake, a milieu in which sex is routinely traded for money, a society in which friendships and alliances are forged to advance the most immoral motives, and in which only fools and martyrs are deluded enough to follow the outmoded promptings of honor, loyalty, and conscience.

Published in 1847, *Cousin Bette* was composed (as always, at breakneck speed) near the end of a prodigiously prolific career that produced nearly a hundred novels, novellas, and short stories. By then, Balzac had mastered the technical skill and the brilliant, glee-ful assurance with which, at the start of *Cousin Bette*, he portrays the meeting between Monsieur Crevel and the Baroness Adeline Hulot—two Parisians with little in common except for the rapidity with which their social status has changed.

The former owner of a perfume shop, Celestin Crevel is a vul-gar opportunist and libertine who has manipulated the fluid politi-cal climate and new atmosphere of social mobility to propel his rise along the shady margins of Parisian society. By the time the novel opens, in 1838, Crevel is already an ex–deputy mayor and wears the ribbon of a chevalier of the Legion of Honor. At once more dramatic and more deserved, Adeline Hulot's ascent has, alas, proved more temporary. For some years after her beauty and dignity persuaded the Baron Hulot to marry her, despite her lowly Alsatian-peasant origins, she enjoyed a brief interlude of marital bliss. But now her beloved husband has succumbed to a tragic flaw that today—when practically every child is conversant with the latest psychological syndromes—would doubtless be diagnosed as a world-class case of sexual addiction.

The baron's obsessive tendency to fall madly in love with, and subsequently enslave himself to, paradoxically cheap and expensive women has brought his family to near ruin. And though Adeline is aware that "for twenty years Baron Hulot had been unfaithful," she has "kept a leaden screen in front of her eyes" and has chosen not to know the details until Crevel visits her at home and puts his terms very plainly: unless Adeline (who, at forty-eight, is still a beauty) agrees to sleep with him, her adored daughter, Hortense, will never marry, because Crevel will let everyone know that the once distinguished, once prosperous Hulots cannot afford to provide her with a dowry. And in case the faithful, long-suffering Adeline wonders how this dire situation came about, the ever thoughtful Monsieur Crevel has come to explain:

Having tired of his lover, Jenny Cadine, whom he corrupted when she was thirteen, the baron has stolen Monsieur Crevel's own mistress, Josépha, the "queen of the demimonde," an insatiably avaricious "Jewess" who has not merely "fleeced" the baron but "skinned" him to the tune of more than a hundred thousand francs. But all is not lost. If Adeline agrees to become Crevel's lover—for ten years!—Crevel will give her the money for Hortense's dowry.

This scene of breathtaking cruelty and blackmail—essentially, a rape in which both parties remain fully clothed—introduces and prefigures the themes that Balzac will develop throughout the novel: heartlessness, self-interest, meretriciousness, greed, revenge, sexual competition. The unnerving conversation between Crevel and the baroness will resonate later in the book, its echo amplified by a series of events that parallel and outdo this one in their sheer awfulness—most notably, another meeting between Adeline and Crevel, three years after the opening scene.

In this variation on the introductory chapter, the now desperate Adeline can no longer afford the luxury of virtue. She tearfully agrees to accept Monsieur Crevel's proposition, only to learn that what had originally inspired the former perfumer was not, in fact, love or lust (motives for which there is much to be said, though perhaps not in this instance) but rather the darker, unhealthier, and even less sympathetic desire for revenge: specifically, revenge on her husband for having stolen Josépha. And now that Crevel has liberally helped himself to the favors of the baron's newest obsession—the scheming, ambitious, and apparently irresistible Madame Marneffe, a civil servant's wife who turns out to be more skillful and greedier than the most successful courtesans—Crevel no longer feels the compulsion to seduce and possess the baron's wife.

Such summaries omit the telling details, the sharp observations, the nearly unbearable conversations, the sudden switches in argument and reasoning that portray precisely the nature of both participants, and the clever parallels that connect apparently dissimilar incidents and characters. Having earlier observed Madame Marneffe completing her calculatedly seductive toilette, we subsequently watch Adeline attempt something similar, only to ruin it when she reddens her nose by crying a torrent of real tears, as opposed to the few attractive droplets that Madame Marneffe would have shed. Correspondences such as these serve as cornerstones in the novel's satisfying and surprisingly (given its interest in the consequences of uncontrolled lust and passion) orderly formal structure.

Summarizing the two parallel scenes helps us see what underlies the architecture and the spirit of the novel: the resolve and, again, the sheer bravery required to begin a book with an example of repugnant behavior and then have the general tone of events and the prevailing standards of conduct go pretty much straight downhill from there. As the plot progresses, vengefulness, greed, and unfeeling ambition are passed, like some sort of evil baton, from one to another of the small but undeservedly successful group of schemers and villains, both minor and major, that populate the novel.

Lurking on the edges of the Hulot family parlor, a room that stubbornly clings to gentility despite the frayed upholstery that Crevel helpfully points out, is Cousin Bette, a vengeful and resentful relative of Adeline's. Unimpressed and unmollified by the sexual, marital, and financial humiliations to which her cousin is at the moment being subjected, the poor relation is utterly consumed by envy of Adeline's privileged existence. Balzac dispatches Cousin Bette in a few swift, brutal strokes:

> Lisbeth Fischer . . . was far from being a beauty like her cousin; for which reason she had been tremendously jealous of her. Jealousy

formed the basis of her character, with all its eccentricities. . . .
A Vosges peasant woman in all senses of the word—thin, dark,
her hair black and stringy, with thick eyebrows meeting in a tuft,
long, strong arms, flat feet, with several moles on her long simian
face—such, in brief, was the appearance of this old maid.

Though she long ago "gave up all idea of competing with or rivaling her cousin . . . envy remained hidden in her secret heart, like the germ of a disease that is liable to break out and ravage a city if the fatal bale of wool in which it is hidden is ever opened."

In fact, Bette proves capable of one of the book's few acts of generosity and devotion: her support of, and attachment to, the gifted and impecunious Polish sculptor Wenceslas Steinbock. Thus she shows herself to be, like so many of Balzac's most memorable characters, full of contradictions, immensely complex, and capable of great extremes—that is to say, she is a recognizable, plausible human, whose humanity we must acknowledge, however much we might wish to disown it.

In any case, when Bette's outwardly disinterested but, at heart, possessive love for Wenceslas is thwarted, the "germ" does eventually break out, and the scorned Cousin Bette unleashes a fury that indeed outdoes hell's. Bette sets in motion her evil plans for the unfortunate Hulot family—a campaign whose chances for success are dramatically improved when Bette's neighbor, Madame Marneffe, realizes that the erotomaniacal Hulot is the perfect stepping-stone to assist her on her way to great wealth and social position, at least in the demimonde.

Thus Balzac demonstrates that greed and wickedness are equal opportunity employers, willing to make use of the services of a pretty married woman, an unattractive unmarried one, and an assortment of male characters, from the insufferable Crevel to the pathetic Monsieur Marneffe, who readily prostitutes his wife in the hopes of a modest career advancement.

From various motives, none of them good, these men and women conspire to impoverish and destroy Baron Hulot and his family. Of course, none of their schemes could succeed were it not for the baron's own weakness. Yet Balzac seems to display a certain, perhaps grudging or involuntary, sympathy for a lover of women whose taste runs the gamut from hardened courtesans to preadolescent girls. Or perhaps the scene in which we watch Madame Marneffe prepare to make her conquests, and the rapidity with which even the uxorious Wenceslas succumbs to her charms, is meant to imply that no male (least of all one like Hulot) can successfully hope to resist the meticulously constructed, accurately targeted sexual allure of certain women.

One almost suspects that Balzac can't help admiring a man who, like himself, possesses monumental appetites and energies, however misdirected. This suspicion reminds us, in turn, of the profound ambivalence that drove Balzac, who may have been the most obsessive shopper, collector, speculator—and (with the possible exception of Dostoyevsky and his gambling losses) debtor—in the history of world literature, to condemn, in novel after novel, a society that overvalues and worships the power of money. Balzac's personal familiarity with the vice against which he most vehemently railed cannot help but add to the reader's impression that the failings of his most unforgivable characters are, finally, only human.

Ultimately, what's most shocking and inspiring about *Cousin Bette* is its sheer relentlessness, the steely mercilessness on the part of the author, which echoes and at moments even exceeds the pitiless schadenfreude of its title character. What hope does the novel offer? Not much, at least not for these individuals and their society. Throughout the book, women steal each other's husbands, men steal each other's mistresses, and everyone—male and female alike—conspires to steal one another's money. Generosity and virtue are repaid with humiliation, betrayal, and the opportunity to discover some devastating piece of personal information. Certainly that is Adeline's fate, from that first interview with Crevel to the book's conclusion, when—having devoted herself to a form of charitable social work that furthers the institution of marriage, an institution that has ruined her life—she receives, as her earthly reward, the chance to see for herself the depths to which her husband has descended.

Nowadays, when critics make sure that the novelist understands the crucial importance of creating characters the reader can sympathize and identify with, approve of and like, when the book-buying public insists upon plots in which obstacles are overcome and hardships prove instructive, in which goodness and kindness are recognized and rewarded, few novelists would have the nerve to author a book as unsparing (and, for that reason, as exalting) as *Cousin Bette*. Reading Balzac's masterpiece reminds us of the reasons why we need great literature: for aesthetic pleasure and enjoyment, beauty and truth, for the opportunity to enter the mind of another, for information about the temporal and the eternal. And for the opportunity to read about things that we may be reluctant to acknowledge but that we recognize, despite that reluctance, as true.

So much of what Balzac tells us has by now become much more difficult, indeed practically impossible (or impermissible), for us to admit to ourselves, or to say: the fact that the poor and the ugly might envy the beautiful and the rich, that our craving for sex and money is so powerful and so anarchic that it can defeat, with hardly a struggle, our better instincts and good judgment. Balzac, who knew about all these things from personal experience, continues to remind us, in novels such as *Cousin Bette*, what we humans are capable of—that is to say, what we are.

5

George Eliot, *Middlemarch*

EVER SINCE *MIDDLEMARCH* WAS PUBLISHED—IN EIGHT
installments that appeared over the course of a year, beginning
in December 1871—George Eliot's magisterial novel has not only
enthralled and delighted millions of readers but has also received
some of literary history's most enthusiastic and passionate tributes
from other writers. When asked what she thought of the book, Emily Dickinson replied, in a letter to her cousin, "'What do I think
of *Middlemarch*?' What do I think of glory?" In an essay on George
Eliot, Virginia Woolf called *Middlemarch* "magnificent . . . one of
the few English novels written for grown-up people"—an often
quoted, though odd, phrase, if only because, as the writer and critic
Rebecca Mead has pointed out, it is a phrase that a child might use
to describe an adult reading experience.

"No Victorian novel," wrote V. S. Pritchett, "approaches *Middlemarch* in its width of reference, its intellectual power, or the
imperturbable spaciousness of its narrative. . . . I doubt if any Victorian novelist has as much to teach the modern novelists as George
Eliot . . . No writer has ever represented the ambiguities of moral

choice so fully." Iris Murdoch praised Eliot's "godlike capacity for so respecting and loving her characters as to make them exist as free and separate human beings."

Julian Barnes told an interviewer from *The Paris Review* that "*Middlemarch* is probably the greatest English novel," while Martin Amis described it as "a novel without weaknesses" that "renews itself for every generation." Indeed, the way in which *Middlemarch* does seem perpetually to renew itself, to take on new meanings that reflect and speak to the experience, the age, and the mood of the reader, is the subject of a book, *My Life in Middlemarch*, in which Rebecca Mead describes first encountering the novel when she was seventeen, then again in her twenties, then returning to it in her forties when, like George Eliot, she found herself caring for stepchildren.

What *is* so captivating and enduring about this sprawling novel of more than eight hundred pages, a novel that is not only physically heavy, and weighty in every other way, but also, as Virginia Woolf points out, partly if not completely lacking in a certain sort of charm? Though the novel contains flashes of wit and humor, it only rarely offers us the fun that we enjoy in the company of Thackeray, Austen, or Dickens. What could Emily Dickinson have meant by "glory"? What *is* a novel for grown-up people? And why, like Mead, do readers keep going back to it and each time find a different book: a novel about a period that had been gone for decades before Eliot brought it back to life on the page, but whose characters are continually having experiences and confronting situations that seem so much like the experiences and situations we may find ourselves facing now?

How, we wonder, does an author who died in 1880 know as much as or more about our inner conflicts and struggles as our closest loved ones intuit, as much as we and our therapists labor to discover?

———

HERE is Virginia's Woolf's crisp, eloquent, sympathetic, and ever so slightly snobbish account of the early years of George Eliot, the pen name of the woman who was born Mary Ann Evans and who would subsequently change her name to, or at least refer to herself as, Mary Anne, Marian, Marian Evans Lewes, and, after a late-life marriage to John Cross, Mary Anne Cross: "The first volume of her life is a singularly depressing record. In it we see her rising herself with groans and struggles from the intolerable boredom of petty provincial society . . . to be the assistant editor of a highly intellectual London review."

One can easily see what Woolf meant about struggle. Mary Ann Evans consistently chose the hard road and bravely followed her principles, regardless of the consequences. She became an unbeliever and was shunned by her devoutly religious father, whom she later nursed when he was dying. With great difficulty, she translated David Strauss's *The Life of Jesus* from the German. She wrote and published sharp criticism and essays, thus becoming the sort of intellectual woman—a bluestocking—guaranteed to earn the contempt of her brother Isaac, with whom she had been close.

Writes Woolf:

> *Though we cannot read the story without a strong desire that the stages of her pilgrimage might have been made, if not more easy, at least more beautiful, there is a dogged determination in her advance upon the citadel of culture which raises it above our pity . . . She knew everyone. She read everything. Her astonishing intellectual vitality had triumphed. Youth was over, but youth had been full of suffering. Then, at the age of thirty-five, at the height of her powers, and in the fulness of her freedom, she . . . went to Weimar, alone with George Henry Lewes.*

Eliot met Lewes, a philosopher and literary critic, in a bookstore in 1851. They could not marry; Lewes already had a wife and children and was unable to obtain a legal divorce. But the couple lived and traveled together, in a harmonious partnership, until Lewes's death, in 1878. Lewes valued and encouraged Mary Ann's abilities, and the start of her life with Lewes coincided with the production of her greatest novels. *Scenes of Clerical Life* was published in 1858. A year later, *Adam Bede* appeared; the year after that, *The Mill on the Floss*. It was followed, within a few years, by the publication of *Silas Marner*, *Romola*, and *Felix Holt, the Radical*.

Eliot began working on *Middlemarch* in the late 1860s, but her work was sporadic and frequently interrupted, most shatteringly by the tragic death of Lewes's son, Thornie, who had returned from Asia with an agonizing and fatal disease of the spine. Eliot's first idea had been to focus on the country doctor who would eventually appear in *Middlemarch* as Tertius Lydgate. But after she began a short story entitled "Miss Brooke," she decided to broaden the scope of her book.

That breadth and depth may have been part of what Emily Dickinson meant by "glory": a view of the world so much wider than the dimensions of the confined space that the New England poet chose to inhabit. The citizens of Middlemarch must have been, in some ways, similar to those of Dickinson's Amherst; the political quarrels, romances, professional hopes and disappointments, the happy and unhappy marriages would surely have resembled their counterparts in a quiet western Massachusetts town.

What a woman of Dickinson's genius, ambition, and psychosocial limitations could not have failed to notice was the courage and invention with which Eliot transcended the personal and autobiographical (despite the fact that she saw something of herself in Lydgate, and in other ways resembled Dorothea Brooke) to portray an entire society: rich and poor, bankers and farmers, men of the church, doctors and auctioneers, male and female, old and young, married and single, liberal and conservative, to say nothing of the endless individual variations of character within those larger categories.

DICKENS and Thackeray had died not long before *Middlemarch* was published. Not many writers, and certainly few women, were announcing their intention to put the whole world, or a fully realized corner of the world, onto the printed page. Yet Eliot was clearly determined to portray the entirety of Middlemarch. Around the time that Lydgate—the ambitious young doctor and outsider—makes his appearances in the novel, a brief consideration of destiny segues into the subject of social mobility in the provinces during the decade in which the book is set:

> *Old provincial society had its share of this subtle movement: had not only its striking downfalls, its brilliant young professional dandies who ended by living up an entry with a drab and six children for their establishment, but also those less marked vicissitudes which are constantly shifting the boundaries of social intercourse, and begetting new consciousness of interdependence. Some slipped a little downward, some got higher footing: people denied aspirates, gained wealth, and fastidious gentlemen stood for boroughs; some were caught in political currents, some in ecclesiastical, and perhaps found themselves surprisingly grouped in consequence; while a few personages or families that stood with rocky firmness amid all this fluctuation, were slowly presenting new aspects in spite of solidity, and altering with the double change of self and beholder.*

So Eliot sums up an era, a place, a political climate—and sets the stage for the remainder of the novel.

This passage occurs almost an eighth of the way through the book, which until this point has been occupied largely with the subject of the fervently idealistic Dorothea Brooke and her marriage to Edward Casaubon, the withered, humorless, pompous scholar who has devoted his life to his magnum opus, *The Key to All Mythologies*—a gargantuan project with which Dorothea imagines that she will provide invaluable help.

Already we understand that this seemingly important and noble work would have a strong attraction for Dorothea. For in the novel's prelude, the brief introduction that many readers page through on their way to the start of what may seem at first (deceptively!) to be the conventional marriage plot, we have been presented with the central problem of Dorothea's life:

> *Who that cares much to know the history of man, and how the mysterious mixture behaves under the varying experiments of Time, has not dwelt, at least briefly, on the life of Saint Theresa, has not smiled with some gentleness at the thought of the little girl walking forth one morning hand-in-hand with her still smaller brother, to go and seek martyrdom in the country of the Moors? . . . That Spanish woman who lived three hundred years ago, was certainly not the last of her kind. Many Theresas have been born who found for themselves no epic life wherein there was a constant unfolding of far-resonant action; perhaps only a life of mistakes, the offspring of a certain spiritual grandeur ill-matched with the meanness of opportunity . . . Here and there is born a Saint Theresa, foundress of nothing, whose loving heart-beats and sobs after an unattained goodness tremble off and are dispersed among hindrances, instead of centring in some long-recognizable deed.*

Rereading this after finishing the novel, we cannot claim that we haven't been warned about the fate of these Saint Theresas everywhere. And yet we begin our reading each time in the hope that the saint, and her more recent incarnations, will be able to strike out on their own, to achieve what they wish, with or without their little brothers in tow.

The novel is almost a hundred pages under way before we meet its second main character, Tertius Lydgate, whose story has numerous connections and parallels to Dorothea's. Arriving in Middlemarch with the plan of using the region as a sort of testing ground and research facility for his scientific theories and modern ideas about medical practice, Lydgate also has something of the Saint Theresa in him: he is idealistic, determined, quasi-fanatical, dangerously flawed.

Eliot allows us to see Lydgate's weak points—his ambition, his vanity, his shallow judgments about women—almost as soon as we meet him. We watch him chatting with the serious, high-minded Dorothea, and, lest we suppose even momentarily that there might be anything between them beyond respectful fellow feeling, Lydgate explains why he has reservations about a woman like Dorothea, whom he finds "a little too earnest . . . It is troublesome to talk to such women. They are always wanting reasons, yet they are too ignorant to understand the merits of any question, and usually fall back on their moral sense to settle things after their own taste." A page or so later, the narrator pulls back from Lydgate's point of view to more accurately diagnose the young doctor's ideas about women: "Miss Brooke would be found wanting, notwithstanding her undeniable beauty. She did not look at things from the proper feminine angle. The society of such women was about as relaxing as going from your work to teach the second form, instead of reclining in a paradise with sweet laughs for bird-notes, and blue eyes for a heaven."

Perhaps this is the time to address the subject of George Eliot's own views on the role of women in society. Though she had close friends who were committed feminists, and though the movement had become more vocal by the time she was at work on *Middlemarch*, Eliot was not among these ardent fighters for equal rights. Here is an incisive summary of her position on women, quoted from Jennifer Uglow's marvelous, brief biography of Eliot, first published in this country in 1987 and now, regrettably, out of print:

The message for the lives of women seems to be that although change must come (preferably gradually rather than suddenly), it must not be at the expense of traditional female values. Although it is wrong for women to be excluded from access to common culture and common stores of power, they should demand them for the sake of partnership with men and for the good of society, not just for their own separate fulfillment . . . Eliot believes partnership is essential for social harmony because there are essential feminine and masculine attributes which derive from biology, cultural conditioning and individual upbringing which encourage contrasting attitudes to life.

What this means in her novels is that "the traditional roles which seem to oppress women most—the submissive daughter, the self-denying wife, the loving and patient mother—become symbols of woman's social mission. The vital thing is not to launch women into a masculine sphere, but to 'feminise' men, because the feminine strengths have for so long been trampled underfoot and undervalued."

Consequently, the domestic contentment that Dorothea achieves by the end of the novel—one of the last things we see her doing is, in effect, arranging a playdate for her child and the children of her sister Celia—is not, for Eliot, a sign of failure. Dorothea's desire to become a modern Saint Theresa was doomed to be at odds with the genuine contribution that Eliot sees her making in the form of a life of service—not service to the bogus work of scholarship on which Casaubon labored, but service to the reformist views and political career of her husband, to the household, the children, the hearth: the moral and spiritual education and improvement of her immediate circle and a few fortunate members of the next generation.

Thoughtful readers will likely suspect that there is something self-contradictory and paradoxical in Eliot giving us a female character who seems unusually forceful, reflective, and intelligent for a woman of the nineteenth century, or, for that matter, of any century—and keeping her at home. What we see by the end of the book is a woman of intense ambition, intellect, passion, and capability who is satisfied and fulfilled by a placid, loving domestic life. This is hardly the life that George Eliot herself led: traveling, receiving the accolades awarded to an extremely famous writer, holding court in her London home, hosting fellow writers and admirers who came to catch a glimpse of her or hear some words of wisdom.

If Lydgate enters into a considerably less than blissful union, it's not—in Eliot's view—because he insists on finding a sufficiently feminine woman who promises "sweet laughs" rather than intellectual companionship. Instead, it's because he chooses the wrong woman, one with no concern for the good of society, no interest in anything beyond prestige and social status, in the luxuries she can acquire, and who demonstrates none of the womanly virtues that Eliot so admired. What Rosamond Vincy—Lydgate's sweetheart and later his wife—*does* offer is one of the greatest portraits of a narcissist in English literature: a woman who believes she is irresistible, that no man can withstand her charms, and that there is no reason she should be denied either the most trivial whim or the costliest desire. She is not only shallow but vain, self-dramatizing, and false: "Every nerve and muscle in Rosamond was adjusted to the consciousness that she was being looked at. She was by nature an actress . . . she even acted her own character, and so well, that she did not know it to be precisely her own." Unlike the straightforward, impeccably honest Dorothea, Rosamond resorts to manipulation, sulking, pouting, and stubborn resistance when she fails to get her way.

As Lydgate falls more deeply into debt, in large part because of furniture and the domestic and personal expenses that Rosamond has incurred, and as his hopes for professional success, fame, and fortune fail to materialize, Rosamond proves that she is not the sympathetic helpmate he imagined, but rather a selfish creature who seems quite willing to cut him loose when it appears that he may be unable to support her in the style to which she has been accustomed.

The Lydgate marriage is not the only unhappy one in *Middlemarch*; the doctor's growing doubts about his wife and the increasing misery and discord in his household parallel that of Dorothea's marriage to Casaubon. Though they could not possibly have found two more different spouses, Dorothea and Lydgate have made similar mistakes: they have married people who will turn out to be quite unlike the people they supposed them to be. Both imagine their prospective spouses to be large-minded and quietly heroic, and subsequently find them to be petty, uncharitable, and, in their separate ways, rigid. Both Lydgate and Dorothea will make disheartening and ultimately shattering discoveries about the true natures that underlie the fantasy creatures they have wed.

READERS may feel that they know all there is to know about the Reverend Casaubon very early on, from his letter of proposal, surely one of the most chilling love letters in literature. But Dorothea's idealism—the quasi-religious enthusiasm she feels at the prospect of aiding her husband in his monumental work—blinds her to the reality of who he is, and of what his work entails, as well as its value.

It is to Eliot's credit that she cannot allow any of her characters—even the odious Casaubon and the maddening Rosamond—to remain one-dimensional. Each is given moments during which we are permitted to see the gap (or, in Casaubon's case, the abyss) between their dreams and what they have been able to achieve. In the middle of an argument during which Rosamond has at last shown her true colors, refusing to empathize with her husband or join with him in contemplating what their financial problems might mean for them both, Eliot gives Lydgate (and the reader) an opportunity, however brief and transient, to consider their descent into hardship from Rosamond's point of view. "Perhaps it was not possible for Lydgate, under the double stress of outward material difficulty and of his own proud resistance to humiliating consequences, to imagine fully what this sudden trial was to a young creature who had known nothing but indulgence, and whose dreams had all been of new indulgence, more exactly to her taste."

Earlier in the novel, during a quarrel between Dorothea and Casaubon, Eliot demonstrates the same insistence on presenting both sides, regardless of how likely we are to favor the beautiful, loving, humiliated wife over the harsh, self-important stick of a husband:

> She was as blind to his inward troubles as he to hers: she had not yet learned those hidden conflicts in her husband which claim our pity. She had not yet listened patiently to his heart-beats, but only felt that her own was beating violently. . . . Mr. Casaubon had a sensitiveness to match Dorothea's, and an equal quickness to imagine more than the fact. He had formerly observed with approbation her capacity for worshipping the right object; he now foresaw with sudden terror that this capacity might be replaced by presumption, this worship by the most exasperating of all criticism,—that which sees vaguely a great many fine ends, and has not the least notion what it costs to reach them.

If we go back and reread Casaubon's chilling letter of proposal, we find a rather complicated mixture of pomposity, self-regard, and insecurity. He begins by citing Dorothea's ability to fill a need in his own life, her capacity for "devotedness," and his hope that she is perfectly suited to help with "a work too special to be abdicated." But he ends by somewhat obliquely acknowledging the difference in their ages and describing the emotions with which he waits for her reply: "I await the expression of your sentiments with an anxiety which it would be the part of wisdom (were it possible) to divert by a more arduous labour than usual. But in this order of experience I am still young, and in looking forward to an unfavourable possibility I cannot but feel that resignation to solitude will be more difficult after the temporary illumination of hope."

With the exception of the unfailingly selfless, patient, and honest Mary Garth and her industrious mother and younger siblings, nearly all the characters in *Middlemarch* have their virtues and their flaws; though, as we may have noticed, in some people the balance tips further toward one side than the other. The vast majority of characters contain a mixture of the admirable and the foolish, the selfish and the selfless, and (in the case of Bulstrode) the penitent, the generous, the secretive, and the reprehensible.

This, too, may be part of what Woolf meant when she said that this was a novel for "grown-up people." Unlike children, with their innocent faith in good guys and bad guys, adults are more likely to understand that to divide our fellow humans into two categories— angelic heroes and devilish villains—is, in most cases, to oversimplify and underestimate human psychology. Often Eliot seems to know more about her characters than they know about themselves, yet somehow this does not diminish them or make them seem lacking in self-awareness, or deluded. She understands how much we can bear to know about ourselves at any one time, and how difficult we find it to admit that we have made serious—and perhaps irremediable—mistakes.

Nearly everyone in *Middlemarch* makes mistakes—yet another truth about adult life that Woolf would have recognized. They marry the wrong people. They champion the wrong side in an argument. They ally themselves with supporters whose patronage is compromised by self-interest or tainted by a past crime that must be hidden, at all costs. And though some of the wrongs can be righted—Dorothea is rescued from her disastrous choice by the death of Casaubon— others (like Lydgate's marriage) are beyond help, incapable of being fixed. Some of the most uncomfortable and painful sections of the novel occur when we watch its central characters realizing how badly they have misjudged a person or a situation—and beginning to fear that they may have ruined their lives.

Unlike other, equally brilliant but rather more charming and comforting novels (the work of Jane Austen comes to mind), *Middlemarch* is a book in which, again with lifelike accuracy, only a small minority of the characters get what they want. And most must settle for some compromise that promises a reasonable measure of satisfaction and happiness, if there is to be any at all.

THE last paragraph of the novel is worth quoting, for its eloquence and for the sheer force of George Eliot's ambivalence about what a person—a woman, in particular—can and should expect from life.

> *Dorothea herself had no dreams of being praised above other women, feeling that there was always something better which she might have done, if she had only been better and known better. . . . [But] no life would have been possible for Dorothea which was not filled with emotion, and she had now a life filled also with a beneficent activity which she had not the doubtful pains of discovering and marking out for herself. . . . Many who knew her, thought it a pity that so substantive and rare a creature should have been absorbed into the life of another, and be only known in certain circles as a wife and mother. But no one stated exactly what else that was in her power she ought rather to have done . . . Her finely touched spirit had still its fine issues, though they were not widely visible. Her full nature . . . spent itself in channels which had no great name on the earth. But the effect of her being on those around her was incalculably diffusive: for the growing good of the world is partly dependent on unhistoric acts; and that*

things are not so ill with you and me as they might have been is
half owing to the number who lived faithfully a hidden life, and
rest in unvisited tombs.

Whatever one imagines that one's life is going to be, how often
one is mistaken, how one's life ultimately turns out—that story, different for each character and each reader, is only one of the stories
for grown-up people that *Middlemarch* tells. Another is the eternally
timely, relevant, and interesting story of the unending conflict between ambition and conscience.

Much of what happens to Lydgate transpires in this arena, and
his decisions about these matters are ultimately more destructive
than his unwise choice of a wife. Rather than spoil one of the novel's critical plot points, I'll refrain from recounting the details of
an essential scene that occurs a little less than a quarter of the way
through—and from which everything that happens to Lydgate
thereafter could be said to proceed. All I will say is that it's an in-
formal election to decide who will get the chaplaincy of the charity
hospital that Mr. Bulstrode plans to establish. There are two candidates. Lydgate has certain reasons (friendship, preference, good
judgment) for voting for one man, and other reasons (a sense of
what Bulstrode wants) for voting for the other.

It's a quiet scene, a vote about a relatively insignificant religious-
political matter, in a country district. But the scene is so well written, so elegantly paced, and, finally, so startling that it may take the
reader a while to recover from what it tells us about Lydgate—and
what it may suggest about us and the people we know. Perhaps that
is partly because grown-up people may recall a similar choice that
occurred in the course of their own lives, or one that they read or
heard about or witnessed. Certainly, such moments are what V. S.
Pritchett had in mind when he wrote of Eliot, "No writer has ever
represented the ambiguities of moral choice so fully."

Middlemarch is rich with plot turns and incidents of this sort. The result is a novel written for grown-up people, thoughtful, complicated, gloriously expansive and old-fashioned, and at the same time as modern and timely as anything we may experience or observe.

6

George Gissing, *New Grub Street*

I WAS HALFWAY THROUGH READING *NEW GRUB STREET*—IN fact, I had brought the book with me—when I happened to sit down for lunch at a neighborhood restaurant in downtown Manhattan. The tables were so close that it took only a few moments for me to gather (it was impossible to avoid overhearing) that the young man and woman at the table beside mine were in the book-publishing business. All through their meal, they exchanged, with breathless intensity, the latest literary gossip: which editor had been hired by which house, which agent now represented which writer, how disappointed a famous biographer was over his new book's lukewarm reception, who had reviewed whose novel (so nastily!) in an influential journal.

There is, as far as I know, no word for the peculiar sensation (it most nearly resembles déjà vu) of having read a passage of dialogue in a novel (especially one written more than a century ago) and going out into the world and hearing that same dialogue issuing from the lips of living, breathing human beings. But such was my experience on that otherwise ordinary afternoon as I eavesdropped on two strangers who were not merely echoing but almost precisely repeating the tropes, the rhythms, the substance of the talks in which George Gissing's characters engage—tirelessly, obsessively— throughout his 1891 novel.

If one purpose of fiction is to remind us of how much remains the same despite superficial changes in manners and customs and regardless of the passage of time, *New Grub Street* fulfills that function perfectly. All these years after its composition, it still seems like reportage, faithful to its moment and descriptive of our own. Gissing's novel is one of those books that confirm our gloomiest suspicions and most dismaying observations about the nature of the larger world in general, and the literary world in particular; and yet there is always something perversely affirming and encouraging about such confirmation. *New Grub Street* is a marvelously brave book in its refusal to equivocate about the darkness it perceives, its vision of the essential baseness of human motivation. The marvel is that it manages to be, at the same time, so engrossing, so entertaining, so well made, and—in its ability to take us out of ourselves and convey us to another realm that so eerily resembles our own—so unexpectedly cheering.

There's something immensely endearing about the person who emerges from the facts of Gissing's biography. The impecunious son of a pharmacist, he received a scholarship to Owens College, Manchester, and seemed headed for brilliant success—a promise he effectively scuttled, at the age of nineteen, by stealing money to help reform a prostitute named Nell Harrison. His impulsive, reckless, youthful behavior suggests the sort of conduct one might expect from any gifted, rebellious, and fiercely idealistic teenager of today. Clearly, no one could have been less like *New Grub Street*'s coldly calculating and self-serving Jasper Milvain than the young Gissing, who, after being expelled from school and serving a month in prison, left for America, where he supported himself by teaching and writing short stories. On his return to England, a modest bequest from an aunt enabled him to marry Nell Harrison—a predictably disastrous union that lasted only four years.

Gissing's literary fortunes were not much happier than his romantic ones. *New Grub Street* was his ninth book, and though it was more favorably reviewed and popular than his previous works, he failed to profit much from its success, having sold the copyright outright to his publishers. It did, however, establish his literary reputation and enable him to write himself out of the grinding poverty he had been enduring. According to his diary, Gissing made seven false starts on *New Grub Street*, then began yet again and managed to complete the novel in two months.

Perhaps that's why the novel has such an air of urgency and immediacy, the sense of an author so eager to tell us what he knows and wants to say that a considerable portion of the book's plot is foreshadowed and encapsulated within the very first chapter. Like the (similarly wicked and sobering) novels of Ivy Compton-Burnett, this one begins at the breakfast table, with what we are led to believe is a typically rancorous conversation between Jasper Milvain and his two sisters, Maud and Dora. It's one of many unpleasant family chats in a novel that fails to provide one single example of domestic sweetness, harmony, or accord, but rather presents us with a virtual panorama of the brutal hells that can—and do—exist between husbands and wives, parents and children, unloving and competitive siblings. The first sound we hear is the tolling of church bells, followed by Jasper remarking, somewhat unnecessarily but with great "cheerfulness," that "there's a man being hanged in London at this moment."

What Jasper—who is not merely a shallow, soulless opportunist but also a consummate narcissist—finds so inspiriting is the thought that this sad fate is not happening to him, a response that Maud correctly diagnoses as symptomatic of "your selfish way of looking at things." Soon enough, the arrival of a letter from Milvain's friend Edwin Reardon turns the conversation to the current situation: this struggling novelist, who—Milvain rather breezily predicts—will ultimately have no choice but to poison or shoot himself. In fact, though Reardon will briefly consider suicide, it will be Harold Biffen—an even more hapless author who, as Milvain says of Reardon, lacks the adaptive and practical skills required to turn writing into a "paying business"—who will eventually poison himself.

After foreseeing this dire fate for his friend, Milvain happily ("The enjoyment with which he anticipates it!" comments Maud) goes on to suggest that Reardon's marriage will come to grief, since his "handsome wife," an acquisition that Milvain envies, has already refused to "go into modest rooms—they must furnish a flat." And lest the reader still fails to grasp the profound and essential dissimilarities between the two friends, Milvain plainly spells them out:

> He is the old type of unpractical artist; I am the literary man of 1882. He won't make concessions, or rather, he can't make them; he can't supply the market. . . . I am learning my business. Literature nowadays is a trade. . . . Your successful man of letters . . . thinks first and foremost of the markets; when one kind of goods begins to go off slackly, he is ready with something new and appetising.

Jasper goes on to espouse his decidedly unromantic view of love and marriage ("When I have a decent income of my own, I shall marry a woman with an income somewhat larger, so that casualties may be provided for"). There follows a somewhat more specific discussion of probable inheritances and financial prospects, and finally a speech that falls somewhere between a rousing, visionary sermon on the subject of the state of literature and the sleaziest sort of self-justification: "I maintain that we people of brains are justified in supplying the mob with the food it likes. We are not geniuses, and if we sit down in a spirit of long-eared gravity we shall produce only commonplace stuff. Let us use our wits to earn money, and make the best we can of our lives."

And there it is; there it all is. For Jasper is not merely a hack writer but a sort of prophet—a man with impeccable instincts about the debased and degraded (though, in his view, glorious) future that awaits him, his family, and his friends. As the novel progresses, events will transpire more or less as he predicts in this initial conversation. The only surprise lies in seeing how it all goes down and in discovering that the reality of *New Grub Street* is even grimier and less attractive than Jasper Milvain's repugnant calculations.

Anyone who has ever written, or considered writing, or who has the faintest interest in literary gossip will find much in *New Grub Street* that is all too familiar. Here, for example, is Whelpdale describing plans for a foolproof moneymaking scheme, a guide to "novel-writing taught in ten lessons":

> *The first lesson deals with the question of subjects, local colour— that kind of thing. I gravely advise people, if they possibly can, to write of the wealthy middle class; that's the popular subject, you know. Lords and ladies are all very well, but the real thing to take is a story about people who have no titles, but live in good Philistine style. I urge study of horsey matters especially.*

Both Milvain and Reardon and their colleagues are almost constantly (if from very different perspectives) discussing the fact that success has less to do with the intrinsic value of a book than with a writer's social position and connections, with the ability to give and attend elegant dinners and parties—the sort of activities that now fall under the rubric of "networking."

Literary ambition, disappointment, rancor, jealousy, and despair are presented with chilling accuracy. Reardon and his creator know exactly how it feels to receive a rejection letter. ("Mr. Jedwood regretted that the story offered to him did not seem likely to please

that particular public to whom his series of one-volume novels
made appeal. He hoped it would be understood that, in declining,
he by no means expressed an adverse judgment on the story itself,
&c." And anyone who has ever worked in magazine publishing will
cringe upon reading Whelpdale's opinion on the best way to ac-
commodate the culture's rapidly shrinking attention span:

> I would have the paper address itself to the quarter-educated . . .
> the young men and women who can just read, but are incapa-
> ble of sustained attention. . . . What they want is the lightest
> and frothiest of chit-chatty information—bits of stories, bits of
> description, . . . bits of statistics, bits of foolery. . . . Everything
> must be very short, two inches at the utmost; their attention can't
> sustain itself beyond two inches. Even chat is too solid for them:
> they want chit-chat.

Yet Gissing's analysis of the literary scene is only part of his
vision of the larger society, a world ruled by greed and money and
wholly determined by the interests and pressures of social class.
His feeling for—and his ability to represent—the nuances of class
difference is pitch-perfect. Indeed, one of the subthemes of the
novel is the inherent difficulty, the problems and perils occasioned
by marrying across class lines, a subject that Gissing presumably
knew about from painful personal experience. Some of the book's
most affecting scenes involve the hideousness of domestic life chez
Alfred Yule, the numerous instances in which Yule (who has married considerably "beneath him") patronizes, punishes, and blames
his innocent, good-hearted, long-suffering wife for the failure of his
own ambitions and hopes. Unsurprisingly, he fears that his daughter, Marian, may be

> infected with her mother's faults of speech and behaviour. He
> would scarcely permit his wife to talk to the child. . . . And so it

came to pass that one day the little girl, hearing her mother make
some flagrant grammatical error, turned to the other parent and
asked gravely: "Why doesn't mother speak as properly as we do?"
Well, that is one of the results of such marriages, one of the myr-
iad miseries that result from poverty.

So *New Grub Street* painstakingly documents the "myriad miseries" of a world in which class snobbery is as powerful—and as
primal—as some sort of alternate life force, a world in which the
struggle for survival hardly, if ever, takes the form of physical com-
bat but rather of scheming, calculation, and, especially, psychological manipulation. Few writers are as attuned as Gissing was to the
ways in which we manipulate one another for our own self-serving
purposes; one of the book's most subtle and artfully orchestrated
scenes is the one in which Jasper rather brilliantly maneuvers Marian into breaking off their engagement.

The ultimate irony of *New Grub Street* is, of course, that a novel
that so gloomily and confidently predicts certain failure for any
work that does not distract, amuse, lie, and flatter its "quarter-
educated" audience has, in fact, not only succeeded and survived
but become a classic. The triumph, for Gissing, was to have written
a book that tells the truth as he saw it—the bitter truth, without
sugarcoating—and to have found so durable and wide an audience.
Even as the novel chills us with its still recognizable portrayal of
the crass and vulgar world of literary endeavor, its very existence
provides eloquent, encouraging proof of the fact that a powerful,
honest writer can transcend the constraints of commerce, can
speak louder than the clamor of the marketplace. How inspiring
and comforting that a voice as clear and pure as Gissing's has managed to rise above the static and buzz that, he seemed to fear, might
keep it from being heard at all.

7

The Collected Stories
of Mavis Gallant

FOR THIRTY YEARS, I HAVE BEEN TEACHING LITERATURE TO college undergraduates and graduate students. And every semester—except on those rare occasions when the subject of the class has been too narrowly focused to include Mavis Gallant's fiction—I have taught at least one, sometimes two, of her stories.

This is partly for selfish reasons. There are few writers whose work gives me so much pleasure to read to a group—in this case, a group of students. What a joy it is to hear, translated into my own voice and rhythms, the crispness and grace of Gallant's sentences; the sparkle of her wit; the accuracy of her descriptions. How satisfying to pretend, if only for a few moments, that the sensible, capacious, no-nonsense humanity of her vision of the world is my own.

In addition, I feel a kind of messianic zeal, which I share with many writers and readers, to make sure that Gallant's work continues to be read, admired—and loved. One can speculate about the possible reasons why she is not more universally known. Though her work appeared regularly and for decades (from the 1950s until the mid-1990s) in *The New Yorker*, where it attracted a loyal and enthusiastic readership, Gallant, who died in 2014, never became quite as popular, as widely recognized, or as frequently celebrated as any number of writers (John Updike would be one example) who published as regularly in the same publication over roughly the same period of time.

Perhaps the simplest explanation is that she was a Canadian short story writer, born in Montreal in 1922, living in Paris, where she worked initially as a journalist, writing in English, and publishing in the United States. It was hard for any country to claim her, to make her a public figure (which she would have resisted), or for readers to classify her as one thing or another. Things (including books) are always easier to describe when they are like something else, and it was Gallant's great strength and less than great public relations problem that her work is so unlike anyone else's. What one extracts from what (little) Gallant has said about her life is the central fact of her wanting to do what she wanted, which was to write.

Finally, the classes I teach (and this has evolved over time) are centered on close reading, on examining every word, every sentence, considering word choice, diction, tone, subtext, and so forth. Most, if not all, serious fiction rewards this, but some writers reward it more than others. And there are some writers who provide evidence for—proof of—what I find myself telling students: some fiction simply cannot be understood—on the simplest level of plot and character—unless you pay attention and concentrate on every sentence, every word.

Mavis Gallant's work demonstrates the technical daring and innovative freedom that, as in a painting by Velázquez, remain hidden unless you look closely, pay attention, and at the same time manage to surrender to the mystery of art, to the fact that it cannot be reduced, summarized, or made to seem like anything but itself. She places a huge amount of faith in her reader's intelligence, a faith that demands and rewards careful reading. But she's also very funny, and a great deal of fun. Her stories are full of satisfying reverses and breathtaking passages of dazzlingly precise, virtuosic writing.

One such story is "Mlle. Dias de Corta," which appears among the stories of the eighties and nineties in the recent reissue of *The Collected Stories of Mavis Gallant*, which was first published in 1962.

In the story, Gallant does a kind of magic trick, introducing us to a fairly unpleasant elderly Parisienne—xenophobic, passive-aggressive, self-involved, sly: a considerable range of unattractive personality traits. The story is framed as a letter addressed (though the letter can never be sent, because the narrator has no idea about what might be the correct address to send it to) to the eponymous young would-be actress who boarded with the narrator and her son decades before, and with whom the narrator's son had a brief, disastrous affair. By the time we have reached the final sentences, our heart is breaking for this woman with whom, in all likelihood, we would prefer not to spend five minutes—unless we managed to persuade ourselves that she is (as indeed she is) a member of a vanishing breed, a subject of anthropological interest.

It is necessary to read closely, to understand what this woman is saying underneath what she appears to be saying: what she wants and needs to say, what she cannot say, and why she so often chooses to say something else entirely. On our second or third or fourth reading, aspects of the story emerge, complications we may have missed earlier—for example, the exact nature of the narrator's worries about her son, Robert, and about the frostiness of their relationship. The way in which his affair with the young actress has divided him and his mother—and brought them together—may be opaque to the reader who skims rapidly through the text. Similarly, the history of the narrator's marriage and the complexities of her worrisome financial situation can be apprehended only if we slow down and attempt to fathom what is being said—and not said.

Among the incisive and revealing passages are excerpts such

as this one, from "The Moslem Wife," the first in the collection. A woman named Netta reflects on the beginning of her childhood fascination with her cousin Jack, whom she later falls in love with and eventually marries:

> *Netta curtsied to her aunt and uncle. Her eyes were on Jack. She could not read yet, though she could sift and classify attitudes. She drew near him, sucking her lower lip, her hands behind her back. For the first time she was conscious of the beauty of another child. He was younger than Netta, imprisoned in a portable-fence arrangement in which he moved tirelessly, crabwise, hanging on a barrier he could easily have climbed. . . . She heard the adults laugh and say that Jack looked like a prizefighter. She walked around his prison, staring, and the blue-eyed fighter stared back.*

Or this one, in which a desperate Paris art dealer named Sandor Speck reflects on the breakup of his marriage:

> *In his experience, love affairs and marriages perished between seven and eight o'clock, the hour of rain and no taxis. All over Paris couples must be parting forever, leaving like debris along the curbs the shreds of canceled restaurant dates, useless ballet tickets, hopeless explanations, and scraps of pride; and toward each of these disasters a taxi was pulling in, the only taxi for miles, the light on its roof already dimmed in anticipation to the twin dots that in Paris mean "occupied." But occupied by whom?*

Line by line, word by word, no one writes more compactly, more densely, with more compression. Great short stories are sometimes said to be as rich as novels. Gallant's are like encyclopedias—of her characters' psyches and lives. In a single paragraph from "Across the Bridge," Gallant tells us much of what we might ever want to know about four characters: the narrator, her parents, and the suitor,

Arnaud, to whom the narrator is engaged and whom she doesn't want to marry because she has her heart set on some totally unsuitable young man in Lille. Gallant paints four portraits so deftly and with such a light touch that we may feel she is telling us something trivial, or perhaps of no importance:

> My mother was a born coaxer and wheedler; avoided confrontation, preferring to move to a different terrain and beckon, smiling. One promised nearly anything just to keep the smile on her face. She was slim and quick, like a girl of fourteen. My father liked her in floral hats, so she still wore the floral bandeaux with their wisps of veil that had been fashionable ten years before. Papa used to tell about a funeral service where Maman had removed her hat so as to drape a mantilla over her hair. An usher, noticing the hat beside her on the pew, had placed it with the other flowers around the coffin. When I repeated the story to Arnaud he said the floral-hat anecdote was one of the world's oldest. He had heard it a dozen times, always about a different funeral. I could not see why Papa would go on telling it if it were not true, or why Maman would let him. Perhaps she was the first woman it had ever happened to.

Each narrative offers us an entire existence (we feel that if a story doesn't illuminate a whole life, Gallant was not interested in writing it) and a whole world, a milieu precisely situated in time and on the map of Europe and Quebec. She builds her fictions with moments and incidents so revealing and resonant that another writer might have made each one a separate story, and she has the nerve to include dramatic and significant events that—as so often happens in life—turn out to have unpredictably minor consequences. In "Irina," the most devastating moment—an old man bursts into tears when he recalls a heartbreak in the distant past—is one that a child half glimpses and doesn't understand. On occasion, the most influential character in the story never appears, like the irascible dead husband—and famous writer—whose oversize personality fills the background of "Irina."

No one provides more concrete and factual information (details of personal and European history and politics, of family, employment; brushstrokes that establish a city, a subculture, or a domestic constellation) while at the same time making you feel as if you suddenly understand something essential about human life, something that perhaps you always knew, though you still can't begin to express it. No one's characters (young and old, male and female, rich and poor, from at least a dozen different countries) are more meticulously rendered. The characters' specificity makes us feel simultaneously delighted, enlightened, and choked up. With a masterful control of tone that allows her to locate the perfect point on the continuum between engagement and detachment, and with a view of character at once scathing and endlessly tolerant and forgiving, Gallant displays an almost preternatural gift for making readers not meet but care profoundly about men and women and children whom they otherwise wouldn't have met and might not have chosen to know. She accepts and reveals our flawed and complex human nature without pretending that our problems have solutions, or that experience—even tragic experience—necessarily changes or improves us.

In an afterword to the *Collected Stories*, Gallant advises her readers: "Stories are not chapters of novels. They should not be read one after another, as if they were meant to follow along. Read one. Shut the book. Read something else. Come back later. Stories can wait." Such advice may be superfluous. When you finish each of Gallant's stories, it's instinctive to stop and regroup. As much as you might wish to resume and prolong the pleasure of reading, you feel that your brain and heart cannot, at least for the moment, process or absorb one word, one detail, more.

The settings of her stories range from the French capital to the

Ligurian Riviera, from Berlin to the Helsinki airport, from a small town in Switzerland to a grand hotel on the Côte d'Azur. Details of geography and local culture are crucial in Gallant's work, despite (or perhaps because of) the fact that so few of her characters come from, or feel at home in, the places where they happen to find themselves. Quite a few are understandably astonished to have wound up poor and adrift in post–World War II Europe, inhabiting the inhospitable border between exile and expatriation, covered with the almost visible film of desperation and the faint squalor that clings to those who feel they have come down in the world and—lacking talent or vocation—must struggle for survival.

Many of Gallant's motley assortment of refugees, fugitives, expatriates, and travelers are displaced persons, scrambling on the margins of a society to which they will never belong and which they regard with the avid longing, curiosity, and clinical objectivity with which the beautifully drawn children in these tales observe the all but inscrutable adults around them. A number of stories tally the costs of dislocation. In "The Remission," a terminally ill, impecunious Englishman brings his wife and three children to a decaying villa on the French–Italian border, where he intends to die. Instead, he survives for three years, long enough for his family to have a series of experiences that will change them far more than his death and absence. "The Latehomecomer" concerns a young German returning to Berlin in 1950 from a term as a prisoner of war in France, a sentence unfairly protracted by a bureaucratic mistake. And in "Baum, Gabriel, 1935-( )," a German-Jewish refugee orphaned by the Nazis supports himself by working as an extra in TV dramas filmed in Paris, a job that eventually obliges him to play a German soldier.

The Second World War and its aftermath shapes or at least shadows many of these narratives. Acutely conscious of history and politics, Gallant's work creates and reflects a milieu very distant from that of contemporary American stories in which the make of a car or a song on the radio may be the only detail that locates the story in time. But Gallant is an artist, not a historian, and she never lets us forget that her focus is not purely on politics, history, and war but on the effect that politics, history, and war have on individual lives. What's painful for the "latehomecomer" is not the memory of his postwar imprisonment so much as the discovery of the vast distance that his mother's life has traveled away from his own during his long absence. The opening of "Mlle. Dias de Corta"—"You moved into my apartment during the summer of the year before abortion became legal in France; that should fix it in past time for you, dear Mlle. Dias de Corta"—is not, as it turns out, principally a means of fixing the story in time, but rather a double-edged sword meant to reopen the wounds suffered by the letter's imagined recipient and by the story's simultaneously unpleasant and sympathetic narrator. So, too, in "The Moslem Wife," the horrors of the Occupation pale beside the dark, unfathomable currents of sexual thrall in which a woman is held by the handsome, shallow husband she has loved since they were children.

Given that there is no "typical" Gallant work, "The Ice Wagon Going down the Street"—among my favorites of her stories—could be said to typify her themes, her style, her strategies, her perspective. Her trademarks: the specificity, the density of detail and incident, the control of language and tone, and her gift for creating a deceptively comfortable distance between the characters and the reader, then suddenly and without warning narrowing that distance, with a force that leaves the reader with the equivalent of whiplash, though the part that has been thrown out of joint is not the neck, but the heart.

As "Ice Wagon" begins, Peter and Sheilah Frazier, a down-on-their-luck but proud and (in their own minds) stylish couple, have returned from Europe to Peter's native Canada, where they are camping out, with their two daughters, in Peter's sister's cramped Toronto flat. Peter is from a "good" Canadian family ruined by

financial scandal, while Sheilah is a British beauty from a lower
social caste.

The opening lines—the continental "peacocks" are lounging
about on a Sunday morning while Lucille, Peter's "wren" of a Canadian sister, has taken the also wrenlike daughters off to church—tell
us all we need to know (or think we need to know) about this brittle folie à deux. Much of our information about the Fraziers comes
through delicate grace notes—ironic word choices ("world affairs,"
"international thing"), the subtle manipulations of tone, the gran-
diosity, mutual consolation, self-congratulation, and faint recrimi-
nation that form the text and subtext of the couple's conversation.

> Now that they are out of world affairs and back where they
> started, Peter Frazier's wife says, "Everybody else did well in the
> international thing except us."
>
> "You have to be crooked," he tells her.
>
> "Or smart. Pity we weren't."
>
> It is Sunday morning. They sit in the kitchen, drinking their
> coffee, slowly, remembering the past. They say the names of peo-
> ple as if they were magic. Peter thinks, Agnes Brusen, but there
> are hundreds of other names. As a private married joke, Peter
> and Sheilah wear the silk dressing gowns they bought in Hong
> Kong. Each thinks the other a peacock, rather splendid, but they
> pretend the dressing gowns are silly and worn in fun.

It is a measure of Gallant's authority and nerve that the name
Agnes Brusen, dropped boldly, without explanation, near the start
of the story, will not reappear or be referred to again until seven
dense and eventful pages later.

Before Agnes can make her formal appearance, we must follow the Fraziers on their nominally fabulous but in fact deeply
sad trajectory through Europe, struggling among all the other
sexy, social-climbing, ambitious young couples who flocked to the

Continent in the aftermath of the war as if it were a Gold Rush town mined with excitement and glamour. Nearly every important event takes place in retrospect. Though everything proceeds smoothly in Gallant's eventful, easy-to-follow narratives, sooner or later it becomes clear how gracefully she dispenses with conventional notions of chronology. Consequently, reading her work is not like being shown how one moment follows another, but rather like watching a hand very slowly pull back a curtain until, inch by inch, everything is revealed.

"Ice Wagon" tracks the Fraziers from Paris, where Peter ruins his nonexistent career during an incident involving a party, a flowerpot, and great quantities of alcohol. From then on, everything that happens to the Fraziers is either a fiasco, an embarrassment, a betrayal, or a disappointment. The family moves to Geneva, where they live in conditions of increasing squalor. ("The flat seemed damp as a cave. Peter remembers steam in the kitchen, pools under the sink, sweat on the pipes. Water streamed on him from the children's clothes, washed and dripping overhead.") Their one talismanic possession is Sheilah's black Balenciaga gown, a symbol of elegance and style that they cling to as a religious couple might treasure the family Bible.

During their time in Geneva, Peter had a job as a file clerk, cataloging photos "in the information service of an international agency in the Palais des Nations" and sharing an office with another Canadian—a homely little mole of a woman by the name of Agnes Brusen.

In Geneva Peter worked for a woman—a girl. She was a Norwegian from a small town in Saskatchewan. . . . Soon after Agnes Brusen came to the office she hung her framed university degree on the wall. It was one of the gritty, prideful gestures that stand for push, toil, and family sacrifice. . . . The girl might have been twenty-three: no more. She wore a brown tweed suit with bone

buttons, and a new silk scarf and new shoes. She clutched an
unscratched brown purse. She seemed dressed in going-away
presents. . . . He was courteous, hiding his disappointment. The
people he worked with had told him a Scandinavian girl was
arriving, and he had expected a stunner. Agnes was a mole.

Almost immediately, Agnes becomes involved in a triangulated
relationship with the Fraziers—not a romantic triangle, but one
including humiliations, disappointments, and misunderstandings.
The Fraziers are appalled to learn that Agnes is a regular visitor
at the home of a couple who have dropped Peter and Sheilah from
their guest list for reasons having to do (Peter thinks) with Sheilah's
class background. Eager to know why Agnes has been admitted to
the lost paradise, Peter and Sheilah invite her to dinner—and to one
of the most excruciating social disasters in literature. At yet another
unfortunate party, this time a costume ball, Agnes, a teetotaler,
gets so drunk that their hostess strong-arms Peter into taking Agnes home. And that night, and the next day, something happens between Agnes and Peter. The something is not sex, but an encounter
just as profound and perhaps more likely even than sex to leave a
man and a woman forever imprinted on each other. For that one
day, the artifice and pretense of Peter's life drop away. But Peter and
Agnes—and the narrator—insist that "nothing happened."

But what were they talking about that day, so quietly, such old
friends? They talked about dying, about being ambitious, about
being religious, about different kinds of love. What did she
see when she looked at him—taking her knuckle slowly away
from her mouth, bringing her hand down to the desk, letting it
rest there? They were both Canadians, so they had this much
together—the knowledge of the little you dare admit. Death, near
death, the best thing, the wrong thing—God knows what they
were telling each other. Anyway, nothing happened.

It would be necessary to read every word of this long, complicated story to get the full import—to feel the force—of its ending. It's as if the eye of the hurricane has been hovering over Agnes and Peter, rather than over Peter and Sheilah, gathering momentum, until in its final paragraphs the story (to extend the storm metaphor) blows the roof off.

Mavis Gallant's work leaves an afterimage that stays with us and that we can conjure up, the way we can close our eyes and see how Velázquez paints an egg. Her fiction has the originality and profundity, the clarity, the breadth of vision, the wit, the mystery, the ability to make us feel that a work has found its ideal form, that not one word could be changed, all of which we recognize as being among the great wonders of art.

8

Roberto Bolaño, *2666*

ALMOST EXACTLY HALFWAY THROUGH ROBERTO BOLAÑO'S
novel *2666*, a seventy-year-old seer and healer named Florita Almada appears on a local TV talk show. Local, in this case, means
Sonora, a state that includes the city Bolaño calls Santa Teresa, and
which is based on Ciudad Juárez, a bleak, industrial desert hellhole
on the Mexican side of the border, where, over the past decade,
hundreds (some say thousands) of women—most of them factory
workers in the multinational maquiladoras—have been raped and
killed in unsolved murders, as they are in Bolaño's book. By the
time Florita makes her television debut, Bolaño has described, in
clinical detail, the discovery of dozens of corpses, but no one in any
official capacity has been much concerned; the police have been
busy trying to catch a madman known as the Penitent, whose illness compels him to desecrate churches.

The litany of dead women and girls (many of the victims are
very young) has exerted an intensifying pressure on the reader.
Why isn't anyone doing or saying anything about the killings?
That pressure will erupt through Florita at the end of an on-air

monologue that goes on for ten dense (there are no paragraph breaks) pages, a speech that seems musical in its flights of melody, its swells and dips and crescendos, like a great operatic aria, but more free-form and improvisational, more like a brilliant jazz solo.

Florita begins by describing the nature and limitations of her gift ("sometimes she didn't see anything, the picture was fuzzy, the sound faulty, as if the antenna that had sprung up in her brain wasn't installed right or had been shot full of holes or was made of aluminum foil and blew every which way in the wind") and goes on to dispense some basic nutritional advice ("a tortilla with chile is better for you than pork rinds that are actually dog or cat or rat"). Next she lists the various schools of herbalism, or "bota-nomancy," including the use of hallucinogens ("Everyone was free to mess with their own heads. It worked well for some people and not for others, especially lazy youths with regrettable habits"). She provides a brisk autobiography, an account of how she cared for her blind mother, and later her blind husband, a dealer in livestock whose habit of bringing home books turned Florita into a voracious reader and autodidact. Next comes a meditation on the childhood of Benito Juárez and the inner lives of shepherds, then an expla-nation of the circumstances that have brought Florita to follow a ventriloquist from Guaymas on *An Hour with Reinaldo*.

Then she glanced at Reinaldo, who was fidgeting in his chair, and began to talk about her latest vision. She said she had seen dead women and dead girls. . . . As she talked, trying to recall her vision as exactly as possible, she realized she was about to go into a trance and she was mortified, since sometimes, not often, her trances could be violent and end with the medium crawling on the ground, which she didn't want to happen since it was her first time on television. But the trance, the possession, was pro-gressing, she felt it in her chest and in the blood coursing through her, and there was no way to stop it no matter how much she

*fought and sweated and smiled at Reinaldo, who asked her if she
felt all right, Florita, if she wanted the assistants to bring her a
glass of water, if the glare and the spotlights and the heat were
bothering her.*

No matter hard how she struggles against it, Florita's vision
takes shape:

*It's Santa Teresa! I see it clearly now. Women are being killed
there. They're killing my daughters! My daughters! My daughters! she screamed as she threw an imaginary shawl over her
head and Reinaldo felt a shiver descend his spine like an elevator,
or maybe rise, or both at once. The police do nothing, she said
after a few seconds, in a different voice, deeper and more masculine . . . but what are they watching? Then, in a little girl's voice,
she said: some are driven away in black cars, but they kill them
anywhere. Then she said, in a normal voice: can't they at least
leave the virgins in peace? A moment later, she leaped from her
chair, perfectly captured by the cameras of Sonora's TV Studio 1,
and dropped to the floor as if felled by a bullet. Reinaldo and the
ventriloquist hurried to her aid, but when they tried to help her
up, each taking an arm, Florita roared . . . don't touch me, you
coldhearted wretches! Don't worry about me! Haven't you understood what I've said? Then she got up, turned toward the audience, went to Reinaldo and asked him what had happened, and
a moment later she apologized, gazing straight into the camera.*

It was at this point in my reading of 2666 that I began impor-
tuning close friends, fellow writers, family members, and casual
acquaintances, urging them to put down whatever they were reading or writing and start Roberto Bolaño's novel. Immediately. My
messianic enthusiasm was at once altruistic—I wanted others to
enjoy and admire the book as much as I was—and also somewhat

self-interested, because to read 2666 is to enter into a parallel world that resembles our world but that exists only between the covers of a novel; it's much like the experience of reading *Moby-Dick* or *David Copperfield* or *In Search of Lost Time*.

One can't help wanting company in those alternate worlds, and (knowing, at that point, only very few people who had read 2666) I wanted someone I could ask about—to take just one of many examples—a subplot in the first of the novel's five sections, "The Part About the Critics." In this story within a story, a painter cuts his hand off because he believes that this will be the ultimate work of art, and he winds up in a mental hospital where he is visited by several of the section's principal characters. Or the parallel insane-asylum story in the second section, "The Part About Amalfitano," a sequence in which the estranged wife of the protagonist (a depressed Chilean academic stranded in northern Mexico) becomes infatuated with a poet with whom she has had semi-public sex at a party in Barcelona, a poet who winds up in a loony bin where his doctor turns out to be writing the poet's biography. And what about the ten-page sermon near the start of the third section ("The Part About Fate") in which yet another protagonist—in this case, Oscar Fate, an African American journalist writing human interest features for a black-interest journal based in Harlem—attends a lecture by a character named Barry Seaman, obviously modeled on the former Black Panther Bobby Seale? Like the larger novel, the lecture is in five sections, the third of which, "FOOD," begins, "As you all know, said Seaman, pork chops saved my life," and segues from a capsule history of the Panthers to Seaman's absurd conversations with his parole officer to a reflection on various Chinese Communist politicians, then back to the aforementioned pork chops—and finally to a recipe for duck à l'orange.

Though what, exactly, would I have asked the obliging friends who (or so I hoped) would read quickly to reach the point I had gotten to in the novel? I suppose I wanted to ask: What's up with those passages? What are they doing in the book? It's a question with no answer, really. They are stations along the circuitous route on which Bolaño had chosen to take us to Santa Teresa. Perhaps I just wanted confirmation for my own sense of the uniqueness, the inventiveness, the sheer ballsy strangeness of what Bolaño is doing. Which is what, exactly?

Four hundred pages in, I thought I was beginning to have some idea of what the book was about, though later I realized how little I'd known. And after two readings, it's still something of a challenge to say what Bolaño is "doing." The five books get steadily more engrossing as they comment and reflect on, refract, deepen, and complete one another—five sections so unlike one another that they suggest different genres, all converging on the dead women lying half-buried or simply tossed aside in the nightmare moonscape and trash heaps of Santa Teresa. On the second reading, I was surprised to notice how often buzzards and vultures are mentioned, because after I'd finished the book it had occurred to me (out of nowhere, or so I had thought) that the shape of the narrative is like the flight of some carrion-eating bird with a wingspan so enormous that to see it take off and soar seems miraculous. Bolaño's terrifying and gorgeous vulture of a novel keeps landing in the same place—Santa Teresa—but the arc of its flight reminds you that evil is like that: it touches down in one country this time, next year in another place. The erratic but relentless flight plan of human evil from one era and continent to the next is, as much as anything, the subject of 2666.

Evidently, Bolaño—who was dying of liver failure while he wrote 2666—wanted this, his last novel, published as five separate books, in the hopes that his heirs might make more money that way. But the sections are clearly parts of a single volume that is nine hundred pages long and crammed with events, plots, subplots, dreams, hundreds of characters, humor, visionary lyricism, stories within stories, pages of compressed, rapid-fire dialogue, switches of pace and tone from academic comedy to something suggestive of a thirties noir thriller, of David Lynch's *Blue Velvet*, of newspaper reports, police procedurals, Orson Welles's *A Touch of Evil*, and all of it culminating in an apocalyptic vision of a war-ravaged Europe that's part history, part Thomas Pynchon, part Kubrick, but mostly Roberto Bolaño. Unless one reads the book slowly, and with a high degree of concentration, it's easy to miss some of its most virtuosic turns—for example, this moment, buried in a long scene during which Harry Magaña, a widowed Arizona sheriff, is having dinner with a Mexican cop:

> Then Ramírez talked about women. Women with their legs spread. Spread wide. What do you see when a woman spreads her legs? What do you see? For Christ's sake, this wasn't dinner conversation. A goddamn hole. A goddamn hole. A goddamn gash, like the crack in the earth's crust they've got in California, the San Bernardino fault, I think it's called. . . . Then came a long story about children. Have you ever listened carefully to a child cry, Harry? No, he said, I don't have children. True, said Ramírez, forgive me, I'm sorry. Why is he apologizing? wondered Harry. A decent woman, a good woman. A woman you treat badly, without meaning to. Out of habit. We become blind (or at least partly blind) out of habit, Harry, until suddenly, when there's no turning back, this woman falls ill in our arms. A woman who took care of everyone, except herself, and she begins to fade away in our arms. And even then we don't realize, said Ramírez. Did I tell him my story? wondered Harry Magaña. Have I sunk that low?

Luckier in death than in his peripatetic and often penurious life, Roberto Bolaño has had the rare good fortune to find not one but two brilliant translators into English: first Chris Andrews, whose version of the stories and short novels is eloquent and fierce, and now Natasha Wimmer, who gracefully follows the book's

switchback turns in diction even as she accommodates the special-
ized vocabularies of every diverse historical and cultural subject
that Bolaño crams into his densely packed suitcase of a novel.

THE first time, I'd had to read the novel's first fifty pages twice to
sort out the characters in a plot that, summarized, sounds like the
first line of the sort of joke to which the novel slyly refers: "An Italian, a Frenchman, and an Englishman are in a plane with only two
parachutes." In *2666*, that joke (which the principals could hardly
take more seriously) involves four academics: a Frenchman, an Italian, a Spaniard, and an Englishwoman. All four share a passion for
a cult novelist, a reclusive German named Benno von Archimboldi,
a collective devotion that helps tie them into knots of romantic and
sexual entanglement. The section struck me as gripping, hilarious, and peculiar, but several times, persuading friends to read the
novel, I found myself telling them not to give up if they didn't like
the first part, because the opening is quite different from the rest
of the book.

I understood why a reader might falter in the midst of the initial section, which (in its charting of a quixotic literary quest) most
resembles Bolaño's earlier novel *The Savage Detectives*. Though I am
a huge fan of Bolaño's short stories and short novels, though I had
begun saying that he was my new favorite writer, I had bogged
down partway through *The Savage Detectives* and quit reading after
its plot turns had spun me out of the novel so often that I'd lost
the energy to work my way back in. The book seemed to me to be
suffering from a sort of attention deficit disorder, contagious to the
reader.

By contrast, the opening of *2666* had me in its spell from those
first pages. Even as the academics are having sex and screwing with
one another's heads in book-filled apartments and at the sort of
hotels that house participants in international German literature

colloquiums, a thrum of disorder and violence is rumbling just beneath the surface. There's a horrifying incident involving a Paki-
stani cabdriver in London, a scene in which Bolaño reminds us—as
he so often does—that you can't predict what any of us will do once
the punching and kicking start.

But only after I had read the last section ("The Part About Archimboldi") did it strike me how inextricably the opening chapters
are connected to the rest of 2666. The book begins in one version of
Europe, the home of Old World high culture, which we leave for
the heavy dose of the New World, with its slave trade, its political,
drug, and sexual violence, its legacy of colonialism, and its ongoing
economic exploitation. Then we head east again for another perspective on the Old World, in case we need reminding that horror
and mass murder are not restricted to the Sonoran Desert.

For a book that begins in the most hypercivilized of venues, the
academic conference, Bolaño's novel may set some kind of record
for sheer carnage. Although the last section is set mostly in Europe
during World War II, the novel is more disturbing than a war novel,
since at least some of the soldiers in Waterloo, Austerlitz, the Polish
front, and Vietnam are—unlike the dead women of Santa Teresa—
conscious combatants, present on their own volition. Besides, those
are historical events, unlike the murders of the women, which go
on for a very long time before anyone much notices or cares.

Among the unusual achievements of 2666 is its ability to make
the reader feel as if the novel is being acted out, cinematically, on
at least two screens at once. On one screen is the latest discovery of
a raped and mangled woman; on the other is the rest of the world,
which doesn't want to watch it.

I'VE mentioned the experience of reading Melville, Proust, and
Dickens—their long novels, it should be pointed out, a form that
Bolaño mentions in a passage that has been cited as a key to his

intentions in writing *2666*. Amalfitano is reflecting on an acquaintance, an avid reader

> who clearly and inarguably preferred minor works to major
> ones. He chose The Metamorphosis over The Trial, he chose
> Bartleby over Moby-Dick, he chose A Simple Heart over Bou-
> vard and Pécuchet, and A Christmas Carol over A Tale of
> Two Cities or The Pickwick Papers. What a sad paradox,
> thought Amalfitano. Now even bookish pharmacists are afraid
> to take on the great, imperfect, torrential works, books that blaze
> paths into the unknown. They choose the perfect exercises of the
> great masters. Or what amounts to the same thing: they want to
> watch the great masters spar, but they have no interest in real
> combat, when the great masters struggle against that something,
> that something that terrifies us all, that something that cows us
> and spurs us on, amid blood and mortal wounds and stench.

The Savage Detectives is full of this sort of thing, half-serious, half-
ironic flights in which a literary fellow makes a case for a certain
kind of literature—usually the kind he writes. But apart from extending a pointless invitation to consider why someone might want
to read "Bartleby the Scrivener" when he could read *Moby-Dick* or,
for that matter, *2666*, Bolaño is on to something—something about
capacity and weight. In those great torrential novels, room and heft
are necessary for the steady accumulation of events and characters
that connect to other events and characters and together form that
parallel fictional world I referred to at the beginning of this essay.

In a series of notes on *2666*, Natasha Wimmer compares Barry
Seaman's lecture to Father Mapple's sermon in *Moby-Dick*, a likeness I hadn't thought of, though one does feel that Bolaño seems
to have had it in mind. In any case, the two novels share a similar encyclopedic impulse, a drive to include everything that can
be known about a subject, as proof that nothing can ultimately be

known about that subject, if that subject happens to be the mystery of evil. In *Moby-Dick*, Melville offers his readers a full course in cetology, containing all the available scientific knowledge about the whale, and we wind up understanding no more than Ahab does about his sworn enemy. *2666* likewise provides us with an encyclopedia on the subject of the dead women of Santa Teresa.

By the time we reach the fourth and longest section of the novel, "The Part About the Crimes," we've followed the literary critics to Sonora, where they've alighted briefly, like butterflies, before flying on, in search of their literary idol. They have introduced us to the academic, Amalfitano, marooned in Santa Teresa, with his daughter, Rosa, whose story carries over into that of Oscar Fate, who in the third section comes to Santa Teresa to cover a prizefight and who learns about the murders but is unable to interest his editor in an article about the killings.

The fourth section begins at what will be the first of many crime scenes:

> *The girl's body turned up in a vacant lot in Colonia Las Flores. She was dressed in a white long-sleeved T-shirt and a yellow knee-length skirt, a size too big. Some children playing in the lot found her and told their parents. One of the mothers called the police, who showed up half an hour later. The lot was bordered by Calle Peláez and Calle Hermanos Chacón and it ended in a ditch behind which rose the walls of an abandoned dairy in ruins. There was no one around, which at first made the policemen think it was a joke. Nevertheless, they pulled up on Calle Peláez and one of them made his way into the lot. Soon he came across two women with their heads covered, kneeling in the weeds, praying. Seen from a distance, the women looked old, but they weren't. Before them lay the body. Without interrupting, the policeman went back the way he'd come and motioned to his partner, who was waiting for him in the car, smoking. Then the two of them returned (the one who'd*

waited in the car had his gun in his hand) to the place where the women were kneeling and they stood there beside them staring at the body. The policeman with the gun asked whether they knew her. No, sir, said one of the women. We've never seen her before. She isn't from around here, poor thing.

This happened in 1993. January 1993. From then on, the killings of women began to be counted. But it's likely there had been other deaths before. The name of the first victim was Esperanza Gómez Saldaña and she was thirteen. Maybe for the sake of convenience, maybe because she was the first to be killed in 1993, she heads the list. Although surely there were other girls and women who died in 1992. Other girls and women who didn't make it onto the list or were never found, who were buried in unmarked graves in the desert or whose ashes were scattered in the middle of the night, when not even the person scattering them knew where he was, what place he had come to.

In his descriptions of the aftermath of the murders, Bolaño manages to combine the stripped-down, just-the-facts account of an autopsy report with the more human tone of a tragic neighborhood story, and finally with something more lyrical and metaphorical. It is a credit to Natasha Wimmer's translation that she succeeds in helping the reader follow these subtle but all-important tonal shifts. In its precision about street names, location, time, the victim's outfit, the order of events surrounding the grim discovery, and the initial impressions of the policemen, the passage mimics the statement that one of the cops might have written.

That is, until we get to the women praying over the body, like mourners in a religious painting, and to their phrase "poor thing," an expression of compassion that effectively turns the mangled corpse back into the body of a person—who, as we now learn, had a name and an age. "The sake of convenience," "the first to be killed," "she heads the list"—such phrases warn and remind us that the list will go on. And then we reach that final sentence, and its reference to the ashes of the women being scattered "in the middle of the night, when not even the person scattering them knew where he was, what place he had come to"—and the language steps up to something more poetic, an evocation of a shadowy killer, lost in the dead of night—something that would never, ever appear in the official report.

The killings continue, and Bolaño gives us every detail about each victim—her name, her age, her history, her job, her domestic situation, what she was wearing, and how she was found. Knowing that very few readers (and not necessarily the kind of readers a writer might want) will stay with a book for several hundred pages of gory crime scenes and wrenching victim bios, Bolaño weaves these sections together with a number of gripping subplots—one about a police detective's love affair with the director of an insane asylum, another about a boy who is recruited from the countryside to work as a bodyguard for a narco's wife, a third about Harry Magaña's ill-fated trip south of the border after an American woman disappears—to keep us reading through the discoveries of the brutalized bodies, the capsule histories and grim fates of the victims. Some of the murders are solved—a few of the women have been killed by their husbands or pimps or boyfriends—but most are not, though throughout there is the suggestion that the killings have something to do with the collusion between the narcos and the police, and the more generalized cruelty and corruption of the maquiladora system, which attracts young women from all over Central America to work, for almost nothing, in the factories. In addition, there is the hint, introduced early on, that Benno von Archimboldi—the critics' darling—might have some connection to the murders. Suspects are arrested and detained, confessions are extorted, and the killings go on, as they have in reality.

ALL of which brings us back to Florita Almada's appearance on
An Hour with Reinaldo and to the possibility that it's Florita—rather
than the obsessed literary critics or the academic Amalfitano, with
his convictions about the "blood and mortal wounds and stench" of
the great torrential novels—who functions as the true stand-in for
the novel's author, and who will finally speak the truth that needs
to be said. Surely it's no accident that her television debut is preceded by the performance of a ventriloquist, or that Florita herself
gives voice to an urgent and impassioned vision of the dead of Santa
Teresa. Every artist has felt, at times—the best times—like some
equivalent of a ventriloquist's puppet, speaking words or creating
images that seem to come from some source outside the self. And
Florita's progression from the general to the specific, from autobiography to history to science to meditation, from the literal to the
metaphysical, is a compressed version of what Bolaño does in *2666*.

For there are some novels—*2666* is one of them, *Moby-Dick* is
another—that make you feel as if some powerful force has moved
through the writer, as if the artist has become the vehicle for the
words of some exalted ventriloquist, or has indeed been possessed
by something, a narrative or a theme, larger than himself. For all
the precision and poetry of its language, for all the breathtaking
complexity of its structure, for all the range of styles and genres
that it acknowledges and encompasses, for all its wicked humor,
its inventiveness and sophistication, *2666* seems like the work of a
literary genius in the ferocious grip of a spirit not unlike the one
that seizes Florita Almada.

Dying, aware that his time was short, Roberto Bolaño gave himself over to the most important of subjects, the eternal and ineradicable
evil that has—for the moment—alighted on the Mexican border; to
the desire to insist that the blameless murdered women of Ciudad
Juárez (or Santa Teresa) were once individual living beings with
names and faces and souls; and to our human need, our obligation,
to cry out, as Florita does: Haven't you understood what I've said?

9

Complimentary Toilet Paper: Some Thoughts on Character and Language—Michael Jeffrey Lee, George Saunders, John Cheever, Denis Johnson

NOT LONG AGO, SARABANDE, ONE OF OUR SO-CALLED *SMALL* independent presses—an adjective that clearly must refer to size rather than to heroism, mission, and conviction—asked me to judge a fiction contest. The winning book would be published.

I agreed, as I have to several similar requests, and, as always, when I put down the phone or sent off the e-mail, I had to lie down, slightly queasy with regret and dread. The obvious anxieties—that I might have to read manuscripts I might not enjoy or that I might make the wrong decision—were compounded by the deeper terror that there would be no right decision to make.

I've heard about several writers, novelists, and poets I admire who have refused to award a prize in a literary contest they were judging because, they believed, no entry deserved a prize. While I respect their integrity, I simply don't have it in me. I say if someone wants to give a prize, they should give a prize. I say if someone wants to publish a book, they should publish a book. Besides, I say, there's no predicting what such an award might do, no telling when recognition, even modest recognition, will reveal, to a merely competent writer, some previously hidden but dazzling vein of talent.

I have, I'll admit, picked winners whose main distinction was that they were the best of a merely competent lot. It felt a little strange, a little inauthentic, I'll admit, but I soon forgot about it, and some writer somewhere got the good news and was happy.

Fortunately, the package from Sarabande contained several strong contenders. But my decision was made when I read a line in Michael Jeffrey Lee's story collection *Something in My Eye*. I recognized at once—correctly, as it turned out—a sentence that would prove hard to beat, because of the way in which it used language to give first life and then dimension to a fictional character.

The narrator of Lee's story "If We Should Ever Meet" has been working (duties unspecified) in a building "so tall that people used to jump from the roof when they became so sad that they wanted to end it all." One day, our hero feels a shadow cross his face, and when he's told that someone has jumped from his side of the building, he lies and says he's seen it. Overcome by guilt at having told a lie, and worried that "the dead person was angry with me for making a memory of him that wasn't true," our narrator spends his days in bed until his employer calls and fires him. Already we have an intimation of something slightly . . . unusual, slightly, one might say, *off*, a sense that is entirely a result of Lee's slightly unusual, slightly *off* syntax and word choice.

The story goes on. We learn that our hero's older brother has been killed in an (again unspecified) war, after spending his military leave leading the family in the evenings, before dinner, in the choral singing of a song he wrote, entitled "If We Should Ever Meet." This "became a little controversial within the family because the lyrics were vague and kind of ominous, and nobody could ever understand why he was singing about a meeting with strangers when there were, all of us around the table, a family and not strangers at all."

After losing his job, the narrator travels to a new town. Getting off the bus, he makes a vow to himself, "that I would try to view each new sentence as independent of previous ones, and make no snap judgments, because although I had visited once before, I was unfamiliar with the people and the customs." The narrator tries to keep this vow, though his resolve is challenged when he drops a cracker and, retrieving it, sees a bloodstain under the bed. Determined to find work, he reads the classifieds like "sacred scriptures," conducts practice interviews with himself, and finds a room in a motel under a freeway and across from a veterans' hospital. Every morning, he showers and shaves and frequently cuts himself shaving.

> *The motel had complimentary toilet paper, so I was able to staunch any of my cuts with little folded scraps before I left my room. One day though, I was in such a hurry that I cut myself under my nose, bad enough that I had to ask the manager nicely for a Band-Aid. People gave me nasty looks on the bus that morning, and I only figured out why, when, after I had filled out an application at the coffee shop and was using the bathroom in the back, I noticed that I had a pretty sizeable amount of blood in my teeth, which I wasn't able to taste because of the cinnamon gum I was chewing.* My brother's song went something like: If we should ever meet, I will kindly take your hand. If we should ever meet, I will cudgel every lamb. If we should ever meet, I will wear my cleanest gown. If we should ever meet, I will set fire to this town. If we should ever meet, I will deny those close to me. If we should ever meet, I will feign to disagree.

Doubtless many readers may still be trying to decipher what the author could have been attempting to communicate with the sheer incantatory weirdness of the dead brother's song. Kindly take your hand? Cudgel every lamb? But let me direct the reader's attention back to the first sentence I quoted. That is, the line that won the prize.

"The motel had complimentary toilet paper." Are there motels that have uncomplimentary toilet paper, for which they charge you extra? Or no toilet paper at all? We know the protagonist has taken a vow to see everything in a new way. But complimentary toilet paper? Has he come not just from another town but from another planet?

On a planet where, it will be noted, they speak a slightly different language. English, but not English. Or English that has been picked up very carefully like a heavy serving platter and moved slightly to one side and set down someplace else—a place created and occupied solely by the character of the narrator. That linguistic transition can unnerve the reader, and whether or not you enjoy that sort of disquiet may determine your response to the story. I like not knowing where a sentence, or a story, is going to wind up, and if the route twists, as it does here, the momentum that propels us forward is the combustive force of language producing a human being. A human who, I should say, may not be to everyone's liking; not every reader may want to spend time in his company, on the page, any more than they would in life. (Myself, I'm delighted to meet him in a book, but not "in the flesh," if I can help it.)

I was shocked when a prepublication review of this book, a work I'd admired and chosen, described its atmosphere as "calculated to be noxious to human health—moral, spiritual, and psychological." But that shock may have been partly inspired by oversensitivity to the uses of language, which, in turn, may have been temporarily intensified by the fact that I had just been reading about the word and imagery choices of the Nazi propaganda machine. My reading had left me with a troubling sense that, historically speaking, it is usually bad news when metaphors of poison and disease are applied to cultural products.

RECENTLY, at a question-and-answer period that followed a reading, I heard the writer George Saunders say that what interests him most about fiction—that is, about writing fiction—is the interior monologues of his characters: specifically, the language of the chatter inside a character's head. He had just read his story "Victory Lap," which is composed entirely of the interior monologue of three separate people who have the misfortune of finding themselves in the same place at the same time: a teenage girl, a boy who lives next door to her, and a stranger who drives up in a van with plans to abduct and murder the girl. Saunders did the three voices expertly, but had we been reading the story silently, to ourselves, the language employed by each voice—vocabulary and rhythm, to choose just two elements of the whole—would have let us know instantly which of the three was speaking, or, actually, thinking. We begin in the voice of fifteen-year-old Alison, who, with her "bigger than all outdoors" hair bow, her "stone age" picture of herself as a little cutie, and her baby deer reverie, could not be anyone else—that is, we would be hard-pressed to imagine that five-year-old boy or sixty-year-old-man whose interior monologue would sound anything like this:

> On a happy whim, do front roll, hop to your feet, kiss the picture of Mom and Dad taken at Penney's back in the Stone Ages, when you were that little cutie right there {kiss} with a hair bow bigger than all outdoors.
>
> Sometimes, feeling happy like this, she imagined a baby deer trembling in the woods.
>
> Where's your mama, little guy?
>
> I don't know, the deer said in the voice of Heather's little sister Becca.

*Are you afraid? she asked it. Are you hungry? Do you want
me to hold you?*

Okay, the baby deer said.

A few pages further into the story, we find ourselves in the
mind of Kyle, the teenage neighbor, whose interior conversation (of
the sort we all have) involves a running imagined dialogue with his
disapproving father:

*Gar, Dad, do you honestly feel it fair that I should have to slave
in the yard until dark after a rigorous cross-country practice that
included sixteen 440s, eight 880s, a mile-for-time, a kajillion Drake
sprints, and a five-mile Indian relay?*

Shoes off, mister.

*Yoinks, too late. He was already at the TV. And had left
an incriminating trail of micro-clods. Way verboten. Could the
micro-clods be hand-plucked? Although, problem: if he went back
to hand-pluck the micro-clods, he'd leave an incriminating new
trail of micro-clods.*

And now the story takes us on a dark excursion into the brain
of a man with a knife—the stranger whose game plan for Alison
fills his mind with a highly concentrated mantra of preparedness
and readiness for any obstacle in the way of the smooth execution
of his psychotically efficient agenda.

*The following bullet points remained in the decision matrix: take
to side van door, shove in, follow in, tape wrists/mouth, hook to
chain, make speech. He had the speech down cold. Had practiced
it both in his head and on the recorder:* Calm your heart, darling, I know you're scared because you don't know me yet
and didn't expect this today but give me a chance and you

will see we will fly high. See I am putting the knife right
over here and I don't expect I'll have to use it, right?

*If she wouldn't get in the van, punch hard in gut. Then pick
up, carry to side van door, throw in, tape wrists/mouth, hook to
chain, make speech, etc., etc.*

What should by now be obvious is that we are never in any
doubt about whose voice we are hearing, and that this certainty is
achieved by the language Saunders uses to portray the way in which
each character is thinking at each given moment. Part of the pleasure
of listening to (or reading) the story comes from wondering what
is going to happen next. At the same time, we are aware that the
outcome—will the would-be kidnapper commit and get away with
his crime?—was not what most interested the writer. When I heard
Saunders explain that what had engaged him had been his characters' interior chatter, I was surprised—though perhaps I shouldn't
have been—because it is something I often say in similar situations.

Actually, I've heard many writers say more or less the same
thing: that narrative and event are merely the armature on which
to hang the layerings of consciousness, the inner monologue imagined and reproduced through precision of diction and word choice.
And I suppose it's what writers mean when they talk about inhabiting a character, about the psychic ventriloquism of understanding
a character on a level so deep and intimate that, when you think
about that character, you seem to hear the language in which that
character thinks.

And while it makes perfect sense to me, it does seem somehow
counterintuitive that writers should want to augment and amplify
and record that interior monologue, when entire religions, meditation techniques, and schools of psychotherapy have been based on
the understandable human longing to mute or silence that chatter,
if only for a few moments of blessed peace.

Perhaps it's this as much as anything—that desire to eavesdrop on the language of what is never said out loud and perhaps cannot be said—that distinguishes the writer from those who have sensibly chosen other professions.

EVEN after all this time, I am still slightly surprised when reviewers or readers talk about the plots of my novels as if plot were the most important element. In fact, plot was only, as I've said, the armature; what I thought I was doing was charting how a character's consciousness changes with each bit of interior or exterior information, and recording the language that accompanies (and comments on) these changes in a person's mental state. Who could have imagined that I'd been engaged by such topics as sexual harassment or academic politics or any of the subjects that readers and critics have seized upon in talking about my novel *Blue Angel*, when the reason I wrote the book was to watch my hero's mind founder and go under and painfully haul itself back to the surface, only to plummet into the hell fires ignited and stoked by his misguided passion for a talented student?

The oddity of this intention, or compulsion, to burrow inside the human mind—rather like the brain worms that were the terrifying mainstay of the science fiction I read as a child—is one reason I never know if people know what I mean when I talk about language as the key that turns the lock of character. Or maybe the problem is that I have been using an unhelpful or confusing illustration whenever I have tried to explain what I mean.

The example from my own experience that most readily comes to mind concerns my desperate efforts to get inside the mind and heart of a character who could hardly be less like me—a young neo-Nazi named Vincent Nolan, who claims, at the start of my novel *A Changed Man*, to have had a radically transformative experience and who, by the end of the book, has actually had one, though the genuine transformation is much more gradual and complex than the pretend one.

In the opening scene, Vincent has just driven in from the country in a stolen truck and is walking through Times Square during an especially crowded lunch hour, on an unseasonably hot day. I could all too easily empathize with Vincent's discomfort, alienation, irritation, with his sense of being threatened and nearly overwhelmed by the crush of unfamiliar humanity and the reek of auto exhaust.

But still it seemed improbable that I would ever understand who this person was. Until (and the really impossible part is trying to fathom where these things come from: obviously from within ourselves, but also, it often seems, from some mysterious "other" place) I found myself writing the following sentence—one of the many thoughts that go through Vincent's mind as he struggles to process, and respond to, and defend himself against the sensory assault of midtown Manhattan at lunch: "While Nolan's been off in the boondocks with his friends and their Aryan Homeland wet dream, an alien life-form has evolved in the nation's cities, a hybrid species bred to survive on dog piss and carbon monoxide."

More than a decade after writing it, I can almost look at the sentence as if it were someone else's, and at the same time I can recall why I found it so encouraging to think of it as I labored to see the world from the point of view of a young man whose worldview is more about hustle than about hate.

I felt that I had cracked a code, that my hero (or perhaps I should say my protagonist) was poised between two worlds, still speaking the language of his immediate past ("Aryan Homeland") but not yet the language of the future into which he was hurtling. He was dismissive of what he'd left behind (the "wet dream" in the "boondocks"), but so intimidated and dissociated from the people around him that they might as well have been visitors from another planet, with wholly different dietary and respiratory needs.

As it was turning out, my character was not stupid but rather intelligent, not self-serious but gifted with an edgy sense of humor, and, most important from my point of view, capable of the kind of sustained metaphorical thinking that could hold my—and, I hoped, the reader's—attention for the next several hundred pages. Of course, one reason I've had trouble explaining why that sentence made me think it was possible to write the remainder of a novel may be that I am the only person in the world who thinks that the phrase "a hybrid species bred to survive on dog piss and carbon monoxide" is an indicator of a gift for metaphor, intelligence, and humor.

In any case, it's always easier to see (or at least to attempt to explain) how other writers use language as a magic charm that makes a character come to life and rise, like a golem or Franken-stein's monster, off the printed page. Not long ago, I met a young woman who had tattooed down the length of her arm a sentence from a story by Denis Johnson—a writer with a particular gift for creating characters who inhabit the margins of society yet whose consciousness thrums with an electrically charged, hallucinatory lyricism that would, or should, be the envy of any established poet.

The sentence that the young woman had running down her arm—"And you, you ridiculous people, you expect me to help you"—appears at the conclusion of Johnson's "Car Crash While Hitchhiking"—the first story in his collection *Jesus' Son*.

In the book, its more or less unnamed narrator takes a wide range of recreational and prescription drugs (without troubling much about possible side effects or contraindications) and gets into (and barely out of) a great deal of trouble. One might think—and the surface of the narrative might lead us to suppose—that the nar-rator is an essentially simple guy: down on his luck, out on a limb, alarmingly vulnerable, open to experience, his consciousness laid bare by vagrancy and desperation and consequently transparent to the reader. But a closer reading reveals a character who's somewhat more complex: high or straight, he's acutely observant, judgmental, and imaginative, and tells us exactly as much about himself as he wants us to know.

The opening story begins with a series of ellipses that use not only language but also punctuation to give us some indication of its narrator's fragmented state of mind: "A salesman who shared his liquor and steered while sleeping . . . A Cherokee filled with bourbon . . . A VW no more than a bubble of hashish fumes, captained by a college student . . . And a family from Marshalltown who headonned and killed forever a man driving west out of Bethany, Missouri . . ."

By the time we've reached the end of the paragraph, we've already gotten some idea that we're hearing from someone whose perceptions are a bit . . . well, out of the ordinary. Beyond the question of content (the alcohol and hashish) is the little matter of *head-on* employed as a verb as well as the haunting redundancy of *killed forever*. And as we focus in on our hero—sopping wet, waiting in the faint hope of getting a ride (who would pick this guy up unless they were too drunk or stoned to know better?) by the entrance ramp to the freeway—Johnson's use of language gives us the first real indications that our hero isn't your ordinary hitchhiker.

"The travelling salesman has fed me pills that made the linings of my veins feel scraped out. My jaw ached. I knew every raindrop by its name. I knew a certain Oldsmobile would stop for me even before it slowed, and by the sweet voices of the family inside it I knew we'd have an accident in the storm." I'd suggest that the conviction of feeling one's veins scraped raw and even of receiving direct and unwelcome communications from the immediate future is somewhat more common (if one were to survey the segment of the population that Johnson's narrator represents) than that of knowing every raindrop by its name. And what would those names be? It's this sentence that puts us on the alert: the interior monologue on which we're being permitted to eavesdrop is a highly unusual one, demanding and deserving of our attention. Like the phrase "complimentary toilet paper," those few words—a single sentence—radically alter and sharpen the quality of attention that we are prepared to pay to what we are being told, and to the person who is telling us.

As daunting as it is to inhabit characters such as the narrators in Denis Johnson's and Michael Jeffrey Lee's stories, or the psycho kidnapper in the George Saunders piece, or my own recovering neo-Nazi, there is also a kind of freedom and exhilaration involved in finding the language that so clearly sets a character outside the parameters of "normal" or "ordinary"—or what we've agreed to call normal and ordinary—interior chatter. I suspect that if we were honest about the thoughts that ran through our minds on a minute-by-minute basis, recognizing and allowing in the ideas and perceptions we've learned to screen out before they can take hold, they might be closer to those of our fictive brothers who are so appreciative of the complimentary toilet paper or on a first-name basis with each raindrop.

But it's a different sort of challenge to find the language in which to portray the interior life of a character who is even better trained than we are to monitor and control the fragments of self that break loose and rise to the surface.

One of my favorite characters in literature, if such a thing could be said about a smug, painfully clueless husband and father, willfully or unknowingly blinded to the truth about his life and those of his mother and siblings, is the narrator of "Goodbye, My Brother," John Cheever's harrowing account of a horrific New England family reunion. Or perhaps it would be more correct to say that the story is one of my favorites to teach, since, in the opening paragraphs, Cheever so masterfully layers the language of class, race, region, gender, and unintentional self-revelation beneath the natter of self-description and mannerly introduction. And because the first-person story is, formally speaking, an interior monologue with dialogue and action, we read this opening with the sense that the narrator is not so much introducing himself to us as crystalliz-ing, for himself, who he is and what he's about.

> *We are a family that has always been very close in spirit. . . . I*
> *don't think about the family much, but when I remember its mem-*
> *bers and the coast where they lived and the sea salt that I think is*
> *in our blood, I am happy to recall that I am a Pommeroy—that*
> *I have the nose, the coloring, and the promise of longevity—and*
> *that while we are not a distinguished family, we enjoy the illu-*
> *sion, when we are together, that the Pommeroys are unique. I*
> *don't say any of this because I'm interested in family history or*
> *because this sort of uniqueness is deep or important to me but*
> *in order to advance the point that we are loyal to one another in*
> *spite of our differences . . .*
>
> *We are four children; there is my sister Diana and the three*
> *men—Chaddy, Lawrence, and myself. . . . I teach in a second-*
> *ary school, and I am past the age where I expect to be made*
> *headmaster—or principal, as we say—but I respect the work.*
> *Chaddy, who has done better than the rest of us, lives in Man-*
> *hattan, with Odette and their children. Mother lives in Philadel-*
> *phia, and Diana, since her divorce, has been living in France, but*
> *she comes back to the States in the summer to spend a month at*
> *Laud's Head. Laud's Head is a summer place on the shore of one*
> *of the Massachusetts islands. . . . It stands on a cliff above the sea*
> *and, excepting St. Tropez and some of the Apennine villages, it is*
> *my favorite place in the world.*

What makes this passage so succinct and so painfully revealing? The regretful acceptance of the term *principal*, "as we say," the public school job description (the narrator teaches on Long Island), in place of the Anglophile prep school *headmaster*. A job, by the way, that our narrator will never get; he just lets *that* pop out. The simple fact of calling one's mother Mother instead of Mom, Mommy, or Mama.

The locutions—"in order to advance the point"—that seem left over from writing (or teaching) the high school essay or coaching the debating team. The genteel understatement of the entitled (the way monumental seaside mansions have been referred to by their residents as *cottages*) and the coded language of "one of the Massachusetts islands"—places that outsiders might be more likely to think of as Nantucket or Martha's Vineyard. The family, the coast, the sea salt in their blood. The fact that what the narrator considers the distinguishing characteristics of the Pommeroys (nose, coloring, longevity) are all physical traits of the sort that might be noted by the eugenicist, rather than deeper qualities: kindness, say, or humor. The telling description of the grown siblings as four children, and the way that judgment and competition (Diana's divorce, Chaddy having done the best) crop up the instant the siblings are mentioned.

We may have to think a minute more to get the implications of a high school teacher (later we will learn that one of his duties is firing the gun at the start of races at the school) telling us about St. Tropez and hill towns in the Apennines.

We must read a good deal further and come back and reread these lines to realize how much of what the narrator says is lies, or at least distortions, untruths that he himself believes, which makes everything all the more complicated. Yes, the family is close in spirit in the sense that they cannot get free of one another; they might as well still be children of their recklessly self-involved, alcoholic mother, and if the narrator doesn't think of the family much, it's hard to say what he does think of. Even the names are freighted with meaning: Diana has the name of a Greek goddess, an association that will become important in the final paragraph; Chaddy is precisely the sort of prep school nickname that one associates with families like the Pommeroys; and as for Laud's Head, one of my students told me that William Laud was the conservative and punitive archbishop of Canterbury, beheaded by order of the court of King Charles in 1645.

As the story progresses, we learn that the despised third brother, Lawrence, has returned to visit the family, and that all the things of which Lawrence is accused by the narrator—pessimism, selfishness, a joyless and judgmental puritanism, disapproval of the family's decadence and excessive drinking—are in fact the narrator's own thoughts, so inadmissible that he can allow himself to think them only by projecting them onto Lawrence.

The cumulative effect of Cheever's virtuoso use of language is that every phrase, every sentence, comes to function as a direct pipeline to the narrator's unconscious, so that the mounting pressure, the explosion of violence, and the final moment of grace are experienced by readers as if we are watching the narrator from the outside and at the same time seeing the world through his cramped worldview, constricted by a lifetime—by generations—of privilege and damage.

The story is a model of the way in which words and sentences are used to construct a character, a family, a history, a plot, a sermon, a story that takes its place in a particular line that connects the Old Testament, Greek mythology, and the fading aristocracy of New England. I could dissect it line by line, but you can do so yourself for a lesson in how many dazzling objects and brilliant perceptions language can juggle at once.

10

Edward St. Aubyn,
The Patrick Melrose Novels

SOME TIME AGO, IN A DINER ON EASTERN LONG ISLAND, I experienced one of those moments to which writers seem especially prone—moments of unseemly over-interest in the people at the next table. Beautifully dressed, sleek and thin as whippets, the young, medicated-seeming mother and her older husband were the sort of parents who transformed each moment with their tiny son into a unique and golden educational opportunity. As the father lectured his squirming child on the proper etiquette required to order a cheeseburger and chat up the waitress, his pedagogical technique had an unmistakable edge of the punitive and mocking.

What made this chilling family scene even more compelling was my vague, unsettling sense that I'd met them all somewhere before. My husband stole a long, sidelong glance at our neighbors. No, he said, we didn't know them. But they were, he pointed out, the real-life counterparts of the main characters in Edward St. Aubyn's extraordinary Patrick Melrose novels.

The first of the Melrose novels, *Never Mind*, begins in the south of France, where the Melrose family lives and where Patrick's father, David, is first seen methodically drowning a colony of ants and calculating precisely how long he must talk to the maid before her arms start to ache painfully from the load of laundry she's carrying. As it turns out, David's barbarous cruelty extends well beyond the insect kingdom and the servants. He rapes his young son, torments his wife, and serves his guests a heady recipe of charm and humiliation.

It's hard to imagine a bleaker domestic landscape, but what makes these novels so extraordinary and pleasurable to read is how beautifully St. Aubyn writes, his acidic humor, his stiletto-sharp observational skills, and his ability to alchemize these gifts into one quotable, Oscar Wildean bon mot after another. What makes the book so moving, as a writer friend of mine said, is that you feel that its hero is trying at every moment, and with every cell of his being, not to turn into the kind of monster his father is: the sadist that he's been programmed from birth to become.

That struggle is ongoing throughout *Mother's Milk*, in which we catch up with Patrick some years after his marriage to the thoughtful and understandably disaffected Mary. He's the father of two sons, and his dying mother, Eleanor, has decided to leave his childhood home in Provence to a sleazy guru named Seamus and his sketchy New Age foundation. The book abounds in visions of motherhood gone wrong, either through monumental self-interest (the awfulness of Mary's mother, Kettle, makes Eleanor seem almost beneficent) or through the sort of quasi-erotic attachment that connects Patrick's wife and their two little boys, and that makes Patrick feel progressively more alienated from that cozy trio.

Few contemporary authors write more knowingly from the point of view of the child who is smarter and more observant than the adults around him imagine. *Mother's Milk* starts, nervily, with what I suppose is called a "birth memory"—in this case, that of Robert, Patrick's older son, recalling his first experience of wrenching separation from his mother. The novel follows the family as the parents' marriage unravels, as Patrick initiates a love affair with a witty and unhappy former girlfriend, and as he flirts with the sort of substance abuse that turned *Bad News* (the second Melrose novel) into a dispatch from the private hell of a damned soul who simply couldn't get high enough to lower the frequency of his own acute, self-lacerating awareness.

Near the end of *Mother's Milk*, the Melrose family decides to cope with their exile from Patrick's childhood paradise by taking a salutary, restorative trip to the United States. By now, the reader can pretty much predict how well this solution will work out, just as we can expect the vacation to provide St. Aubyn with yet another chance to display his gift for making us recognize a volley of hilariously barbed and enraged perceptions as the flailings of a character struggling not to drown in a sea of despair.

Here, to take one example, are the anxious young Robert's musings on the "hysterical softness" of his fellow passengers boarding the flight from Heathrow to New York, strangers displaying

> a special kind of tender American obesity; not the hard-won fat of a gourmet, or the juggernaut body of a truck driver, but the apprehensive fat of people who had decided to become their own airbag systems in a dangerous world. What if their bus was hijacked by a psychopath who hadn't brought any peanuts? Better have some now. If there was going to be a terrorist incident, why go hungry on top of everything else?
>
> Eventually, the Airbags dented themselves into their seats. Robert had never seen such vague faces, mere sketches on the immensity of their bodies. Even the father's relatively protuberant features looked like the remnants of a melted candle.

However much we may love our parents, filial affection only rarely trumps our fear that we may grow up to become them. This unease is closer to terror for Patrick Melrose, whose anxiety is understandable, given that his father, David, is a pedophile and a rapist, while his mother, Eleanor, is a dotty do-gooder whose telescopic philanthropy makes Dickens's Mrs. Jellyby seem a paragon of maternal solicitude, and who, in a fit of misguided charity, gives away Saint-Nazaire, the beloved house in the south of France, the only place where Patrick ever felt at home.

The Patrick Melrose novels can be read as the navigational charts of a mariner desperate not to end up in the wretched harbor from which he first embarked on a route that has steered him in and out of heroin addiction, alcoholism, marital infidelity, and a range of behaviors for which the term "self-destructive" is a euphemism.

Summarizing these novels can make them sound like yet another account of wretched family dysfunction, brightened by copious infusions of lively table talk and British-American expat high-society glamour. Indeed, that society is so high that *Some Hope* features a country-house party at which the guest of honor is Princess Margaret, portrayed here as a figure of jaw-dropping idiocy, petty snobbishness, and blinkered self-involvement.

But in order to understand what makes these novels so extraordinary, one should open them at random to marvel at the precise observations, the glistening turns of phrase, the dialogue witty enough to make one's own most clever conversations sound like . . . well, like St. Aubyn's Princess Margaret at her most platitudinous. Patrick's sons, Robert and Thomas—whose protected childhoods could hardly be less like the tormented boyhood Patrick endures in *Never Mind*—are as astutely observant as their father. *Mother's Milk* suggests that children not only are smarter than we might imagine, but they are, almost from birth, wise to their parents' foibles. Ultimately, Thomas's sage observation that the mind exists to be changed will help rescue the newly orphaned Patrick from the dismal straits in which we find him at the beginning of *At Last*:

*It was all very well for the Oliver Twists of this world, who
started out in the enviable state it had taken him forty-five years
to achieve, but the relative luxury of being brought up by Bumble
and Fagin, rather than David and Eleanor Melrose, was bound
to have a weakening effect on the personality. Patient endurance
of potentially lethal influences had made Patrick the man he was
today, living alone in a bedsit, only a year away from his visit
to the Suicide Observation Room in the Depression Wing of the
Priory Hospital. It had felt so ancestral to have delirium tremens,
to bow down, after his disobedient youth as a junkie, to the shattering banality of alcohol.*

These books are at once extremely dark and extremely funny.
In *Bad News*, Patrick visits New York, where his father has just
died. "It was hot, and he really ought to take off his overcoat, but
his overcoat was his defence against the thin shards of glass that
passers-by slipped casually under his skin, not to mention the slow-
motion explosion of shop windows, the bone-rattling thunder of
subway trains, and the heartbreaking passage of each second, like
a grain of sand trickling through the hourglass of his body. No, he
would not take off his overcoat. Do you ask a lobster to disrobe?" A
minor character in *At Last* is described as having three drawbacks
as a guest: "She was incapable of saying please, incapable of saying
thank you and incapable of saying sorry, all the while creating a
surge in the demand for these expressions." Meanwhile, the humor
is deepened by our sense that Patrick's banter and the dazzling py-
rotechnics of his interior monologues are a source of pain for him,
as he hears, in his own witticisms, chilling echoes of the "pure contempt" of his father's mocking humor.

In *At Last*, Patrick comes to see that these aspects of his personality have insulated and distanced him from the life around
him. "He was doing what he always did, under pressure, observing
everything, chattering to himself in different voices, circling the

unacceptable feelings." Irony, he tells a friend, "is the hardest addiction of all. Forget heroin. Just try giving up irony, that deep-down need to mean two things at once, to be in two places at once, not to be there for the catastrophe of a fixed meaning."

It's possible to read *At Last* without knowing the earlier novels, but it is a bit like paging straight to *Time Regained* and skipping the rest of Proust, especially if Marcel had discovered the equivalent of what Patrick learns: the linden tea was laced with hemlock and the madeleines were poisoned. Without having met David Melrose's old friend Nicholas Pratt—whose manic rants evoke the specter of Noël Coward on crack—in his prime, it's hard to understand why his surprise appearance at Eleanor's funeral should affect Patrick (and us) rather like Carrie's arm shooting out of the grave at the end of the Brian De Palma film. Most of the characters have long and tortuous shared histories, and secrets to which we are privy, so that the most minor event—a little boy watching a gecko—reminds us of a similar, significant incident in the past.

Without having witnessed Patrick's suffering, we are inadequately equipped to fully appreciate the magnitude of the realizations he arrives at in the final and most meditative of the Melrose novels.

It's a credit to St. Aubyn's delicacy that the passages inspired by Eleanor's death strike us as belonging less to the realm of psychology than to that of metaphysics.

> *What would it be like to live without consolation, or the desire for consolation? He would never find out, unless he uprooted the consolatory system that had started on the hillside at Saint-Nazaire and then spread to every medicine cabinet, bed and bottle he had come across since; substitutes substituting for substitutes . . . What if memories were just memories, without any consolatory or persecutory power? Would they exist at all, or was it always emotional pressure that summoned images from*

what was potentially all of experience so far? Even if that was the
case, there must be better librarians than panic, resentment and
dismembering nostalgia to search among the dim and crowded
stacks.

I wonder if the novel's end might seem more purely optimistic
had we not observed Patrick's earlier victories over his past and
subsequent relapses. If this is, as St. Aubyn's publisher claims, the
"culmination" of the Melrose cycle, we can only wish Patrick well
and be thankful that his travails have furnished the material for
some of the most perceptive, elegantly written, hilarious, and important novels of our era.

11

Paul Bowles,
The Stories of Paul Bowles
and *The Spider's House*

"TEN OR TWELVE YEARS AGO THERE CAME TO LIVE IN TANGIER a man who would have done better to stay away." This wickedly portentous sentence, which begins Paul Bowles's story "The Eye," could just as easily serve as the opening of most of his novels and stories—especially if we expand the list of ill-advised travel destinations to include nearly all of Morocco and a virtual Baedeker of hellish jungle outposts in Latin America and Asia. For Bowles's obsessive subject, to which he returned again and again, and which he wrote about brilliantly, was the tragic and even fatal mistakes that Westerners so commonly make in their misguided and often presumptuous encounters with a foreign culture.

One can hardly imagine a more timely theme, one more perfectly suited to the poisonous and perilous world in which we find ourselves. Yet, strangely, Paul Bowles's name never (as far as I know) appeared on those rosters of writers one saw mentioned in the aftermath of September 11, classic authors whose work appears to speak across centuries and decades, directly and helpfully addressing the crises and drastically altered realities (terrorism, violence, our dawning awareness of the hidden costs of colonialism and globalization) of the present moment. Perhaps it's because the books that were commonly cited (*War and Peace, The Possessed, The Secret Agent,* and so forth) seemed, even at their darkest, to offer some hope of redemption, some persuasive evidence of human resilience and nobility, whereas Bowles's fiction is the last place to which you would go for hope, or for even faint reassurance that the world is anything but a senseless horror show, a barbaric battlefield.

Frequently, Bowles begins his fiction in ways that seem to promise (or threaten) the sort of narrative we might expect from other writers who have focused on the confrontation between East and West, from novelists as dissimilar as Conrad and Waugh, Naipaul and Forster, from works in which a naive colonial sightsees his way into one heart of darkness or another—and lives to regret it. But soon we can watch Bowles part company with his fellow authors and enter territory that he has claimed as uniquely his own, a moral universe that few, if any, of us would willingly choose to inhabit—which is not to say that Bowles's lifelong residence in that bleak and harsh (though often grimly hilarious) landscape seems voluntary, exactly.

In his characteristically distanced, clinical, quietly confident, and authoritative tone, employing a rigorously unadorned, quasi-journalistic prose style, Bowles approaches his material and his characters in a way that seems relentlessly anthropological, scientific, distanced, unbiased by either contempt and derision on the one hand or sympathy and affection on the other—or by any powerful or particular tribal loyalties of his own.

Writing about expatriates and Moroccans warily coexisting in the crowded medinas, wealthy suburbs, and desert encampments of North Africa, he depicts all these groups acting badly, even brutally. Every community seems capable of committing any crime, no matter how mindless or vile—willing and able to do anything, that is, except understand one another. What mostly (if not entirely) exempts Bowles from the charges of racism that his portrayals of brutal and scheming Moroccans have, at times, occasioned is the fact that his dispatches from the various frontiers of savagery and bad behavior are so evenhanded and broadly inclusive. It's not at all clear that the merchants in his story "The Delicate Prey," who take revenge on the man who murdered three of their kinsmen by burying the killer up to his neck in the desert sand and leaving him there to die, are any better or worse than the Frenchmen in his remarkable 1955 novel *The Spider's House* who round up all the young males in the medina of Fez (boys who have done nothing to them, men they don't even know) and bring them into the police station to be tortured and perhaps killed. "As far as I can see," said Bowles in a 1981 *Paris Review* interview, "people from all corners of the earth have an unlimited potential for violence."

Readers accustomed to parsing literature for clues to the personal history of a writer or for instruction on how to live may be puzzled by the discrepancies between a body of work that seems to advise against ever leaving home and the facts of Bowles's unusually peripatetic existence. An avid and intrepid traveler, Paul (a dentist's son from Queens) abandoned a promising career as a composer and spent much of his early adulthood in Paris and Germany, North Africa, Mexico, Guatemala, Sri Lanka, and Thailand. From the 1940s until his death in 1999, he was a more or less permanent resident of Tangier, where he lived with his famously eccentric and fascinating wife, Jane, author of the dazzlingly original novel *Two Serious Ladies*. He also formed a series of intimate relationships with Moroccan men and translated books of Maghrebi oral narratives.

Bowles was immensely proud and fiercely territorial about his knowledge of North African customs, music, and folktales, his familiarity with Islam, his fluency in Maghrebi, his ability to understand the North Africans around him, or at least (unlike most foreigners) to admit, and know why, he would never understand them.

Near the beginning of *The Spider's House*, there's an incisive and revealing passage in which an American writer named Stenham (the character who, one might argue, most nearly seems like a stand-in for the author) considers the possibility that his own fondness for making such statements "gave him a small sense of superiority to which he felt he was entitled, in return for having withstood the rigors of Morocco for so many years. This pretending to know something that others could not know, it was a little indulgence he allowed himself, a bonus for seniority. Secretly he was convinced that the Moroccans were much like any other people, that the differences were largely those of ritual and gesture."

The Spider's House should top those lists of novels that speak to our current condition. Set in Fez during the first upheavals that announced a more radical and violent phase of the Moroccan struggle for independence from the French, the book seems not merely prescient but positively eerie in its evocation of a climate in which every aspect of daily life is affected—and deformed—by the roilings of nationalism and terrorism, by the legacy of colonialism, and by chaotic political strife. It's chilling to hear its characters speculate on the root causes of insurrection ("If people are living the same as always, with their bellies full of food, they'll just go on the same way. If they get hungry and unhappy enough, something happens"), on the grim satisfactions of terrorism ("the pleasure of seeing others undergo the humiliation of suffering and dying, and the knowledge that they had at least the small amount of power necessary to bring about that humiliation"), and on the sources of anti-American sentiment in the Muslim world: "The arms used against the Moroccan people were largely supplied by your government," a nationalist tells Stenham. "They do not consider America a nation friendly to their cause." Yet another agitator speculates on the most efficient means of getting American attention. "Once we've had a few incidents directly involving American lives and property, maybe the Americans will know there's such a country as Morocco in the world. . . . Now they don't know the difference between Morocco and the Senegal."

What makes this all the more intriguing, and all the more convincing, is that Bowles never thought of himself as a political writer—and, perhaps as a result, few readers see him that way. In the preface to *The Spider's House*, he wrote:

> *Fiction should always stay clear of political considerations. Even when I saw that the book that I had begun was taking a direction which would inevitably lead it into a region where politics could not be avoided, I still imagined that with sufficient dexterity I should be able to avert contact with the subject. But in situations where everyone is under great emotional stress, indifference is unthinkable; at such times all opinions are construed as political ones. To be apolitical is tantamount to having assumed a political stance, but one which pleases no one. Thus, whether I liked it or not, when I had finished, I found that I had written a "political" book which deplored the attitudes of both the French and the Moroccans.*

The last sentence is particularly telling. To be a political writer (as the term is generally understood) suggests strongly held opinions, a polemical agenda, a taking of sides—something that would have been not merely aesthetic anathema but a characterological impossibility for the exquisitely detached Bowles. The novel's characters (both Moroccan and American) repeatedly express their contempt for those fanatics who would willingly sacrifice individual lives to gain political objectives. Moreover, what Bowles tells us at the start (and what subsequently emerges) is that his initial impulse for writing the book derived from his fear that the medieval city of Fez (and, by extension, the rest of Morocco) would be changed and modernized beyond recognition—an anxiety that he wisely mistrusts as stemming from the most self-indulgent sort of romanticism.

As Stenham realizes, "It did not really matter whether they worshipped Allah or carburetors . . . In the end, it was his own preferences which concerned him. He would have liked to prolong the status quo because the decor that went with it suited his personal taste." Throughout Bowles's work, you can watch the author battling his own inherent romanticism (one of the characters in *The Spider's House* calls Stenham "a hopeless romantic without a shred of confidence in the human race") and straining to see the world and its denizens as they really are—without romance, without sentimentality, without blinders.

However unintentional, the political subtext of his fiction proves that when you write accurately and comprehensively about human beings, politics inevitably comes into your story, since—it hardly needs to be said—politics exerts such an enormous influence on every aspect of our lives. Even Chekhov, whom we also tend to think of as a largely apolitical writer (in contrast to, say, Dostoyevsky or Tolstoy), frequently established or clarified the nature of his characters by informing the reader about their political sympathies. How peculiar it suddenly seems to mention Chekhov and Bowles in the same paragraph, or even the same essay! Were there ever two more dissimilar literary sensibilities?

With his apparent cold-bloodedness and lack of empathy, his chilly skepticism, his refusal to demonstrate an even passing interest in the process of spiritual transformation or individual redemption, Bowles strikes us as the anti-Chekhov. Which may be why he seems, right now, as necessary as Chekhov, equally valuable in his contribution to the chorus of voices that constitute our literary heritage, and no less essential in his ability to remind us of who we are, of how we live, and of what we can—and inevitably will—do, in accordance with our nature.

In an era in which circumstances much like those that inspired *The Spider's House* force us, whether we like it or not, into an often passionate political engagement, we would do well to be aware, and wary, of the dangers and pitfalls of such an engagement: dogmatism, intolerance, the unshakable conviction of one's own righteousness and blamelessness. What Paul Bowles reminds us of, what he won't let us forget, is that all of us, regardless of nationality or religion, are capable of acting from highly suspect, compromised, "primitive" motives and of behaving in ways that, we would prefer to think, we could never even imagine.

12

Patrick Hamilton, *Twenty Thousand Streets Under the Sky: A London Trilogy; The Slaves of Solitude; Hangover Square: A Story of Darkest Earl's Court*

BOB, A WAITER AT THE LONDON PUB FROM WHICH PATRICK Hamilton's 1929 novel *The Midnight Bell* takes its title, has saved—from tips, in shillings and pence—eighty pounds. On his days off, Bob likes to stroll past the bank that houses the fortune that, he imagines, will someday enable him to quit the bar and become a writer. But Bob's plans for the future are disrupted when he falls in love with a young, beautiful, ferociously unredeemable prostitute, Jenny Maple. Unlike Bob, the reader soon intuits that Jenny will wind up with most, if not all, of those eighty pounds. But before we can think, *Oh, that story*, Patrick Hamilton has us too busy worrying about Bob—and about his bank account in particular. As the balance drops and drops again, to finance generous "loans," to purchase a new suit, and to pay for a holiday trip to Brighton, we find ourselves anxiously subtracting these increasingly reckless sums from the original eighty as Hamilton evokes (in the reader, if not in his hero) the most upsetting financial panic in literature since Emma Bovary frantically counted and recalculated her debts.

With their intense, and intensely mixed, sympathies for the men and women who haunted the pubs and walked the streets of London's tawdrier districts just before, during, and after World War II, Patrick Hamilton's novels are dark tunnels of misery, loneliness, deceit, and sexual obsession, illuminated by scenes so funny that it takes a while to register the sheer awfulness of what we have just read. In *The Plains of Cement* (1934), the third novel in the trilogy *Twenty Thousand Streets Under the Sky*, all of which concern the Midnight Bell and its unhappy patrons, Ella, the barmaid at the pub, adores the handsome Bob. But she is insufficiently pretty and manipulative to attract the sort of self-destructive man at the center of Hamilton's fiction.

Only Mr. Eccles, a patron of the bar, appears to see something in Ella. A nattily dressed older gentleman who spends the first part of their courtship mashing his face into Ella's and the second phase lecturing her on his many tedious opinions and quirks, Mr. Eccles has snagged Ella's attention with the hint that he might be planning to propose marriage.

Ella knows she cares only about his money, but she is tempted by the most pitiful promise of pleasure. An evening at the theater and dinner at a Lyons Corner House are enough to make her seriously consider the grim stability of a future with Mr. Eccles. But Mr. Eccles's fantasies are more immediate and more carnal. At the end of their first date, he decides to collect what's owed him. When he insists on walking her home, Ella must fend off his advances:

> *"It was ever so kind of you," she tried, and since she could shirk it no longer, she turned her head and met his eyes.*
>
> *"What?" said Mr. Eccles, gazing at her in a hypnotized, semi-squinting way, and all at once she felt his arm round her waist.*
>
> *His face was now so near to hers that she found herself squinting back. "I don't know," she said, blindly, in complete prostration of the intellect.*

But this was no answer for Mr. Eccles.

"M'm?" he said, and then again, as his hold round her waist was made firm, "What?"

"You shouldn't be doing this, you know," said Ella. "Should you?"

"M'm?" said Mr. Eccles. "What?"

Could the unfortunate murmuring man say nothing but "What?" Hysteria would seize her in a moment and she would start giggling.

"I said you shouldn't be doing this," she said. "Should you?"

"What?" said Mr. Eccles. "What?"

It was no good. Mr. Eccles was in a trance, and would go on saying "What" till midnight and beyond if left in peace. She definitely would have to leave him.

Ella's problems are exacerbated when her boss's young grandson is obliged, by an illness going around his school, to spend a few days hanging around the pub. Bored and out of sorts, the "healthy yet loathsome" child tortures Ella with his intellectual superiority. "Unable to refrain from seizing any and every opportunity to wipe the floor with her," Master Eric asks if she knows the H_2O content of the bottles she's putting away. (Taunting the hired help is a favorite pastime in Hamilton's fiction; the snobbish Mrs. Plumleigh-Bruce in *Mr. Stimpson and Mr. Gorse* [1953] jollies up her Irish servant girl by speaking in a fake Irish brogue.)

Sensing a trap, Ella dodges Master Eric's question, only to have him ask her what H_2O is. Ella knows the answer, but as the boy badgers her, she begins to doubt herself. Finally, she says that it's water, but her tormentor still wins when he makes her admit she doesn't know what the letters stand for. It never occurs to the deeply conventional Ella that it might be possible (let alone permissible) to dislike a child, so she cannot even identify the emotions that their unpleasant exchange has inspired.

Such scenes evoke situations you may feel you've observed in life—first dates gone awry, exchanges between nannies and their truculent charges—and yet you cannot recall similar passages in fiction. Hamilton's novels are unlike anyone else's, though at moments you catch glints of other writers: Charles Dickens, William Trevor, Henry Green, Patricia Highsmith. In their simultaneously purposeful and almost giddy malevolence, some of his characters recall the principals in Jacobean tragedy, which seems fitting, since, in addition to his novels, Hamilton was also the author of two popular melodramas, *Rope* and *Gaslight*, both of which were made into films.

The latter may be one of the few literary titles to have become a verb. "To gaslight" is now commonly used to describe the willful undermining of someone's sense of reality in order to drive that person mad, a malign scenario often enacted in Hamilton's fiction. Along with alcohol, loneliness, and romantic obsession, the abuse of power—the small but all-important degrees of dominance conferred by class, gender, status, and beauty—is Hamilton's great subject. For Hamilton's heroes, falling in love entails surrendering their autonomy to undeserving women who mistreat their abject suitors, partly because it is the only power these women will ever have, and partly because they enjoy it.

At the start of *The Siege of Pleasure*, the second novel in the *Twenty Thousand Streets* trilogy, Jenny Maple has just finished breaking Bob's heart and blowing the last of his savings. Now she looks back on the social and moral descent that began when—poor, alone, dependent on her so-called betters—she worked in the suburbs as a live-in servant, entombed with two ancient sisters and their gaga brother. How little she would have sold her soul for, or, for that matter, her body. A car ride seemed exciting. Tea in a tea shop! A movie! A drink! Especially a drink. Jenny blames her downfall on a single glass of port, which led to another glass of port. Here is how Hamilton describes alcohol's seductive and ultimately successful assault on her virtue:

A permeating coma, a warm haze of noises and conversation,
wrapped her comfortably around—together with something
more. What that something more was she did not quite know.
She sat there and let it flow through her. It was a glow, and a kind
of premonition. It was certainly a spiritual, but much more em-
phatically a physical, premonition of good about to befall. It was
like the effect on the body of good news, without the good news.

Much of Patrick Hamilton's fiction was based loosely on personal experience, a biography that involved considerably more alcohol than good news. Few literary families (excluding, perhaps,
the Trollopes) produced as long a list of books and plays as did Patrick Hamilton's. Both of his parents were writers, his brother Bruce
a prolific novelist, his sister Lalla a singer, actress, and playwright.
Patrick's second wife, Lady Ursula Stewart, a relative of the Earl
of Shrewsbury, also wrote and published novels, several of which
focused on the unhappiness of women who marry beneath them.

Hamilton's father, Bernard, was a disputatious drunk whom
his wife and children dreaded, a womanizer who squandered the
legacy he inherited from his Scottish military clan. The setting of
Bernard's first novel, *The Light?*, ranged from ancient Egypt to the
Battle of Waterloo. For other novels, he chose Danton and Colum-
bus as heroes, and in life he was a passionate admirer of Mussolini.
That Bernard's first wife was a prostitute is worth noting, since Patrick's own fascination with prostitutes would become a theme in
his fiction. Bernard's snobbish, class-conscious second wife, Nellie,
the mother of Patrick and his siblings, was the author of two novels, daring for their era, on topics that included erotically frustrated
wives. Like her predecessor, she committed suicide. Throughout
Hamilton's fiction, his parents make frequent cameo appearances,
thinly disguised as bullying blowhards with military backgrounds
and blowsy parvenus who capriciously mistreat their employees.

Born in 1904, Hamilton spent his childhood in and around

Brighton and in Chiswick, a western suburb of London, navigating the steep slope of his family's downward mobility. It's easy to see why he found a kindred spirit and a literary model in Dickens. He left school at fifteen and briefly attended a commercial college in London, where his sister Lalla was performing on the stage and where his brother-in-law got him a job as an actor and an assistant stage manager.

Like several of his main characters, Hamilton knew early on that he wanted to be a writer. His first novel, *Monday Morning*, published when he was nineteen, takes its title from the day when, the hero promises himself, his life as an author will begin. His second book, *Craven House*, was set in a boardinghouse much like ones he lived in with his family during periods when they were especially strapped for cash. One of his ambitions, he told his brother, was to describe the hideous existence of prostitutes and servants.

In 1929, *Rope*, a thriller with marked similarities (a resemblance that Hamilton denied) to the Leopold and Loeb murder case, was a West End hit. That same year, he published *The Midnight Bell*, which was enthusiastically received and sold well. At twenty-five, Hamilton went from penury to wealth and success. "I am known, established, pursued," he wrote to his brother Bruce. "The world, truly, is at my feet."

Hamilton's demons seemed to have pursued him even more assiduously than the admiring world. Over the years, his alcoholism worsened to the point that he was consuming three bottles of whisky daily, an expensive habit in wartime. He spent his royalties on alcohol and on the prostitutes with whom he had ruinous, obsessive affairs. His first great love of this sort was Lily Connolly, who wrote him letters that he gave Jenny to send Bob in *The Midnight Bell*. In *Patrick Hamilton: A Life* (1993), Sean French astutely notes the many small edits that Hamilton made in one of Lily's letters, so that her fictional counterpart would seem less affectionate and kindhearted than her real-life model.

Later, Hamilton was fascinated by a doctor's speculation that alcoholism might be an inherited condition. Yet by that point he'd had plenty of reasons, beyond the genetic, to seek solace in drink. In 1932, he was hit by a car that jumped the pavement while he was walking near Earl's Court Road. He suffered multiple fractures and lost much of his nose. Concerns about his altered appearance may have aggravated the sexual problems that had plagued him since youth. His long first marriage, to Lois Martin, whom he met at J. B. Priestley's house, most likely remained unconsummated. With characteristic tact, Bruce Hamilton refers to "the idiosyncratic deviations from absolute normality that Hamilton shared with almost every normal man (though few admit it) and which with him was a mild form of masochism."

Patrick reported to Bruce that his first "unequivocal lovemaking" followed directly upon his horrified response to seeing Alfred Hitchcock's version of *Rope*, with its obvious homoeroticism. That "unequivocal" experience was shared with Ursula Stewart, for whom Hamilton left Lois and began a marriage so tempestuous that he frequently retreated back to the undemanding comforts of Lois's household. He continued to migrate between the two women until the end of his life.

His political views would become as extreme as his father's, though at the opposite end of the spectrum. A committed Marxist, he was one of the few members of his circle (a group that included the journalist Claud Cockburn) to remain untroubled by the Hitler-Stalin Pact. After Stalin's excesses were admitted, Hamilton switched his allegiance to Khrushchev, and, in his final years, veered to the right and voted Tory.

Eventually he fell into a depression so profound that, in a letter to his brother, he compared himself to a small boy forced by his parents to stand in the corner of a locked and empty room all day and all night for a year. Electroconvulsive therapy abated his depression, along with the last vestiges of his desire to write. In failing health, he consented to experiment with various treatments and cures, yet managed to drink heavily even while in residence at a dry-out clinic. He died of liver and kidney failure in 1962. By the time of his death, Hamilton's novels were rarely read or talked about.

In recent years, he has been the subject of a documentary produced by the BBC, which also broadcast an adaptation of *Twenty Thousand Streets Under the Sky*. And five of his novels are again in print, for the first time in decades.

One can all too readily find possible explanations for the eclipse of Patrick Hamilton's reputation. His success as a melodramatist may have been responsible for an occasional, unhelpful reliance on artifice, and for certain antiquated strains in the structure of books such as *The Siege of Pleasure* and *Hangover Square*. The darkness of his vision and the escalating horrors of his protagonists' debasement can become oppressive. His ambivalence about his characters is frequently extreme; it's hard to think of another writer who so thoroughly despises the weaknesses of the very same men and women he so desperately and compassionately longs to save from themselves.

At times his view of humanity seems positively Manichaean. Half of his characters are consumed by shame and regret, while the other half feed on the tender, foolish emotions of the first half. He allows his characters to descend to a level of degradation so low that you might assume they'd hit bottom unless you'd read enough of Hamilton's work to expect them to sink further as they anguish over every major slight and minor decision. He may be among the earliest authors to chart the infernal arithmetic of telephoning the beloved: when to call, when to call back, how soon to call again.

Hamilton is often seen as the darkly comic bard of alcoholism, but drunkenness was only a subset of what engaged his interest. He was fascinated by consciousness in all its forms, ordinary and altered, pathological and normal. The last writer one might think

to compare him to is Virginia Woolf, but in fact the proportion of
exterior to interior action in his work is at times reminiscent of *Mrs.
Dalloway*, and there's a similar recognition of how little it requires
to send someone hurtling down a rather rocky path of memory and
reflection.

Our introduction to George Harvey Bone, the hero of *Hangover
Square*, involves the alarming attacks he suffers, brief neurological
blips—perhaps a combination of petit mal seizures and alcoholic
blackouts—during which the life around him suddenly stops and
turns mute, until the action and sound resume:

> *It was as though one had blown one's nose too hard and the outer
> world had suddenly become dim and dead. . . . It was as though
> a shutter had fallen. It had fallen noiselessly, but the thing had
> been so quick that he could only think of it as a crack or a snap.
> It had come over his brain as a sudden film, induced by a foreign
> body, might come over the eye.*

Hamilton was no less engaged by, and no less skillful at describing, other psychological states. On the morning after her date
with Mr. Eccles, Ella awakes in her bedroom above the Midnight
Bell, and we get this account of the shifting moods that so often
accompany the start of a new day:

> *The deceptive juice Sleep, while it no doubt actually reconstructed
> and refreshed Ella's nervous resources, always gave the appear-
> ance, first thing in the morning, of having wrecked them. . . . So
> soon as she was conscious her mind would go stalking anxiously
> through the debris of yesterday, certain of signs of calamity and
> wreckage, and seeking to discover what precise shape they had
> taken, and for what she was to be indicted by herself. Never
> did she fail to fix upon something to make the jagged worst of,
> moved by a hateful yet deliberate impulse. As the day wore on*

the streams of health and positiveness flowed once more in the dried-up channels, and she was her proper self.

When Hamilton's work is at its best, his preoccupations—consciousness, power, obsession, sex, and social class—converge, and their combined weight gives the fiction a momentum that moves it above the sooty streets of Earl's Court and the cheap Brighton hotels. Whenever history enters the novels, it's like a window shade snapping up, flashing a spike of bright light through the dreary pubs, and showing us that we have been watching something more complicated than the regulars drinking too much and hurting themselves and each other.

Like *The Midnight Bell*, *Hangover Square* has, at its center, a man with the bad luck to fall for a woman who does not return his affections. The oafish but fundamentally decent George Harvey Bone is madly in love with Netta Longdon, a beautiful would-be actress who turns out to be shallow, grasping, abrasive, and lazy. The book takes place in 1938, in the shadow of Munich and Chamberlain's concessions, and though one never experiences George and Netta's endless pub crawl as a parable, one can't help noting the gleeful determination with which the powerful trample the weak, or simply those burdened with a functioning moral conscience. Halfway through the novel, we learn that Netta is not merely a parasitical fraud, but a Nazi who harbors "a feeling for something which was abroad in the modern world, something hardly realised and difficult to describe."

This something, which she could not describe, which was probably indescribable, was something to do with . . . blood, cruelty, and fascism. . . . In secret she liked pictures of marching, regimented men, in secret she was physically attracted by Hitler; she did not really think that Mussolini looked like a funny burglar. She liked the uniforms, the guns, the breeches, the boots, the swastikas, the shirts. She was, probably, sexually stimulated by these things in the same way as she might have been sexually stimulated by a bull-fight. And somehow she was dimly aware of the class content of all this: she connected it with her own secret social aspirations and she would have liked to have seen something of the same sort of thing in this country.

If *The Slaves of Solitude* (1947) is arguably Hamilton's most formally and emotionally satisfying novel, it's partly because its setting ("intense war, intense winter, and intensest black-out in the month of December") enables him to give a deeper sense of a claustrophobic milieu, and partly because its heroine, Miss Roach, is the most sympathetic, resourceful, and complex of Hamilton's creations. Unlike Bob, Ella, and George, she's more intelligent than her tormentors and therefore more capable of outwitting their machinations; perhaps one reason that Hamilton allows Miss Roach to prevail is that war (and not erotic longing) is the force that has flung her into their treacherous orbit.

Driven from her London home by the air raids, Miss Roach has found shelter in a suburban boardinghouse, the Rosamund Tea Rooms, where she comes into contact with two of Hamilton's most thrillingly awful bullies: Mr. Thwaites, whose principal weapons are language (he speaks a maddening faux-Elizabethan, faux-Scottish patois) and merciless, hounding repetition, and Vicki Kugelmann, a German woman Miss Roach befriends until she learns that there is nothing to which the scheming Vicki will not stoop. Like Netta Longdon, these two have a soft spot for the Nazis. Mr. Thwaites is secretly a "hot disciple" of the Führer, while Miss Roach will have cause to wonder:

Were not all the odours of Vicki's spirit—her slyness, her insensitiveness—the heaviness, ugliness, coarseness, and finally cruelty of her mind—were not all these the spiritual odours which had prevailed in Germany since 1933, and still prevailed? . . .

Was not this woman one who would, geographically situated otherwise, have been yelling orgiastically in stadiums, supporting S.S. men in their ambitions, presenting bouquets to her Fuehrer? . . .

In fact, if one interpreted Vicki Kugelmann in the light of some aspects of Nazidom, and if one interpreted some aspects of Nazidom in the light of Vicki Kugelmann, were not both illuminated with miraculous clarity?

The answer is, quite definitely, yes. As we read *The Slaves of Solitude*, the assaults, deprivations, and sufferings occasioned by the war become nearly indistinguishable from the power grabs and petty cruelties that the residents of the Rosamund Tea Rooms inflict upon one another. To fully appreciate the miraculousness of that clarity—the light that the behavior of the amateur bully sheds on that of the bullying dictator—it's helpful to have read not only *The Slaves of Solitude*, but other Patrick Hamilton novels, and to know something about his difficult life. With the perspective that such knowledge provides, Miss Roach's low-key resistance and modest triumph (she manages to rid herself of both Thwaites and Vicki) seem, without ever appearing transparently allegorical or reductive, a major victory, not only for herself but for people like Bob and Ella and George, and for the innocent victims of the private and public incarnations of Netta Longdon, Vicki Kugelmann, and Mr. Thwaites.

At the end of *The Slaves of Solitude*, Miss Roach, "knowing nothing of the future, knowing nothing of the February blitz shortly to descend on London, knowing nothing of flying bombs, knowing nothing of rockets, of Normandy, of Arnhem, of the Ardennes bulge, of Berlin, of the Atom Bomb," slips peacefully out of wakefulness into a sort of benign piety: "At last she put out the light, and turned over, and adjusted the pillow, and hopefully composed her mind for sleep—God help us, God help all of us, every one, all of us."

This final benediction seems all the more affecting when we reflect that its author was an atheist with little interest, and less belief, in the efficacy of prayer, in the consolations of religion, or in the power of faith to protect us from a future that we, like Miss Roach, may be better off not knowing.

13

Isaac Babel

LIKE ALL THE STORIES IN ISAAC BABEL'S MASTERPIECE, RED *Cavalry*, "My First Goose" is set among the horse soldiers of General Budyonny's Red Army during the bloody Polish-Soviet War of 1920. Its narrator is an idealistic young intellectual who finds himself riding with the Cossacks—thugs who have nothing but contempt for a bespectacled law graduate from St. Petersburg. A sympathetic quartermaster suggests that the way to win his comrades' respect is to "ruin a good lady."

But as it turns out, any living creature will do. Hungry, tormented by cooking aromas, our hero kills his landlady's goose by cracking its skull under his boot—and orders the old woman to cook it. This impulsive brutality convinces the Cossacks that the narrator might, after all, be a worthwhile human being. They invite him to share their pork-and-cabbage soup, and allow him to read to them Lenin's speech from *Pravda*. Later, "we slept, all six of us, beneath a wooden roof that let in the stars, warming one another, our legs intermingled. I dreamed: and in my dreams saw women. But my heart, stained with bloodshed, grated and brimmed over."

Naturally, this brief summary omits much of what makes the story great: details such as the landlady's magnificently despondent line "I want to go and hang myself," repeated twice in the narrative, and, more important, the story's subtext, which is sex—an erotic charge ignited by the first paragraph's description of the division commander, Savitsky ("His long legs were like girls sheathed to the neck in riding boots"), and exploded in the final lines, in that tangle of sleeping male bodies.

I was eighteen, a college sophomore, when our writing instructor read us the whole of "My First Goose." This was at Harvard, in 1966, and we—aspiring novelists all—were great admirers of Hemingway, with whom Babel shared much in common: a similar interest in storytelling, in themes of warfare, courage, and violence, an obsession with style, extreme compression, and economy, and a commitment to revitalize the written language through a precise, elegant fidelity to the spoken vernacular.

Hearing "My First Goose," we intuitively understood that we were listening to something resembling Hemingway—but stripped of his romance and sentiment, and without that failure of nerve caused by the longing (so damaging to a writer) for the reader's admiration and affection. If Hemingway told us that wars happened and brave men fought them, Babel suggested that violence was sexy, that something in human nature liked it—even required it. No Hemingway hero would pray for what the soldier in Babel's "After the Battle" asks from fate: "the simplest of proficiencies—the ability to kill my fellow men." And if Hemingway wrote about "men without women," Babel matter-of-factly, with neither titillation nor alarm, zeroed in on the homoerotic nature of army life.

Our instructor told us a few facts about Babel, culled from Lionel Trilling's introduction to the 1955 edition of *The Collected Stories*. Born in Odessa in 1894, Babel moved to St. Petersburg to become a writer and published a story in a magazine edited by his mentor, Maxim Gorky, who advised him to go out and experience life and work on his prose style. He joined the czar's army, then the Soviet army, and, like the hero of "My First Goose," rode with the Cossacks in the Budyonny campaign—an odd choice, since Babel was Jewish and the Cossacks were known for their murderous anti-Semitic rampages.

After his stories began to appear in the 1920s, he became an international success. *Red Cavalry* was published in this country in 1929. His personal life was complex; he fathered three children by three different women, and habitually obfuscated and mythologized his past.

After his wife and daughter emigrated to Paris, Babel lived with Antonina Pirozhkova, an engineer whose touching memoir, *At His Side*, describes his final years. Under pressure from the government to voice the current party ideology (in an address to the 1934 Soviet Writers Congress, he praised Stalin's literary style), he wrote less and less. In 1939 he was arrested by the secret police, and, it was said, he died in a labor camp two or three years later.

Now we know that Babel was never sent to a labor camp but was shot in prison eight months after his arrest—a fact that the government chose to hide from his family until decades later. Some of the mysteries surrounding Babel's life and death have been cleared up. But questions remain, among them the riddle of why, exactly, he was killed.

Despite his relatively modest output, he is considered by many to be one of the most important writers of this century. Maxim Gorky called him "the great hope of Russian literature." Harold Bloom has edited a book of essays about his work. According to Cynthia Ozick, "If we wish to complete, and transmit, the literary configuration of the twentieth century—the image that will enduringly stain history's retina—now is the time (it is past time) to set Babel beside Kafka." Novelists, poets, and serious readers speak of his work with an intense—and almost cultlike—respect and devotion. So why is Babel's work not more widely read by the general public?

The above summary of "My First Goose" suggests some probable causes. Babel is one of the least reassuring or politically correct of writers—which is not to say that his work is unrelievedly grim, or that it isn't frequently lively, charming, and funny. He is, however, unrelenting in his refusal to editorialize, to moralize, to interpret. As Lionel Trilling wrote, "One could not at once know just how the author was responding to the brutality he recorded, whether he thought it good or bad, justified or not justified. Nor was this the only thing to be in doubt about. It was not really clear how the author felt about, say, Jews; or about religion; or about the goodness of man." Babel's heroes are gangsters, whores, and soldiers, as well as boys and young men in the process of finding out that the world is populated by gangsters, whores, and soldiers.

Countless writers have linked sex and death, violence and art, but few have made that linkage seem so raw and unromantic. Sex, in Babel's stories, is raucous, juicy, compelling, and dirty; he accomplishes in a few allusive sentences what Henry Miller required a trilogy of novels to convey. "Guy de Maupassant," a tale about an aspiring writer who trades on his literary abilities to get laid, ends with the hero returning from a night of drunken passion with his voluptuous, married translation student and reading the biography of his hero, Maupassant, who, in the final stages of syphilis, cut his throat and was confined to a madhouse, where he crawled about on all fours, devouring his own excrement. Indeed, it's hard to think of a writer of equal genius whose work runs so directly counter to the prevailing popular taste for sympathetic characters and an affirmative worldview. If our culture prefers (or demands) sincerity and transparency, Babel's work, to quote Trilling again, is "heavily charged with . . . intensity, irony, and ambiguousness."

For a while I stopped teaching Babel. This was the result of a class in which I used the instructive and remarkably different two versions ("My First Fee" and "Answer to an Inquiry") of the same narrative. The plot concerns a young man who is infatuated with a prostitute who takes him home, where he realizes that he has no money to pay her. Inspired by ardor, he invents a sad tale about having been the kept lover of a homosexual Armenian, a lie that convinces the whore that she and the kid are colleagues, and that moves her to offer him a night of love for free. Several of my graduate students were offended by what they considered the damaging stereotype of the whore with a heart of gold, as well as by an author who tacitly condoned a hero who would deceive an oppressed female sex worker. But their horror was nothing compared with that of my class of University of Utah undergraduates, most of them Mormon, whom I assigned to read Babel's "The Sin of Jesus."

Cast as deceptively lighthearted folktale, the story concerns a hotel servant, Arina, who keeps getting pregnant by a succession of men. After she prays for help, the Lord sends her an angel named Alfred to be her husband and protector, with strict instructions to remove Alfred's fragile wings before going to bed at night. But one evening Arina gets drunk, and in a fit of lust she rolls over on the angel's wings and crushes him. Of course, Arina is soon pregnant again, and at the story's conclusion she berates Jesus for having pushed her beyond her limits. When the Savior, suitably chastened, falls to his knees and begs her pardon, Arina replies, "There's no forgiveness for you, Jesus Christ . . . No forgiveness, and never will be." My students were appalled, I think, not merely by the blasphemy but by the vision behind it: that is, by Babel's view of a universe without sense or order, a world in which, if we are to love one another at all, we must first admit that we often behave no better than animals—and, in fact, often worse.

14

Lolita, Just the Dirty Parts:
On the Erotic and Pornographic

IN THE SPRING OF 2001, ON THE FINAL NIGHT OF A GERMAN
book tour during which I had become convinced that, evening after evening, in city after city, I was reading to a group of cataton-
ics who had bused in from the local mental hospital, I was staying
at an appropriately eccentric hotel on a hilltop high above Zurich.
The hotel—founded (or so I was told) in the previous century by a
group of Swiss women's-temperance health nuts who had arranged
matters so that twenty-first-century guests still couldn't get a
drink—seemed like the perfect culmination of a Kafkaesque travel
experience.

It was late. My husband and I were flying home the next morning, and we couldn't sleep. We flipped through the TV channels,
past the badly dubbed Steven Seagal action films and the ultra-
boring, deliriously pompous French talk shows, until at last we
found an "adult" station broadcasting from Bavaria that seemed to
offer some promise.

First came a sort of slide show of blonde women, built like

Wagnerian heroines, with escort-service phone numbers bannered across their prodigious breasts.

This menu of local beauties was followed by a film clip. In the film, two go-go girls were dancing in a bar, both blonde and shirtless, both with a zombie-like affect, both wearing tiny leather miniskirts, which they kept lifting as they danced, and under which they were naked. This went on for quite a while, skirts up, skirts down, until it became as tedious as the French talk shows, only seedier and more depressing.

Except that there was one interesting . . . detail, you might say, an element that riveted our insomniac attention.

In the background, behind the dancing girls, was a recording, playing over and over, of Martin Luther King delivering his "I Have a Dream" speech.

Was the film erotic or pornographic? I would have to say: neither. It certainly didn't seem to reflect some sexy, sensual welling up of the life force, and quite frankly—though you'll need to take my word for this—after seeing the film, the last thing in the world that anyone (excepting, I suppose, a few Bavarian maniacs) would want to do was have sex.

LIKE many distinctions, the border between the erotic and the pornographic has been blurred and redefined, not by the natural evolution of language and culture but by capitalism's imperative to help the consumer readily locate the product he wants to buy. Beyond any meaning they once possessed, beyond the connotations that still reward consideration, which I'll consider in a moment, the words *erotic* and *pornographic* have by now become niche-marketing tags, designed, like the film-rating system, to answer the logical questions any potential customer might sensibly ask. How naked? How deep? Which orifices? Most important is the unspoken inquiry beneath every purchase decision: What do my desires reveal about who I am?

Erotic now means R-rated, perhaps edging toward NC-17, while *pornographic* suggests X and the more alarming XXX, a cautionary designation that (like the new meaning of *adult*) hardly requires a Roland Barthes to deconstruct its semiotics. The harried office worker stopping by the bookstore for something to enliven a solitary weekend might be drawn to a volume entitled *Best Erotic Fiction* but might shy away from an anthology of the year's *Best Pornographic Fiction*, just as the business traveler, returning to the hotel after a day of stressful meetings, may hope to order up some straight-up porn—as opposed to erotic cinema—on the pay-per-view channel.

Meanwhile, the nuances distinguishing the erotic from the pornographic have effectively been reduced so that both locutions suggest nothing more than different degrees and intensities of sexual content and arousal, much as those tiny chili peppers on the Szechuan menu promise or warn of heat and spice. Do you want your twice-cooked pork with the one-pepper icon or two?

What's been lost in the process is the broader meaning of *Eros* and *erotic*, words that have always included the sexual but have also suggested the mysterious, even metaphysical connection between sex and life, between sex and pleasure, between the origin of life and the celebration of life—between the way that life begins and the will to live. If I were asked to design the curriculum for the junior high sex-education class of the future (obviously, a wishful fantasy predicated on a future that permits sex education), I might begin by telling students about the contrast, in Greek culture, between Eros and Thanatos, between the realms of life and death.

Some vestiges of this wider understanding have managed, against all odds, to survive. One could still claim that the dinner scene in Fielding's *Tom Jones* is erotic in its depiction of gastronomy as foreplay. Indeed, the erotic is regularly (and most often preciously) invoked in food writing. A restaurant critic might claim that the effect of the fish lightly kissed with a tomato-licorice foam is positively erotic, without (let's assume) confessing he wants to have intercourse with the halibut on his plate. One can say that the warmth of the sun on the skin, on a cool autumn day, is erotic, again conjuring up the atmosphere of sex but not, specifically, the mechanics of sex.

By contrast, *pornography* is all about the mechanics, and has always been less about aesthetic content than about physiology. The Greek origin of the word (where it meant "writing about prostitutes") obviously implies a narrower focus than a word derived from the name of Eros, the god of love. Erotic literature or art can be judged by a wide range of criteria (Is it beautiful? Is it true? Does it reflect the viewer's own experience of sex or love or pleasure?), whereas the requirements and standards for assessing pornography are, by contrast, simpler: Does it, or does it not, succeed in getting its audience hard?

As in the case of everything remotely or directly related to sex, the most puritanical and hypocritically moralistic elements of our society (a group that, sadly, includes our lawmakers) have managed to surround pornography with such an aura of evil and condemnation that, for many, it has become inextricably associated with sexual violence against women. (My own feeling, or hope, is that pornography does little to incite the would-be rapist; on the contrary, ready access to enough effective porn might prevent the potential attacker from making it out the door to commit his crime.)

The consequence—since we are speaking at least partly of language here—is that the pejorative connotation of the word *pornographic* has expanded to include the voyeuristic, the invasive, and any text or image that provides the reader or viewer with an inappropriate buzz of suspect curiosity or twisted gratification. I myself have employed the word *pornographic* to describe news photos of massacres, crime scenes, and accident scenes, pictures in which the victims necessarily have no say about how they are viewed, but in retrospect, I regret having settled for such a simultaneously sensational and approximate locution.

I can't help wishing I'd held out for something more precise and less loaded. Harking back to its origin, the word has also become associated with exploitation, just as it has become a loosely (too loosely) used synonym for anything creepy, displeasing, or distasteful. It is also, like *erotic*, used about food—namely, food that is, in quantity and complication, excessive. "That platter of baby lamb's tongues at the banquet was positively pornographic."

By that definition, despite its being a sexual turnoff, the film of the two Bavarian women dancing to Martin Luther King was pornographic in the extreme.

IN his essay "On a Book Entitled *Lolita*," written in 1956, the year after his novel's publication, Nabokov offers a characteristically incisive description of pornographic fiction:

> In modern times the term "pornography" connotes mediocrity, commercialism, and certain strict rules of narration. Obscenity must be mated with banality because every kind of aesthetic enjoyment has to be entirely replaced by simple sexual stimulation which demands the traditional word for direct action upon the patient. . . . Thus, in pornographic novels, action has to be limited to the copulation of clichés. Style, structure, imagery should never distract the reader from his tepid lust. The novel must consist of an alternation of sexual scenes. The passages in between must be reduced to sutures of sense, logical bridges of the simplest design, brief expositions and explanations, which the reader will probably skip but must know they exist in order not to feel cheated . . .

It was similarly characteristic of Nabokov to want to define the terms of the conversation, then current, about his novel—specifically, about whether or not *Lolita* was pornographic. Doubtless there are learned societies devoted to the details of Lo and Humbert's sex life, academic conferences assembled to hear Lacanian readings of what the runaway couple did and didn't do behind the closed doors of their motel rooms.

Today, the book's actual sexual content would seem mild (probably not even earning an NC-17 rating) compared with what is "out there." On the other hand, its nominative subject matter (Humbert Humbert's pedophilia) is fully as controversial as it was in the 1940s and '50s, perhaps even more so, now that it is so often among the first things we think of when we see a priest's cassock or a coach's whistle or a Boy Scout troop leader's chest festooned with merit badges.

In any case, the fact is that most readers—or so I'd be willing to bet—tend not to remember the "dirty parts" in Lolita. For whatever reasons, the first tentative gropings and fumblings, and the scenes in which Humbert possesses his adored Lo, are not what lodge in our minds.

I myself have read the novel several times. I've retained in memory Humbert's childhood love affairs, his meeting with Lolita and his courtship of her mother, Charlotte Haze, Charlotte's convenient accidental death, Lo and Humbert's cross-country trips, Lolita's ditching Humbert for the mysterious Clare Quilty, the lower-class incarnation of his beloved that Humbert tracks down to Coalmont, "a small industrial community some eight hundred miles from New York City," where he finds her, pregnant and living in squalor with her husband, Dick.

And I could hardly forget the chaotic, protracted, exhilaratingly messy scene in which Humbert murders Quilty, a section that—when

I was Lolita's age, more or less—I heard read by Nabokov on the radio. (At the time, I didn't know what book the passage was from, or who the author was, but nonetheless I somehow understood that it was extraordinary.) In addition, because I had once participated in a marathon reading of *Lolita*, I remembered the chapter I was assigned to read aloud, the hilarious school-admission interview in which Humbert, who is of course sleeping with his pretend daughter, is lectured by the bluestocking, "progressive" principal, Miss Pratt, who believes she has all the most liberal—the most shockingly revolutionary—ideas about girls and sex and so forth.

I remembered that Humbert was hyperaware of how many beds there were in the motel rooms in which he and Lo stayed. I knew that the couple was having sex, but I simply couldn't remember any scenes in which they did.

When I mentioned this to a friend, he said, "Are you kidding? Check out the section, early in the book, in which Lo has her legs across Humbert's lap."

During that scene, as some readers (though not, evidently, this one) will recall, Humbert contrives to sing a popular song (in which "Carmen" rhymes with "barmen") as the pressure of Lo's legs (she is munching on an apple) against his groin arouses him.

Suspended on the brink of that voluptuous abyss (a nicety of physiological equipoise comparable to certain techniques in the arts) I kept repeating chance words after her—barmen, alarmin', my charmin', my carmen, ahmen, ahahamen—as one talking and laughing in his sleep while my happy hand crept up her sunny leg as far as the shadow of decency allowed. . . . And because of her very perfunctory underthings, there seemed to be nothing to prevent my muscular thumb from reaching the hot hollow of her groin—just as you might tickle and caress a giggling child—just that—and: "Oh it's nothing at all," she cried with a sudden shrill note in her voice, and she wiggled, and squirmed, and threw her head back, and her teeth rested on her glistening underlip as she half-turned away, and my moaning mouth, gentlemen of the jury, almost reached her bare neck, while I crushed out against her left buttock the last throb of the longest ecstasy man or monster had ever known.

Is the moment erotic? Obviously, the force of Eros is what inspires and rewards Humbert's faux-innocent and apparently harmless encounter with Lo. Nabokov refers to the "erotic" scenes near the start of his novel, passages that persuaded certain (subsequently disappointed) readers "that this was going to be a lewd book." But is it pornographic? Gentlemen of the jury, I'd argue that the passage is too cerebral, too humorous, too whimsical, too ironic, and, above all, too giddily verbose to function as pornography. The dazzle of language distracts us from the concentration that sexual excitement provides and requires; it's rather like having one's partner begin to prattle, in the midst of lovemaking, about the weather or the stock market or the undone household chores. It's hard to imagine the reader whose level of titillation would not be significantly lowered by phrases such as "the hidden tumor of an unspeakable passion" or "the corpuscles of Krause were entering the phase of frenzy."

There is also the scene in which Humbert first has sex with Lo. Ever since the start of their journey (or flight) in the aftermath of Charlotte Haze's death, Humbert has been planning to drug Lolita with some sort of sleeping pill and (to employ a Humbert-like locution) have his way with her, but—as is so often the case—things turn out rather differently from what our hapless narrator has in mind:

I had thought that months, perhaps years, would elapse before I dared to reveal myself to Dolores Haze; but by six she was wide awake, and by six fifteen we were technically lovers. I am going to tell you something very strange: it was she who seduced me. . . .

If we limit our definition of pornography to that which leads more or less directly to sexual arousal, there are, one can only assume, or perhaps hope, a limited number of readers for whom these scenes will function as pornography—who will feel a rush of desire in response to a heavily ironized account of a middle-aged sleazeball (however charming) attempting to drug and rape a child. Or to the subsequent passage in which Humbert fondles Lo while she is picking her nose and reading the comic pages. Or to the shorthand with which Nabokov describes the lovemaking that precedes the illicit couple's discovery by two nymphet hikers and their chaperone: "Venus came and went."

Defending his novel from the charge that it was pornographic, Nabokov focused on its form—on the ways in which the novel's structure differs from that of the conventional pornographic narrative. But just as important, clearly, is the question of content. In making a case for *Lolita* as art, erotic in its opening chapters and then increasingly less so as Humbert's lust is increasingly transmuted into desperation and self-loathing, let's return for a moment to the wider way in which *pornographic* is currently defined: voyeuristic, exploitative, decadent. I remember using the word to describe the popular TV series *To Catch a Predator*, which ran from 2004 to 2007, a "newsmagazine" program in which obviously ill sex offenders were lured, via Internet chat rooms, into confusing their fantasies with reality. That thirteen-year-old of their dreams wanted them! She was home alone, waiting for them, right now!

Then, exposed and busted by a suave anchorman—on national TV—they were tackled, flung down, and handcuffed, usually on the front lawn of the house in which the sting had occurred.

It's hard to understand who, exactly, found this spectacle entertaining. But sadly, one can all too easily imagine audiences consciously or (more likely) unconsciously turned on by the vice-cop-on-pervert wrestling matches with which these unfortunate encounters culminated, and by the romance of power and violence they represented.

I'd prefer not to believe that I am living in a culture in which TV viewers got actual hard-ons watching the shaming and sadistic struggles that ended with the perp hog-tied, facedown. But sexuality is a mystery, as individual as our fingerprints, so how can I know whether the satisfaction my fellow Americans took in these performances was putatively "moral," or physiological, or both?

Among the qualities (beauty, intelligence, grace, complexity, facility of language, and wit, among countless other literary virtues) that distinguish *Lolita* as a work of art is the fact that it functions as the opposite of—the antidote to—*To Catch a Predator*. It deepens our well of compassion and sympathy, whether we like it or not. The predator is caught, all right, but first Nabokov's novel charms and badgers, irritates and delights us into seeing the world through the eyes of the perp.

That near-miraculous process reminds us of a near-miraculous fact: that great art manages to coexist in the same world in which, in a studio somewhere (let's say, Bavaria), a cameraman shoots some footage of two hapless junkies (I forgot to mention the disturbing close-ups of the needle tracks on the women's legs) gyrating to techno-pop, and then someone adds, on the audio, the sly, knowing joke. Ha ha, these grinding white girls are Martin Luther King's dream.

If Eros is the life force, then *Lolita* is—for all its ironic remove and tragic desperation—Eros between the covers, Humbert Humbert's loopy, unpleasant, celebratory, obnoxious human voice erupting like a jack-in-the-box each time we open the book, even now, especially now, at this moment in our history when it so often appears that Thanatos has Eros pinned like those perverts on the front lawn.

15

Gitta Sereny, *Cries Unheard*

IN THE SPRING OF 1968, IN THE SLUMS OF NEWCASTLE, England, an eleven-year-old named Mary Bell killed four-year-old Martin Brown in a ruined house; nine weeks later, she murdered three-year-old Brian Howe in a vacant lot near a munitions plant that the children called the Tin Lizzie. Soon after, she was tried, convicted of manslaughter, and sentenced to reform school and then prison, from which she emerged, somewhat unsteadily, in 1980.

By the time she reached her forties, Mary Bell had become the responsible, attentive mother of an adolescent girl. Profoundly changed by her love for her daughter, she was attempting, at great personal cost, to come to terms with the person she was, and had been.

No one could be better qualified to document these costly efforts than Gitta Sereny, whose *Cries Unheard* tells Mary Bell's chilling, cautiously redemptive story—her gruesome childhood, her crime, her scandalous trial, her incarceration, and the "mystery of transformation" that turned a violent, disturbed girl into a "morally aware adult." A Hungarian-born journalist living in London, Sereny is best known here for her powerful, unique researches into the evolution of conscience, and into our capacity for succumbing to—or resisting—evil at its most extreme and persuasive. *Into That Darkness* (1974) is a book-length interview with Franz Stangl, the happily married family man who served as the commandant of the Treblinka extermination camp. *Albert Speer: His Battle with Truth* (1995) painstakingly attempts to fathom how a brilliant, thoughtful man could have thrown himself so wholeheartedly into the job of being Hitler's chief architect and engineer.

What makes her books so controversial, so profoundly threatening—and so unlike anyone else's—is Sereny's unconventional and immensely brave refusal to demonize her subjects. She stubbornly insists on viewing them as complex human beings with histories, quirks, virtues, flaws, and needs—not unlike our own. (The Speer book begins, provocatively, "Albert Speer, whom I knew well and grew to like . . .") Convinced that little is to be gained from exploring the reasons why monsters behave monstrously, she focuses instead on the desires, petty self-delusions, and equivocations that seduce sentient, apparently "normal" people into making unconscionable compromises and decisions.

Confronting these penitent or unrepentant sinners without prejudgment or condemnation, Sereny has devised a singular strategy, so simple and so brilliant that it's hard to understand why no one else has employed it in quite the same way: she listens carefully, calmly, asks for repeated accounts, compares competing versions, monitors her own responses, and interviews the sort of collateral figures (Stangl's wife, Speer's secretary, Mary Bell's probation officers and fellow prisoners) with whom conventional historians never bother. Sympathetic, unsentimental, alert to the vagaries of memory and to the possibility of manipulation, Sereny describes the excruciating self-examinations occasioned by her patient interrogations—and in the process she denies us the easy consolations and comforts of convincing ourselves that these criminals and mass murderers belong to an alien species.

Sereny has also written extensively about the moral lives of abused children; her book *The Invisible Children* is a study of child prostitution in Europe. In 1972, she published *The Case of Mary Bell*, an account of the little girl's trial, which Sereny attended. She writes in *Cries Unheard*:

> It seemed very obvious to me that there were elements of Mary Bell's story that were either unknown or hidden from the court. And as she grew up in detention and was repeatedly mentioned in the press, I found myself hoping that one day Mary Bell and I could talk. By finding out not from others but from her what had happened to and in her during her childhood, I felt we might take a step toward understanding what internal and external pressures can lead young children to commit serious crime and murder.

In 1995, she heard that Mary's mother had died and that Mary wanted to write "a serious book" about her life—and so their intense and often painful collaboration on *Cries Unheard* began.

Cries Unheard is structured rather like a detective story, an inquiry into the mystery of why the hapless eleven-year-old reached the breaking point, an explosion preceded and accompanied by a series of troubling incidents (Mary attacked other children, broke into the local preschool, ran away from home) that might have broadcast her wish to be stopped or caught—if anyone had been paying attention or been qualified to interpret her behavior.

The book begins with the trial at which Mary was sentenced to life imprisonment. Her codefendant and best friend, thirteen-year-old Norma Bell, was acquitted of all charges, though Norma undeniably knew about—and was perhaps complicitous in—the killing of Brian Howe. But the slow-witted Norma had the advantage of a demonstrably loving family, while Mary, far more intelligent and disturbed, came from a more problematic and (at least to the jury) less sympathetic background. Her biological father's identity was unknown, and her mother, Betty, was a prostitute whose "specialty" involved whips, as well as a delusional sociopath who acted out at the trial, took suggestive photographs of Mary while she was in detention, and hawked personal information about her daughter to the tabloids.

Only after reading about the arraignment of the bewildered child (whom the press described as "a freak of nature" and "a bad seed") do we learn the details of the criminal investigation that began after Brian Howe's body, strangled and marked by peculiar scratches, was discovered between two cement blocks in the Tin Lizzie. Gradually, the detectives' suspicions collected around Mary and Norma, who had been behaving bizarrely since Martin Brown's death, nine weeks before. A few days after Martin was found, Mary "rang the Browns' doorbell and, smilingly, asked Martin's shocked mother to let her see the little boy in his coffin." The girls protested their innocence until their inconsistent and improbable stories— and their eerily accurate knowledge of unpublicized aspects of the murders—pointed to their involvement, and they were arrested.

Sereny tracks Mary's thorny, circuitous route from imprisonment to parole, a journey that began at Red Bank, an enlightened reform school for boys, headed by a compassionate former naval officer whose kindness first suggested to Mary that an adult could be trusted. But the progress made at Red Bank was rapidly undone in prison, where Mary responded to her rehabilitation with escape and suicide attempts, violence, and her endlessly inventive uses of sex and personal charisma to manipulate her surroundings.

In these sections, as in the rest of the book, Sereny is less engaged by facts of biography than by questions of consciousness and of epistemology. What was Mary's experience of the crimes, the trial, and her detention? And what does she remember and understand in the light of what she subsequently learned? *Cries Unheard* has not even a vague familial resemblance to a "true crime" story, but is instead a profoundly philosophical and reflective psychological study of culpability and innocence, conscience and redemption.

Throughout, the tragic narrative of damage and misunderstanding is interrupted by interviews and encounters in which the adult Mary fearfully inches toward the truth of what she did, and what was done to her.

> She invariably lost control of her emotions when trying to talk about the actual killings. In the early weeks of our talks, her distress at these disclosures would be so intense that I sometimes became afraid for her and urged her to lie down and rest or even to go home. . . . Her recovery from these terrible bouts of grief, however, was astoundingly quick, and at first these rapid emotional shifts raised doubts in me. After a while, though, I came to realize that they were part of the internal pattern that governs all of her feelings and her conduct. She has an exceptional range of opposing needs, all of which are constantly acute: her needs for disclosure and for hiding, for sociability and isolation, for talking and for silence, for laughing and for crying. Only one thing overrides them all: the discipline she has created inside herself in order to give her daughter a normal life.

Like many children, Sereny believes, Mary and Norma only dimly comprehended the finality of death. As Mary says of Martin's killing, "I told him to put his hands on my throat and I put my hands on his. . . . Obviously, I must have been messed up inside, but I never associated it with the afterwards. . . . I think to me it was: 'You'll come around in time for tea.'" In addition, Mary and Norma were genuinely dumbfounded by the gap between the gritty realities of police custody and the glamorous fantasies of chase and escape they'd constructed from watching old westerns and hearing about the latest high-profile bank heists. "For children," writes Sereny, "for whom there is a wide separation between what they should know or are believed to know and what they do feel and understand, the evidence that proves their crimes, once obtained, should become almost irrelevant. The only thing that should count is human evidence—the answer to the question 'Why?'"

The *why*, in this instance, is quite obviously Betty Bell, whose initial, instinctive response to her newborn daughter was "Take the thing away from me!" Early in the narrative, Sereny informs us that when Mary was "between the ages of four and eight, her mother, then a prostitute, had exposed her to one of the worst cases of child sexual abuse I have ever encountered." But, cannily, she waits almost until the book's end—till we have come to know Mary, to see her through Sereny's eyes, to recognize "Mary's two best qualities, compassion and humor"—to disclose the specifics of Betty's attempts to poison her and give her away, and of the appalling sexual uses to which Betty and her clients put the little girl.

Our sympathy for Mary and our outrage at her mother are further intensified by the fact that Sereny reveals the full history of their catastrophic relationship immediately after the very different, and very moving, account of Mary's own labor and delivery: "Then they said, 'It's a little girl. You've got a little girl,' and I burst into tears and I held her and they said they had to take her away to clean her up. . . . And then they brought her back all swaddled and I held her to me . . . and I said, or I thought, 'Hello, I've been waiting a long time to see you.'"

At a cultural moment when so much in our society—criminal defenses based on histories of childhood abuse, the growing popularity of the notion that past suffering absolves the victim of moral responsibility—persuades us to blur or eradicate the line between compassion and forgiveness, both Mary Bell and Gitta Sereny are fiercely meticulous in drawing and maintaining the all too rarely made distinction between sympathy and absolution. *Cries Unheard* reminds us that understanding and accountability can coexist, that we need not choose between them. While Mary's abysmal

childhood helps explain her violence and catastrophic disassocia-
tion, it does not excuse her crimes. Thus, when Sereny asks Mary
whether she ever associated Martin Brown's death with a vicious
physical fight that she had with her mother on the day of the murder, Mary recoils from what she interprets as an attempt to diminish
her culpability: "'I didn't ever want to say it. Not today either. . . .
It sounds too much . . . too much like . . .' I waited. She couldn't,
wouldn't say the word. 'Nothing can justify what I did,' she finally
said. 'Nothing.' Mary knows her guilt is permanent. Nothing can
remove it, nothing can allay her sadness for what she has done. But
her dream—a modest one, I feel—is to work, to study, to live in
peace, to be allowed, as she puts it, 'to be normal.' . . . She allows
herself no mitigation, and in her despair for an answer has repeatedly said, 'There are many unhappy, very disturbed kids out there
who don't end up robbing families of their children.'"

Sereny's journalistic—and, one wants to say, spiritual—
disposition serves her well in a project that is in itself an ethical
minefield. Preemptively, she raises the vexing moral questions
even before they occur to the reader.

> There has not been a day in the two years I have worked on
> [the book] when the two little boys—who would now have
> been thirty-five and thirty-four years old—have not been in my
> mind. And there has not been a day, either, when I have not
> asked myself whether writing this book was the right thing to
> do . . . for Mary Bell, from whom, with great difficulty and
> agonizingly for her, I extracted her life, for the families of the
> children she killed, and for her own family, above all her child,
> who now is her life.

Regardless of her private apprehensions, Sereny is certain about
her motives for writing the book, confirmed in her faith that

*if anyone could ever help us one day to understand, firstly, what
can bring a young child to the point of murder, and second,
what needs to and can be done with and for such children, Mary
would be able to . . . If Mary's painful disclosures of a suffering
childhood and appallingly mismanaged adolescence in detention
succeed in prompting us . . . to detect children's distress, however well hidden, we might one day be able to prevent them from
offending instead of inappropriately prosecuting and punishing
them when they do.*

Evidently, too, Sereny has weighed the implications of Mary's
participation in the project—as have the British tabloids, which
swarmed all over the fact that the convicted killer was paid for her
cooperation. Unrelenting and sensational media attention helped
whip up the frenzied scandal that has greeted the book's publication in Great Britain. In 1998, reporters tracked Mary Bell to the
house in which she was living with "Jim," her partner of many
years, and her fourteen-year-old daughter, who had been unaware
of her mother's past until the press besieged them. ("'I knew there
was a secret,' the girl said. 'But Mum, why didn't you tell me? You
were just a kid, younger than I am now.'")

Such passages are extremely painful and troubling to read,
but—as in all of Sereny's books—these harrowing, probing, and
empathetic glimpses of her subjects' psyches and domestic intimacies are essential for her method, and her purpose. They compel
us to examine and deconstruct our received or simplistic notions
of innocence and wrongdoing, and to confront the complicated,
discernible humanity of the very people we are most eager to despise and dismiss. In Gitta Sereny's competent hands, the faces of
the guilty become distorting mirrors in which we are forced to acknowledge skewed but still recognizable versions of the faces we
have seen, and lived with, all our lives.

16

Andrea Canobbio, *Three Light-Years*

ANDREA CANOBBIO'S REMARKABLE NOVEL *THREE LIGHT-YEARS* begins with the sort of metaphor, the kind of sweeping statement, that in the work of a less gifted author might warn readers to brace themselves for the onslaught of something sententious and bogus. But the paragraph that follows is so artful and intriguing that it dispels whatever unease its opening sentence might have inspired: "Memory is an empty room. Gone are the bookshelves littered with journals, gone are the chairs and table, the paintings, the calendar, and the computer screen filled with words. My father is gone, too, effaced by thousands of identical moments, deleted by the same repetitive gestures day after day, as he sat there tapping the keys."

Even as we are parsing this passage, and already admiring the deftness (how apt that word choice: *deleted*) of Anne Milano Appel's exemplary translation, the novel has rushed past us. The narrator's father, a repressed, middle-aged Italian doctor named Claudio Viberti, is working at the computer in the pediatricians' lounge of an urban hospital when, entirely by chance, the beautiful Cecilia—a stranger in a white lab coat—bursts into the room. "Her

eight-year-old son had been admitted to the ward a few days earlier
and she was looking for a doctor, or at least someone dressed as a
doctor, who could persuade him to eat."

Given this scenario, a lesser talent might fashion a novel resembling a script for a TV medical drama. But Canobbio, whose
previous novel that appeared in English was *The Natural Disorder
of Things* (2004), avoids the obvious pitfalls, largely as a result of
his acuity and inventiveness, of the specificity and density of his
detail, the elegance of his style, and the depth of his psychological insight. These virtues are apparent early on, in this account of
what Viberti observes and intuits after he agrees to help Cecilia
and drifts through the children's ward, feigning an interest in the
young patients' charts.

> A sullen-looking little boy occupied the bed near the door, and a
> child with a mop of red hair had the one next to the window. A
> woman, presumably a mother, was sitting in the far corner, knit-
> ting. There were still women who knitted, then; you saw them
> in waiting rooms, in the wards, mysterious and comforting like
> childhood scars you rediscover on your skin from time to time.
>
> Cecilia's son was watching the red-haired boy maneuver two
> dinosaurs on the bed in a noisy, never-ending battle. He looked
> a lot like his mother; his face was hardly sunken, he didn't seem
> emaciated. On the bedside table, next to a bottle of mineral wa-
> ter and a glass, four toy cars rested on a sheet of graph paper on
> which the diagram of an angled parking lot had been drawn with
> great precision. My father thought the child must love things that
> were done just so, that he must love any form of order.

The boy, Mattia, who has been hospitalized for an eating disorder, is reading a book called *Supercars*, in which Viberti finds a
picture of an old Aston Martin, like the one driven by James Bond.
After a brief chat about Agent 007 and the villains he outsmarted,

Viberti asks the red-haired boy about his dinosaurs and the sulky boy about the music he has downloaded onto his iPod. Viberti avoids looking directly at Cecilia's son, but he notices that Mattia, whose reflection he glimpses in an IV bag suspended between the beds, has begun to eat.

Cecilia is also a doctor, an emergency room physician who will turn out to be the love of Viberti's life. *Three Light-Years* tracks their long, intense, and tormented affair, a romance blighted by the lovers' crippling reserve and their painful personal histories, by the competing claims (children, parents) on their affections, by their inability to decide what they want or to act on their desires, and ultimately by bad timing and bad luck.

The mother of two children, Cecilia is separated from her husband when Viberti meets her and is subsequently divorced; the breakup of her marriage and the crisis that precipitated it have done considerable psychic damage. And Viberti ("the shy internist," Cecilia calls him) has reached what appears to be a terminal impasse; a creature of habit and routine, he is stuck living in the same apartment building as his ex-wife, her new family, and his elderly mother.

Viberto and Cecilia continue meeting for lunch even after Mattia is released from the hospital. They talk mostly about work, and Viberti is

> *amazed by the accuracy of her diagnoses, and by how sound and sensible her treatments were. He thought that sooner or later, at least once in a lifetime, a doctor like him (diligent, caring, mediocre) was bound to meet a true natural talent. There was no envy, it was pure admiration. . . . The only resource he could claim, experience, could be measured by age; it was less mysterious than talent, but more bitter, because to a great extent you earned it by making mistakes.*

Early on, Viberti realizes that he is in love with Cecilia.

He would have liked to see a face like that every morning when he opened his eyes (my father thought for the first time). No, that wasn't right. Not a face like that—that face. Sudden, overwhelming desire: he wanted to leap down from the windowsill—swoop down like an angel in an ex-voto—and wheel around her, glide down to grasp her and snatch her away, save her from an impending danger. . . . Of all the faces in his life, why that one?

But almost a year goes by before he can bring himself to make an ardent declaration of love, a confession so awkward that it rapidly devolves into a consideration of the fine points of language.

"I know you don't feel the same attraction, I would have noticed, but in the last few months you've become a kind of torture, so I thought that if I told you maybe I'd be able to stand it, I don't know, maybe it's a stupid idea, I'd like to get over it." He immediately regrets using the word "torture," but he didn't prepare the little speech he's giving now. "Well, torture is an exaggeration, sorry, I meant fixation, obsession, in a positive sense." . . . He's complicating his life, making things worse. He takes a sip of water.

Such passages make one acutely aware of the challenges that Appel must have faced—and finessed—in rendering Canobbio's Italian into English.

Cecilia pretends not to have suspected the depth of the shy internist's feelings. (In truth, she'd estimated that there was an "eighty percent chance" that he was in love with her.) And she tells him that she doesn't think of him that way. What follows is perhaps one of the most extended, beautiful, and excruciating descriptions

in literature of how a woman can be deeply in love with a man—
and not know it. When Cecilia is apart from Viberti, she constantly
imagines talking to him, sleeping with him, watching television
with her head on his shoulder; her fantasies about him are alternately sisterly and sexual. She tells him, "When I have to think
about something wonderful and good I think of you, at night I
think of you and calm down and fall asleep." To which Viberti replies, "Well, better me than a benzodiazepine."

The couple attempt to make love in Viberti's car—with comic
and embarrassing results. They see each other and their affair
grows more passionate and intimate. They decide to stop seeing
each other and then have "relapses." (Unsurprisingly, they employ
the vocabulary of medicine and disease in talking about their affair.) "He'd started calling them relapses to make her smile, so they
could laugh about it together, because their relationship was a re-
curring illness, because they were doctors unable to cure it, but
now it was no longer funny."

Throughout the novel, Cecilia and Viberti keep important
secrets from each other, but Canobbio's readers know what they
are concealing, because the point of view shifts from character to
character, revealing every facet of the lovers' deepest emotions—
and everything they hope to keep hidden. The narrative frequently
circles back to an event about which we've already read in order to
show us the incident from a new vantage. These refractory, changing perspectives function like a series of dramatic plot turns and
reverses, drawing us through a book in which not all that much
happens, or, to be more accurate, much of what happens occurs
within (and *only* in) the characters' minds.

A critical scene in which Viberti accidentally meets Cecilia
while she is having lunch with her sister Silvia is replayed three
times and becomes, in effect, three different stories, with contrasting preludes, beginnings, and endings, all depending on whose
experience of this chance encounter is being reported. Almost a

hundred pages after Viberti announces his love, Cecilia contemplates (and partly explains) her response:

> When the day of his declaration came, Cecilia thought about how blind she'd been, how strongly she wanted everything to remain as it was, for nothing more to happen in her life, for each day to be like every other, each action indistinguishable from that of the day before, for the children to always be children. . . . Without doing anything to discourage him, she had soaked up that silent worship, had fed on his ever-deepening love. So when he seemed to have exhausted his speech (if it had been prepared, it was badly prepared and even more poorly delivered) Cecilia thought: What have I done?

This tale of passion, doomed forever by self-consciousness, confusion, and cowardice, may remind us of nineteenth-century Russian fiction: of the mushroom-picking scene in *Anna Karenina*, in which two would-be lovers fail to overcome their reserve; of Chekhov's stories ("About Love") and his plays, among them *Uncle Vanya*, its characters forever stalled between timidity and yearning.

In fact, Chekhov is mentioned several times in *Three Light-Years*. Viberti's mother, Marta, retells a "scandalous" story that, her son believes, is by either Chekhov, Maupassant, or Tarchetti. "The name of the protagonist (who may have been Russian, French, or Italian) was Cecilia, and the chance appearance of that name on his mother's lips seriously upset Viberti, though the story left him somewhat indifferent (some kind of incest)—especially since his mother's narration was even less consistent than usual."

Later in the book, the real Cecilia refers to this incident, which Viberti has mentioned; she is curious about Marta's story. Though we have assumed that Viberti only dimly heard his mother, we now learn that he'd been listening quite closely indeed. He tells Cecilia a preposterous tale about a dying man who asks his daughter

(Cecilia) to have his watch repaired by a particular watchmaker, a request that will result in her marrying a man who, unbeknownst to her, is her brother. This time it's Viberti's lover who is distracted; in the middle of the story about the incestuous brother and sister, Cecilia makes a resolution about how to deal with her own son and daughter, whose relationship puzzles and disturbs her: from time to time, she decides, she'll keep the siblings apart.

Later still, Viberti asks his mother if she feels that she hasn't really lived, and by way of reply she recalls a performance of *The Cherry Orchard* that she and Viberti attended when he was in high school. She mentions a character in the play, a sad man who sounds (to the reader) rather like Viberti. Does Viberti recognize the resemblance? Does it irritate him? Does Viberti really not remember the play, though Marta is the one who is supposed to be losing her memory? And does anyone but the author and the reader understand that Viberti feels irritation toward his mother partly because the mention of a cherry orchard reminds him "about cherries, about *sakura*, about Japanese cuisine"—and of a Japanese dinner he recently ate with Silvia, and about which he feels vaguely guilty?

He doesn't remember, he doesn't care. He stands up and says, "Mama, are we sure you have a memory problem? It seems to me you remember everything clearly."

Marta reaches out her arm, as if to introduce herself, extends her open hand. Viberti shakes it. He will continue shaking hands with her as long as she lives, she clinging to him, and he clinging to her, in her few remaining years, until the day comes when, seeing a close-up of the Pope on television, she'll ask softly, "Why is he looking at me?" Until the day she scratches out people's eyes in the old family photos, until she becomes convinced that her caregivers want to kill her, until she hurls insults at him, calling him a "little toad" because she doesn't want him to give her an

injection, until she no longer gets out of bed and she widens her
blue eyes without speaking, and stares into his.

Even if Chekhov's name weren't invoked, we might think of him when we read Canobbio. Among the qualities they share is a gift for finding the perfect illuminating or clarifying detail; it's what Nabokov calls "the magic of the trifles [Chekhov] collects." In Canobbio, these apparent trifles are often employed to explain or emphasize some aspect of a character's personality. Mattia's interest in parked cars, which Viberti analyzes in the opening scene, outlasts the boy's hospital stay, and reappears later in the novel, with painful consequences for Mattia, his mother, and his older sister. And like Chekhov, Canobbio often uses humorous details to lighten a passage that might otherwise seem ponderous. Consider, for example, the snack that concludes the following paragraph:

She awoke in the night seized by the darkest anxiety; she wasn't
in love with the shy internist, she didn't want to begin a relation-
ship, being with him that afternoon, kissing him, letting herself
be undressed in the car like a teenager had been a mistake, a ter-
ribly selfish outburst . . . She got up an hour before the alarm
went off, paced back and forth in the kitchen so as not to wake the
children. She ate two packets of mascarpone spread on rice cakes.

Both Chekhov and Canobbio are fascinated by (and endlessly sympathetic to) the tortuous and often maddening convolutions of an unhappy love affair. Both dangle before the reader the slim, unlikely chance that the lovers' story will have a happy ending. Both writers excel at what fiction accomplishes better than any other form of art, which is to anatomize human consciousness, to show us how the world looks through the eyes of a particular human being, to record each minute shift in awareness and understanding, the revisions and corrections of what that person feels and thinks in response to the information that is, every moment, being received from the world.

This sort of fiction has consciousness as its subject, and Canobbio's ability to engage us in the consciousness of his characters is what keeps us enthralled by the advances and reverses of Viberti and Cecilia's neurotic love affair. We inhabit the novel's characters; we hear their opinions about marriage, medicine, family life, and the films of Almodóvar; we temporarily inherit their worries, their uncertainties, their nostalgias. We know what they are really thinking—even or especially when they are mysteries to themselves and to the people they love.

Canobbio is unusually adept at depicting the ways in which people can hold two disparate subjects in mind more or less at once (Cecilia's attentions are perpetually tracking back and forth between thoughts of her lover and her children) and simultaneously inhabit the present and the past. From its opening sentence, the novel announces that its subject is memory, which will prove to be the obsession, refuge, and nemesis of each character. For Viberti's mother, memory has become a tricky path to navigate without losing her balance; keeping up the pretense that her recall remains sharp has become a game. Much of Viberti's memory is occupied by three towering figures: his mother, prone to depression when he was a boy, his father, who died young, and his father's friend, a doctor who stepped in to fill the absence left by Viberti's lost parent. Cecilia's day off, at the beach, is both enhanced and spoiled by her intense longing for the bygone, paradisiacal time when the children were younger and completely *hers*, more like affectionate puppies.

> *Especially nice to see the children playing in the distance, having fun and yelling excitedly. Even nicer when they ran back now and then, taking turns. But that happened rarely now. At one time, when they were little, those return visits were the most delightful*

part of a day at the beach. Every twenty or thirty minutes, one of
them would race back and collapse on top of her, clinging to her.
And she'd pretend she was tired and that they were heavy, all the
while smiling as she pretended to be impatient and somewhat
irritated. Now she would give anything for one of those appear-
ances, and when it happened she had to contain her joy.

It is also at the beach that we first meet Silvia, unmarried,
childless, lonely, difficult, a nonstop talker and a fantasist—another
reminder of Chekhov: the loaded gun onstage that will go off by
the end of the play. She is the less pretty, the less successful, attractive, and accomplished sister. With her signature black headband,
which makes her hair puff out so that her head looks like a mush-
room, she reminds us of a creature in a children's book: the resentful fairy who hasn't been invited to the christening party. Silvia
works alone at home as a copy editor. "At times of sinking self-
esteem she feels like a cleaning lady venturing into other people's
pages . . . She spends hours at the stupidest job in the world, she
checks to see that she's made all the revisions, spelling the words
out on the screen, tapping them out, as if she were knocking to
find out who's behind them."

Of all these forlorn men, women, and children, Silvia is the
saddest. Even a pleasant evening out with friends is basically bleak:

She recalls many shameful things her friends have told her, but
she isn't sure she remembers all the shameful things she's told
them about herself. They laugh, but they're really not joking, be-
cause the questions that fascinate them are questions of life and
death: a life they're afraid they won't live, a life that hasn't be-
gun, a love life, a professional life. They fear the lack of strong,
passionate feelings and exciting, long-lasting careers, or an ex-
cess of tenuous feelings and precarious careers. An absence of life
that is fear of death; that is always there.

With her inability to forget the one lover who came closest to (and still remained far from) being "the right man," her unrelenting grief for the dead father she adored, her attachment to her troubled adolescent niece, and her stormy relationships with her mother and sister, Silvia is a slightly more extreme, slightly more frustrated funhouse-mirror version of the other characters. When, in the last third of the novel, she emerges as an important figure, the book undergoes a tonal shift and becomes more manic, and darker. Her intercession—or interference—in her sister's love affair has dramatic consequences that not only affect Cecilia and Viberti's future, but alert the reader to the fact that we (like the novel's characters) have somehow misunderstood the most important things; we've jumped to conclusions and gotten it wrong. In fact, the story being told to us by the narrator—the son whose doctor father, Viberti, wanted him to be an architect and who became a writer instead—is significantly different from the one we assumed we were reading.

These final sections not only provide the principal characters with an ingenious (if not entirely desired or desirable) means of rescue from the mire into which we have watched them sink, but they allow Canobbio to maintain, until the book's conclusion, a delicate, even precarious balance between gravity and levity, between the comic and the tragic. The last few pages remind readers of what the preceding ones have made clear: how impossible it is to understand ourselves, let alone anyone else, and how we can be held hostage by obsession and self-doubt until fate intercedes and sets us free, or until some combination of chance and character makes our decision for us.

17

Diane Arbus: *Revelations*

AMONG THE OMINOUS HALLUCINATIONS THAT TERRIFY THE little boy who tricycles manically through the deserted hotel in Stanley Kubrick's *The Shining* is a pair of female twins whose appearance, posture, and affect are a quotation from, or an homage to, Diane Arbus's photograph "Identical Twins, Roselle, New Jersey, 1967." The little girls in the film are harbingers of the hotel's gory past and the boy's violent future, and the vision of Kubrick's eerie sisters, superimposed upon our own memory of Arbus's portrait, not only telegraphs its sinister import with the eloquent concision of a Chinese character but provides an extra somatic jolt, a shiver of apprehension.

If, however, you actually study the picture—included, in several variant versions, in *Diane Arbus: Revelations*, a new collection of her photographs and biographical material—the girls hardly seem like candidates for cameo roles in a horror film, no matter how nuanced and brilliant. The news they bring is not about death but birth; they're poster children for DNA, witnesses to heredity's power to send us into the world fully formed—doubled, if that's our luck. It would seem naive to deny the fact that there's an inherent strangeness about twins. But like all serious art, Arbus's work resists generalization to focus on the specific, or, more accurately, arrives at a general truth by examining a highly particular reality.

And so, if you look closely, what seems strangest about these specific twins (aside, perhaps, from their Siberian-husky pale eyes) is that they're dressed and coiffed so identically, like the two halves of a Rorschach blot; even their bobby pins are in the same places. Arbus began her career as a fashion photographer and, everywhere in her portraiture, she intends details of dress, hairstyle, makeup, and gesture (the way someone holds a cigarette, for example) to communicate as articulately as they do in life. At one point, she remarked that fashion photography didn't interest her because the people in the pictures weren't wearing their own clothes. What engaged her far more was how people select their outfits, their chosen methods of self-presentation—and the ways in which their personalities affect (and seem to rub off on) what they wear.

Unlike the Kubrick image, which flashes by at a speed that manages to evoke the instincts of those cultures that credit twins with necromantic powers, the Arbus photograph gives us time to study the twins' faces, which are actually quite lovely and not menacing or freakish in the least. The significant differences in their facial expressions would be (if only we could interpret them) keys to the deepest mysteries of individual personality; and whatever secrets they harbor seem less like sources of horror than causes for their own bemusement.

"Identical Twins" has, like numerous Arbus photos, become an icon—which may not be the most fortunate fate to befall a work of art. Because when we call something "iconic," part of what we mean is that we assume we can see it without looking. And once we can summon an image from memory, reconstruct it in our minds, interpret it in ways that become convenient substitutions for the image itself, we may lose our motivation to revisit the actual object as often—and to study it as closely—as we should. We stop returning to it for the periodic soundings that it can provide on the subject of how we, and the world around us, have changed with age and maturity, and in the course of time. (One could argue that the worst thing that can happen to a work of art is to wind up on a cocktail napkin, as have Monet's water lilies and Georgia O'Keeffe's poppies; happily for Arbus fans, it's hard to imagine her portraits of the transvestite in curlers or three geriatric Russian midgets becoming the sorts of icons that decorate drink coasters.)

One of the most welcome and corrective aspects of *Revelations* is that it brushes off the obscuring patina of iconography and invites us to see Arbus's art in fresh ways, amending and deepening our own partial memories and surface impressions. *Revelations* features, along with more familiar works, scores of less famous and previously unknown photographs, contact sheets, and variant prints of single images. The book includes essays by Sandra S. Phillips and by photographer Neil Selkirk, the exclusive printer for Arbus's estate since her death. Jeff Rosenheim, a curator at the Metropolitan Museum of Art, has contributed capsule biographies of the friends, family members, and colleagues who surrounded and influenced Arbus. Finally, there is the engrossing and, as it were, revelatory *Diane Arbus: A Chronology*. Compiled by Elisabeth Sussman and by the artist's daughter Doon, it lists the major events in Arbus's life, contains quotes from her letters and notebooks, and includes biographical documents and artifacts ranging from family photos to grant applications, from her high school report card to her autopsy report.

The fascinating assemblage of history, jottings, and detritus that makes up *Chronology* hangs solidly on a structure built from the facts of Arbus's life, and from the many photographs in which she herself always looks beautiful and wholly different each time, until her last years, when exhaustion evidently slowed the mercurial shifts in appearance. The biographical material contradicts the myths that have come to surround her, the aura that has had a great deal—too much—to do with her suicide, in 1971. For it seems to be the particular fate of female artist suicides—Virginia Woolf and Sylvia Plath naturally come to mind—that self-murder lends a sort of romantic and even ghoulish luster to their reputations and causes their art to be seen, selectively and often inaccurately, through the narrow prism of the manner in which they died.

BORN in 1923 to the wealthy owners of a Manhattan department store, Diane Nemerov led a cosseted childhood, attended private school, and, at eighteen, married Allan Arbus, whom she'd met when she was fifteen. An extremely close couple with a palpable sexual charge, the Arbuses collaborated on fashion photographs for such venues as *Vogue* and *Glamour*.

Increasingly frustrated by the restrictions of her day job, Arbus—who by then had two daughters—separated from her husband and quit the studio in order to pursue her own work. Her inclusion, along with Garry Winogrand and Lee Friedlander, in the 1967 *New Documents* show at New York's Museum of Modern Art boosted her reputation, and from then on she enjoyed a combination (more common then than it is now) of artistic celebrity, popular notoriety, and penury. She received a Guggenheim grant, published in magazines such as *Esquire, Harper's Bazaar, New York*, and the London *Sunday Times Magazine*, won an award from the American Society of Magazine Photographers, and sold work to numerous museums. Nonetheless, she was always scrambling for money, and she spent her final years living in Westbeth, a fortress-like subsidized-housing complex for artists in the far West Village, where tenancy required that residents earn no more than $8,400 a year.

The admirable, hardworking, resilient, and gifted woman who emerges from these pages bears only intermittent resemblance to the spectral depressive seeking risky thrills on the dark side and having casual sex with strangers—that is, the Diane Arbus one encounters in the popular imagination and in such books as Patricia Bosworth's respectful 1995 biography. It's true that, in Arbus's occasional writings, the word *gloomy* and profound doubts about her self-worth recur with increasing and chilling frequency over the years, as do accounts of physical illness, rejection, and alternating periods of elation and depression.

"Energy, some special kind of energy, just leaks out," she records, "and I am left lacking the confidence even to cross the street."

Despite daunting health and financial problems, she worked continuously. The list of professional assignments that sent her to cover events—ranging from Tricia Nixon's wedding to an antiwar demonstration—is dizzying, and the urgency and gratitude with which she sought and received commissions makes more sense when you realize that, at the time, top dollar for a magazine shoot was a few hundred dollars. She interacted productively with several generations of photographic colleagues, from MoMA curator John Szarkowski, Walker Evans, and Helen Levitt (who wrote Arbus's first Guggenheim recommendation) to Bruce Davidson and Joel Meyerowitz, and she recorded her responses to influences such as Lartigue, Brassaï, August Sander, and her teacher and mentor, Lisette Model.

Driven by the exacting demands of her unique vocation, she nonetheless seems to have had limitless love and energy for her children and a genuine, passionate interest in their individual personalities. Her postcards and notes to them are chatty and sparkling; in one letter to her daughter Amy, Diane bravely, if not entirely convincingly, portrays a grim hospital stay (for hepatitis) as a glorious adventure. Yet, lest we mistake Diane Arbus for a respectable single mother, supporting herself as an artist, with a taste for eccentric folk, there is one especially jaw-dropping image amid a series of contact strips. The repeated subject is a couple, two lovers:

a handsome, bare-chested black man in a pair of white pants, and a white woman, naked or wearing a transparent nightgown. The caption states simply, without elaboration, "In the frame second from the top of the center strip Diane is lying across the man's lap in place of the woman." There is no point noting the obvious: that the photographer is naked. This, and the inclusion of several photos of the same models, among them a blonde transvestite with terrific cleavage and a "young Brooklyn family," taken in different settings and apparently on different occasions, acknowledges that Arbus's relationships with her subjects were often more intimate, intense, and prolonged than those of other photographers—for example, Weegee.

All of this enhances whatever conclusions we might draw from Arbus's own comments, made during one of the interviews that form the text of her 1972 Aperture monograph, about the fact that she was naked when photographing nudist colonies: "You think you're going to feel a little silly walking around with nothing on but your camera. But that part is really sort of fun."

In its austere shorthand of document, date, and quotation, *Chronology* portrays one of those artists who seem to have ordained what they would eventually accomplish. A high school paper on Chaucer reads like a prescient analysis of the preoccupations that would animate Arbus's work:

> *His way of looking at everything is like that of a newborn baby; he sees things and each one seems wonderful . . . simply because it is unique and it is there. When he describes the nun's daintiness, it doesn't seem as if he thinks that that is a standard of good conduct . . . rather he turns separately to each one and looks at them as a whole miracle not as compounds of abstract qualities.*

She was, from early on, an avid reader, and the book is filled with references to writers ranging from Plato to Rilke to Italo

Svevo. She herself wrote beautifully, had a great gift for narrative and description, and for reflecting on her process in ways that are often witty, incisive, and as tantalizingly elusive as the work itself. "I think I must have been brought up to be a sort of magic mirror who reflects what anyone wants to believe because I can't believe they believe it, like Atlas holding up a bubble and groaning." She thought in grand, ambitious terms, planned future projects, mapped avenues of investigation, and made simultaneously encyclopedic and idiosyncratic lists of subjects to explore: "a certain group of young nihilists, a variety of menages, a retirement town in the Southwest, a new kind of Messiah, a particular Utopian cult who plan to establish themselves on a nearby island, Beauties of different ethnic groups, certain criminal types, a minority elite."

Even as *Chronology* expands our view of the artist herself, the hundreds of familiar and unknown images collected here, and the elegance and exactitude with which they are printed, refute and dismantle the half-truths about, and knee-jerk responses to, her work. In its crudest possible form, one notion of Arbus's oeuvre describes a limited palette: high-contrast, confrontational portraits of tormented freaks—a categorization that could be applied, just as unhelpfully, to the majority of Gogol and Dostoyevsky characters. Included is a quote from a memoir by Diane's brother, the poet Howard Nemerov, in which he expresses something uncomfortably close to this received opinion of the work of his sister: "a professional photographer, whose pictures are spectacular, shocking, dramatic, and concentrate on subjects perverse and queer (freaks, professional transvestites, strong men, tattooed men, the children of the very rich)."

As *Revelations* argues, little could be more reductive, or more unfair. In fact, her range was wide, and included not just portraits but landscapes, such as the surrealistic "Clouds on Screen at a Drive-in, N.J., 1960," and the simultaneously ironic and romantic "A Castle in Disneyland, Cal., 1962." Her subjects were not only sideshow performers but dancing couples and newborns, not just anonymous women with unfortunate relationships to cosmetics but celebrity heartthrobs such as Marcello Mastroianni, not just retarded inmates but geniuses such as Jorge Luis Borges, not just sword swallowers but pretty kids.

Reminiscent of certain of Helen Levitt's pictures, "Two Boys Smoking in Central Park, 1962" radiates admiration for the insouciant style and beauty of the boys. If the light and the lens—and an eye for composition—are a photographer's principal tools, *Revelations* proves that Arbus could, at will, make her technique invisible or, conversely, achieve theatrically virtuosic effects. Two photographs of a movie screen showing the film *Baby Doll* and another shot of a darkened theater in which a movie is being shown are dazzling visual dissections of how cinema deploys darkness and light. You don't have to understand the full implications of what it means to print on pre-cadmium purged Agfa Portriga-Rapid paper developed in a solution of Dektol and Selectol Soft to grasp how Neil Selkirk's essay informs what we can plainly see in the photos—namely, that Arbus knew what she was doing and what she wanted, not only on the street but also in the darkroom. She knew how to let the light locate and pick out telling, glittering details: the wedding-cake-like trophy that a muscle builder displays in his Brooklyn dressing room, or the Asian knickknacks, shiny dress, jewelry, coffee cup, and pill bottle of a widow in her Manhattan apartment.

The contact sheets in *Revelations* function as a primer on Arbus's working methods and on photography in general. The remarkably contradictory information conveyed by each separate frame dispels any notion that photography is about uncovering and telling "the truth." Or perhaps it argues that there is no such thing as a single truth about a complex human being. In only one shot does the sweet, eager-to-please, fussily dressed little boy reveal the twisted maniac Arbus depicted in "Child with a Toy Grenade in Central Park, 1962." And the different and fleeting moods caught in multiple images of a single sitting reveal the intelligence and the compositional sense that inspired Arbus to choose the version of "A Jewish Giant at Home with His Parents in the Bronx, N.Y., 1970" that shows the two (comparatively) normal-size parents grouped on one side of their son, staring up, in apparent wonder, at their prodigious offspring. Other shots, in which the giant stands between his parents with his arms draped around their shoulders, are merely a joke about size—and not, like the final version, a metaphor for the astonishment parents feel toward the fully grown beings they can barely believe they created.

IN an afterword to *Revelations*, Doon Arbus writes that a photograph should be allowed to speak for itself, without explanatory, contextual, or biographical data. And indeed, we hardly need a word of text in order to respond, cerebrally and viscerally, to the intricate mysteriousness of what Diane Arbus is showing us. We can, without help, track the visual and thematic obsessions that last throughout her career, her fascination with the tension between how people wish to look and how they actually appear (what she called "the gap between intention and effect"), as well as with ambiguities of all types: with people whose appearance confounds whatever we had assumed to be the signal divisions between male and female, young and old, beautiful and ugly. Without reading the Guggenheim application in which she outlines a project involving rituals and ceremonies, we intuit that she was drawn to the rites that establish a community's hierarchies and tighten the bonds of a common identity. Without learning that she worked on journalistic projects on the themes of love and the family, we gather that these subjects were of consummate interest to her, objects of a curiosity that grows in proportion to the distance between her family constellations and our traditional assumptions about how these groups should look. And even without noting how references to mirrors recur in her notebooks, we can tell how profoundly she identified with her subjects, how she was always looking for something of herself in them, and how that identification and that search prevent her pictures from seeming exploitative, clinical, superior, or judgmental.

But even if we ourselves believe in the primacy of the work itself, in the centrality of the object that nimbly eludes any attempt at summary or interpretation, still we can't much suppress our appetite for those works and documents—Woolf's diaries, Chekhov's letters—in which an artist steps out from behind the scrim to comment directly on matters of art, the self, and the world. And so it is with the text of *Revelations*, in which Arbus's own words function as guides of a sort, tactful and unobtrusive, but nonetheless encouraging us to notice things that we otherwise might have overlooked.

One such helpful prompting arises from the fact that many of the extracts from Arbus's writings—indeed, most of the ones set in a larger typeface and given pages of their own—employ the vocabulary of religion and of spiritual autobiography. Scattered throughout are references to conversion, God and the devil, Adam and Eve, divinity, blasphemy, and faith. The book's title and its epigraph are taken from an Arbus quote: "And the revelation was a little like what saints receive on mountains—a further chapter in the history of the mystery . . ." She writes about Mae West, whom she photographed, hearing the voice of God and longing to lift the hemline of the unknown, and describes a roomful of baton twirlers as practicing "a most ascetic mystic moral discipline."

Once you allow your thoughts to be nudged ever so gently in that direction, it becomes easy to spot, along the way, images that evoke the classic tropes of Western and Eastern religious art: the kitschy "Buddhist" altar decorating the Manhattan widow's living room; a nudist Adam and Eve, holding hands in a forest glade; the windblown crucifixion of the "Albino Sword Swallower at a Carnival, Md., 1970"; the benediction offered in "Bishop by the Sea, Santa

Barbara, Cal., 1964," by a white-haired old woman who apparently called herself the Bishop, and who is shown wearing a silvery robe and a goofy homemade miter, extending her arms and holding, in one hand, a cross patterned with smaller crosses. In one of the volume's most moving images, a dominatrix embraces a customer, extracting a moment of tenderness from a presumably ritualized cash transaction and enacting a tableau reminiscent of any number of paintings in which saints (this one improbably clad in a bustier and patterned panty hose) are clothing the naked or comforting the sick at heart.

All this cannot help but influence our sense of what Arbus was searching for in her art. Not unlike Flannery O'Connor, she employed the grotesque as a staging ground in her quest for the transcendent. She remarked that there were things that no one would see unless she photographed them, and it's obvious, even banal, to note that by taking pictures of people from whom we might instinctively turn away, she was not only allowing us to stare, but insisting that we look beyond the jarring physiognomies of what she termed "singular people." Studying her portrait of Ronald C. Harrison, you first register "The Human Pincushion," but then you may find yourself trying to look beyond the needles—to remove them from his face, by sheer force of imagination, in order to figure out what the guy actually looks like.

IN *Chronology*, one of Diane Arbus's friends refers to the photographer as being headed "to the absolute inside of the inside." Contemplating her unblinking, fearless portraits, we register all the details of self-presentation and milieu, and yet we keep checking this information against whatever agreement or demurral we read in the subject's eyes, as if this time we will succeed in seeing beyond them.

Looking through *Revelations*—revisiting the icons, as it were, in the new light of the artist's writings—I began to contemplate the existence of something deeper than the psyche and the trappings of personality, more powerful than fear, desire, or aspiration, more formative than the residue of personal history and experience. If there is such an entity as the soul, it could be argued that it is the ultimate object of Arbus's explorations. Even as we grow more restive with conventional religion, with the intolerance and even brutality it so frequently exacts in trade for meaning and consolation, Arbus's work can seem like the bible of a faith to which one can almost imagine subscribing—the temple of the individual and irreducible human soul, the church of obsessive fascination and compassion for those fellow mortals whom, on the basis of mere surface impressions, we thoughtlessly misidentify as the wretched of the earth.

18

Helen Levitt, *Crosstown*

ONE OF THE CLEVER CONJURING TRICKS THAT A WORK OF art can perform is to transform the visible world into the work of the artist. Read a Balzac novel and everyone around suddenly seems to be feverishly social climbing, or contesting a will. Watch a Fellini movie and the neighbors swell up, larger than life, freakish and endearing. Study a van Eyck painting and the people outside the museum organize themselves into saints and sentries, madonnas and magdalenes, auditioning for bit parts as extras in the crowd at a Netherlandish Nativity.

Look at a Helen Levitt photo and the city streets, the subways and rooftops, become pure Helen Levitt. Encountering Helen Levitt's pictures, taken mostly between 1930 and 2000, mostly around Manhattan, is like taking off your sunglasses, or cleaning your spectacles, or just blinking—which is only appropriate, since so many of them seem to have been taken in a blink—and to picture something that will be gone, that *was* gone, a blink after it was taken. These photographs radically readjust our visual fine-tuning to remind us of how rapidly everything changes, of how large a fraction of what we see won't exist, in its present form, only a heart-beat from now. It's impossible not to notice that the beautiful gypsy kid, caught in mid-motion in the doorway of his apartment, was disappearing even as his portrait was being taken.

What makes these pictures so unusual is their instinctive, un-stagy, natural grasp of what adds layers of meaning and beauty to a visual image. All decisions about subject and composition have been made unconsciously, on the fly, in a few seconds or less, since these pictures' subjects, like the photographer, were lively and on the move, people and animals, adults and children, not still lifes of driftwood, flowers, and fruit—though there is the occasional wall decorated with chalk drawings that are also transitory, finite, a life span that can last only until the next rain, the downpour that will inevitably erase the public announcement that BILL JONES MOTHER IS A HORE.

Helen Levitt's eye, her visual judgment, is like a great drafts-man's line, and one can only admire the acuity of vision that al-lowed her to catch the moment when so many different, disparate events were happening at once, and playing out against such iron-ically suitable backgrounds; one can only marvel at the focus that enabled her to see the ways families arrange themselves in solid pil-lars of flesh, spanning generations; the quickness that alerted her to a woman in a checkered outfit standing beside a checkered cab; the sureness that let Levitt capture a sandlot baseball player at the most guided moment of his swing, an act that happens to be taking place in front of a wall mural, painted on brick, of a guy playing ball.

The photographs in *Crosstown* seem so effortlessly right that it's only when you think for two seconds, or recall all the bad doc-umentary photography you've seen, or pause to marvel at the high-wire act they're performing even as they focus steadfastly on the ground, that you realize how frighteningly simple it would be to get all of this terribly wrong, to make the children cute and the old ladies darling. Helen Levitt's work is never sentimental; it never aestheticizes or objectifies, never turns its subjects into art objects, never distorts them into noble heroes of poverty and desolation; it is never falsely, preemptively elegiac or nostalgic. You never feel the artist calling attention to herself or to the breadth and compassion of her vision. Everything is happening too quickly—and too interestingly—for anything remotely resembling self-conscious artiness or narcissism.

Here, as always, humor helps, waging its sly guerrilla war against the pious and sentimental. Many of these photos are hilarious, but the (never easy or obvious) jokes are subtle, and difficult to summarize or re-create apart from the image; it is impossible, for example, to explain why the nuns looking out at the river against the skyline make us feel so lighthearted and giddy. The cardboard box with legs and the mother disappearing into her small son's stroller (and in the process transforming the stroller into a vehicle equipped with both wheels and human torso) suggest that *surrealism* should have been a term invented for certain especially felicitous examples of naturalistic street photography. The little kid in the window with the painted face, mustache and beard, and Frankenstein scar makes us laugh out loud, but laughter is only the image's way of getting our attention—attention that stays on the photo, as it does on all of Helen Levitt's pictures, as we try to see and process everything in the frame (the curtain, the woman, the contrast between the baby's perfect comfort and ease and the essential precariousness of a baby in the window) and to imagine all the other moments that came before and surrounded the moments in which the picture was taken.

How much complex information these seemingly straightforward images convey, with their mysterious intimations of nuanced Chekhovian situations: the drama of the overweight girl, mooning, helplessly infatuated with her heartbreakingly handsome young neighbor, of the woman with the flashlight calling out for help, of the game of hide-and-seek. And the image of the woman and her children stuffed into a phone booth says more—in shorthand, more

entertainingly and affectionately—about the coziness and claustro-
phobia of family life than many novels or plays do.

After looking at Helen Levitt's photographs, the street and the
city seem, to put it simply, more interesting. For what has come
through the pictures is not the artist's personality, but rather the
quality and quick intensity of her interest, her instant compre-
hension of her subject. In some inexplicable way, you feel that she
instinctively grasps—she gets—the life transpiring around her.
Among the qualities that distinguish Helen Levitt's photographs
from anyone else's is the particularity of her lively, bemused,
cool admiration for the life of the neighborhoods she depicts—
never idealized fantasy or false appreciation, but rather a genuine
pleasure in tiny details of self-presentation (a swagger, a detail of
makeup or coiffure), of costume (a funny hat, a headscarf, a stylish
fedora), a gesture. How could we have imagined, before we saw
these photos, the nuances and range of what can be communicated
by a comforting hand placed on a neighbor's shoulder, or by the bal-
letic grace of an old man sitting sideways in his chair and describing something to a friend, his hands as expansive and expressive as
those of an orchestra conductor. Levitt's eye is drawn to subjects
who are self-dramatizing, who play to the crowd, even when no
one is looking—like the guy declaiming from his seat on the front
bumper of a truck.

What keeps snagging her attention is a sort of paradoxically
unself-conscious theatricality: the drama of the little girl in her
church clothes grabbing the old man around the waist, the mysterious contretemps between the reverend or priest and the girls in the
doorway, the scenario that the young woman with the milk bottles is enacting for the entertainment and torture of her contemp-
tuous pregnant friend, the cinematic series of events involving a
guy, a baby carriage, his neighbors, and a cigarette. Her subjects
are theatrical even when they're asleep: the man napping on the
hood of the car beside his bunches of unsold bananas. And, not to

be outdone, the animals—a horse, a Dalmatian, a black cat, a mini-flock of chickens—seem likewise gifted with a particular flair for the pictorial and the dramatic. The pigeons (not what we usually think of as the most intelligent of creatures) seem here to know something important, which they have wisely elected not to tell us.

These photographs are action-packed; there are no static tableaux. Even when taken on the subway, a place where one might think the opportunities for movement (except, of course, the train's rocking and forward motion) are limited, the pictures capture charged, intensely animated, and highly mobile transactions. Men and women embrace, regard each other, wary or entranced; parents hold their children; each glance or touch conveys a lifetime's worth of experience. Often, the connections among these subway passengers are so profound that they seem to function on a biological or cellular level, and the pictures offer hilarious, insightful glosses on the way that family members start off—or wind up—physically resembling one another.

What goes without saying is how much of the city pictured here—the buildings, the street life, the neighborhoods, the physical types—no longer exists. Helen Levitt's city is (unlike the cities that other photographers have given us) neither a futurist construct nor a dreamy, romantic American version of Atget's Paris, nor an abstract wonderland of geometric form, but instead—and always—a theater and a playground. Even the broken record is having fun (and entertaining its nonexistent audience, or, rather, the audience of one) as it rolls across the street. Helen Levitt has become known as a photographer of children, but what appears to attract her is not so much children as action in general, and play in particular. Dressed up in their Halloween masks and costumes, cross-dressing as women or as some fantasy version of a foreign legionnaire (a fashion model that no contemporary kid would dream of imitating), dancing, pirouetting, fondling or brandishing toy guns, children are simply more likely than adults to be acting and playing.

Like the photo of the baby with the painted face in the window, many of these pictures evoke the innate, unconscious fearlessness—the natural courage—of kids who haven't learned any better than to trust the world, children who have confidence in their own bodies, their own grace and strength, and who know beyond a doubt that they will live forever. They scramble up trees and across the lintels of doorways (or, when they are older, flank the doorway, like handsome caryatids), they catch rides in the backs of trucks, they drive their bikes through a frame from which the mirror has been removed, and in the process they shatter everything we think we know about conventional ideas of child safety—and conventional notions of photography. In their nerviness, their assurance, and the risks they take, the children resemble the photographer who is taking their picture, and who is engaged (like them) in a parallel, split-second defiance of the seemingly unbreakable laws of gravity, and of time.

Also in defiance (in this case, of the ways in which our culture devalues, undervalues, and commodifies sex), the photographs in *Crosstown* are extraordinarily sexy. It's not just the obvious candidates—the lovers on the subway, the sharply dressed couple in front of the luggage store, the gorgeous young woman in her mother's lap, the young man leaning, flamingo-like, against a parking meter—who strike us that way, but also the old and the young, the men and women well outside the range of what we're encouraged to think of as charismatic and attractive. What's more, it's the photographer's interest in them—in their unself-conscious grace and self-confidence, in the way they inhabit their bodies, in their faces, their eyes, their skin, their irreducibly complex selves—that makes them seem vital, interesting, beautiful, worthy of the second—and third—look. There's even something paradoxically sexy about the solitude of many of these photographic subjects, about the quiet insistence with which they have managed to create a tranquil private space for themselves amid the swirl and bustle of the street.

In picture after picture, Helen Levitt's photographs compel us to pay a closer, a more bemused and studious attention to the city, to the world, and to our fellow humans, which is, finally, among the most important things that any sort of naturalistic art can do. They make us aware of how much can happen in an instant, they console us for the loss of what is constantly disappearing, and they remind us of what is, just as constantly, arriving to take its place. Each one of these lively, spirited, and immensely beautiful images represents a feisty, spirited, irrepressible victory over (and a celebration of) the inexorable forces of change and the passage of time.

19

Mark Strand, *Mr. and Mrs. Baby*

IMAGINE, IF YOU CAN, A KAFKA WITH A ROBUST AND FORGIVING sympathy for the absurdity of human relationships and a lighthearted appreciation for the female body; a Bruno Schulz who leaves his Polish town to find romance and adventure in Australia and Machu Picchu; a Calvino who chooses his characters for their likeness to Hollywood B-movie stars; a Beckett with a soft spot for the tenderness between mothers and sons; a Borges with a fondness for childish jokes.

It is impossible to envision these literary masters altered in ways that would have made them unrecognizable to us and to themselves. Impossible, that is, unless we read the remarkable stories in *Mr. and Mrs. Baby*, stories that allow us to hear distant echoes of these writers—the dark comedy of Kafka and Beckett, the lyrical imagination of Calvino and Schulz, Borges's attraction to the cerebral, insoluble puzzle—filtered through the utterly original and unique sensibility of Mark Strand.

In Strand's stories we find the beauties of style and the complexities of subject matter that we have come to associate with his poems. Death and the melancholy that accompanies loss—and even the premature anticipation of loss—hover lightly (or not so lightly) over these fictions. For much of its length, "The Tiny Baby" evokes those cheesy horror films whose protagonists, shrunk to the size of mice, cower in terror from the rampages of the family cat. Until, at the story's conclusion, we meet the tiny baby grown into "a smallish woman." And the delicate irony of the final sentences changes our understanding of what we have been reading, which now seems not merely comedic but metaphysical:

> *Her thin legs crossed, the tips of her shoes hardly reaching the ground, she suddenly, in barely audible tones, sings a song about rain falling and a man on a bicycle, hurrying home. The man's wife leans from a window, watching him, but is distracted by the noisy appearance of sea gulls. The smallish woman gets up. The train has left. The day keeps echoing around her. Everything is priceless, she thinks. Death will not have me. That is the story of the tiny baby.*

Among the lures that seems to have drawn the poet Mark Strand to the narrative is its potential for depicting unlikely transformations. In "More Life," the narrator's father returns first as a fly, then as a horse. Finally his spirit inhabits his fiancée, Helen—alarming to her if not to our hero, who is not only astonished but thrilled to meet his father speaking to him in the voice of a terrified woman. Retired from the wars, the hero of "The General" turns into an elderly child, playing with toy soldiers, imagining the clamor of battle, and reliving historic victories.

The title story is characteristic of how beautifully written—how sad, how funny, how unsettling—the fictions in this collection can be. In this portrait of a marriage, the ennui, the disappointments, the isolation and loneliness that are an inescapable part of being human govern the ebb and flow of affection between Mr. and

Mrs. Baby. On their way to a party, "the urgency of promised adventure was so palpable that the neighborhood seemed to murmur with pleasure. And when they walked to the party, they were almost overcome with the magical intimacy of leaves saturating the air with the odor of green, the sweet seasoning of summer." But, perhaps predictably, reality turns out to be something of a letdown: "Nothing was happening. The Babys stayed only as long as they had to and then walked home."

I suppose it could be argued that, to a certain extent, every poem is about poetry. But in these fictions, Strand meditates at once more openly and more ironically on the poetic impulse and the nature of poetry than is his custom in his poems—excepting, of course, such masterpieces as "Eating Poetry." In "The President's Resignation," the leader of the country reveals himself to be attentive to, perhaps even obsessed by, changes in the weather—in other words, a character who may remind us of the poet Mark Strand.

> Who can forget my proposals, petitions uttered on behalf of those who labored in the great cause of weather—measuring wind, predicting rain, giving themselves to whole generations of days—whose attention was ever riveted to the invisible wheel that turns the stars and to the stars themselves? How like poetry, said my enemies. They were right. . . . I have always spoken for what does not change, for what resists action, for the stillness at the center of man.

Moved by a sudden moment of illumination, Bob Baby discovers poetry:

> Brought outside by a restlessness whose source was obscure, he was likewise brought out of himself by a spacious aura of epiphanous light, into an openness of being that took him by surprise. With a knowledge almost too deep for tears, he saw all things

*ablaze with the glory of their own mortality. He lingered until
the world around him suddenly resumed its normal aspect, then
he went inside and began to pace on the green living-room rug.
He wondered why he was here and not there, why he had chosen
the life he had instead of the life he hadn't, why he felt as he did
and, sometimes, as he didn't. Thus it was that Bob Baby wrote
his first poem and decided to say nothing about it to Babe.*

And in "The Killer Poet," a man about to be executed for mur-
dering his parents reflects on the origins of his literary career:
"Though my meditations were filled with the self-regarding pomp
of adolescence, something important was taking hold of me—the
privileged and ponderous assessment, for the first time, of my own
mortality. The beauty and mystery of death beckoned, and I began to write. My anguished humming into the empty corridors
of the future, my plangent dialogues with absence, were all that
sustained me."

What's hardest to describe, but what I hope has come through
in the passages I've quoted above, is what makes these stories at
once so touching—and so funny. The plot of "True Loves" derives
its comedy from a series of repetitions with variations—the structure of a sort of morose shaggy-dog joke. A married man keeps
falling in love, under the most impossible and often risible circumstances, with strangers, women who not only fail to return his passion but who excite an unrealizable longing that only succeeds in
torpedoing each of his five marriages.

Much of the humor that runs through the collection results
from Strand's ability to use language—the most elegant, the simplest yet most brilliantly metaphorical language—like the air with
which the narrator is blowing up a balloon, the dirigible of a story.
And then something goes too far, crosses over the edge, the mem-
brane of the narrative reaches its limits—and explodes. Consequently, the delight that these fictions generate in the reader is the

joy of a child watching the explosion take place—an at once amusing and melancholy reminder of the eternal and the transient, the absurd and the incisive, the silly and the profound. Those contradictions are what make these stories so rewarding to read—and so satisfying to return to, to reread, knowing that each rereading will yield more pleasure, more amusement, more meaning. More life.

20

Karl Ove Knausgaard, *My Struggle*

FEW OF US, WHILE ON A LONG-DISTANCE FLIGHT, ARE GLAD to be seated next to a loquacious stranger who ignores the signal we try to send with our open book, our earbuds, the sleep mask we pull down over our eyes. Imagine, then, that the traveler beside us is a craggy, middle-aged Norwegian determined to tell us everything that ever happened to him in his life, every boyhood memory, every random association and metaphysical speculation, every song he listened to, every book he read, every detail he can recall about his parents, his first friendships, his three children's personalities, the diapers he changed, the meals he cooked, the highs and lows of his second marriage. It's not all that difficult to imagine, but what seems far more improbable is that we become so riveted by our companion's story that we begin to wish the flight could continue for as long as his monologue lasts—or at least until we figure out why we are so enthralled.

That unlikely scenario vaguely approximates the unusual experience—and the mystery—of reading Karl Ove Knausgaard's *My Struggle*, a dense, complex, and brilliant six-volume work, totaling more than thirty-five hundred pages, that could, I suppose, be described as a cross between a memoir and an autobiographical novel were it not unclassifiable: a genre of its own. The book has been a critical and popular success in Europe, where it has won literary prizes. It was a sensation in Norway, its notoriety boosted by Knausgaard's nervy decision to borrow the title (*Min Kamp*, in Norwegian) of Hitler's literary call to arms, and by the media scandals that erupted when his ex-wife and uncle objected to the ways in which they are portrayed in his work.

In a masterful translation by Don Bartlett that follows Knausgaard's tonal shifts from the colloquial to the conversational to the lyrical, *My Struggle* has gained a sort of cult following that has gradually broadened to include a larger base of readers, most of whom agree that there's nothing else like it, and also that it is difficult to explain just how the book works its particular magic. Why are we so interested in the minutiae of this guy's life?

The third volume, "Boyhood," is—like the first half of "A Death in the Family"—an account of the author's childhood: his loving but distant mother, his tyrannical father, his adored older brother, Yngve, his pals, teachers, grandparents, and neighbors, the local girls who become the objects of his first romantic obsessions. What "Boyhood" shares with its predecessors is not simply Knausgaard's (by now) familiar voice, its alternations between narration and essayistic rumination, between passages of lyrical elegance and scenes of dialogue, or even its setting and cast of characters, but, more important, Knausgaard's determination to include everything, no matter how banal, trivial, embarrassing, or personal. This volume poses the same questions as the previous books: How do we construct a self from each experience and impression, each moment of our lives? And how can the ghosts of the past be not only recaptured (as in Proust, to whom Knausgaard has been compared) but exorcised, so that a father need not repeat the mistakes his father made in raising him?

Long after we stop caring how much of this is "true" and how much has been embellished, we remain intrigued by the challenge of explaining why, given the memoir-novel's unexceptional subject matter and its author's encyclopedic approach to his personal history, we are unable to put the book down. Why is it so *hypnotic*, a word that keeps cropping up in reviews of Knausgaard's books and among his fans? Why do we follow, with breathless excitement, the seventy-page account, in "A Death in the Family," of the teenage Karl Ove's Herculean efforts to procure beer for New Year's Eve? Why are we so engaged by the depiction (in the second volume, "A Man in Love") of the super-crunchy children's birthday parties and nursery school classes to which Karl Ove reluctantly takes his son and two daughters, after he moves from Norway to Stockholm? And why do we so happily follow his recollections, in "Boyhood," of how he liked his breakfast cereal?

In Book Three, Karl Ove could be Everyboy. A ragtag gang of Scandinavian Huckleberry Finns, he and his friends search for the pot of gold at the end of a rainbow; they play soccer, start fires that briefly threaten to burn out of control, visit the local dump to watch some guys shoot rats. They learn to swim, go fishing, pore over a treasured cache of porn. They grow older and compete on the playing field, in their classrooms, and in a school election. Karl Ove joins a terrible rock band, with the generationally perfect name Blood Clot, and falls in love with a succession of neighborhood girls who ditch him for more attractive and popular boys. He wrecks an early romance by persuading his sweetheart that they should try to break the local record for length of time spent kissing; he is mocked by the other kids when his mother buys him a swimming cap decorated with flowers; a family crisis erupts when he loses a sock. His father, a high school teacher, is transferred. The family moves to another town. And Knausgaard reflects on the beauties of the lost-forever world in which he came of age:

Landscape in childhood is not like the landscape that follows later; they are charged in very different ways. In that landscape every rock, every tree had a meaning, and because everything was seen for the first time and because it was seen so many times, it was anchored in the depths of your consciousness, not as something vague or approximate, the way a landscape outside a house appears to adults if they close their eyes and it has to be summoned forth, but as something with immense precision and detail. In my mind, I have only to open the door and go outside for the images to come streaming toward me. The gravel in the driveway, almost bluish in color in the summer. Oh, that alone, the driveways of childhood!

Ultimately, very little happens to Karl Ove that might not have happened to countless other middle-class boys living on the outskirts of a Scandinavian town (or, for that matter, in a small American town) during the 1970s—or at least to every other boy who was terrified of his father. In the first volume, we witness Karl Ove's Pavlovian response to his father's presence: just the sound of Dad's footsteps on the stairs is enough to inspire a watchful unease, perpetually on the brink of tipping over into panic and fear. In Book Three, the boyhood idylls screech to a halt whenever Dad comes onstage to perform the petty acts of cruelty, impatience, injustice, and rage that make the child—and the reader—feel a jolt of anxiety whenever Dad's car pulls into the driveway. The party's over.

As stern, omnipotent, and implacable as the Old Testament God, Dad is uninterested in details like the difference between intentional and accidental, between disobedience and carelessness, innocence and guilt. Who cares if Karl Ove didn't mean to break the TV he was specifically instructed not to turn on, or if it's true that he got a five-kroner coin from an old woman he and his friends helped by moving a fallen tree lodged in a stream? The punishment—slaps, ear pulling, shouting, humiliation—is the same as if the boy had been lying.

When Dad's enraged, capricious unfairness makes the child cry, his tears not only shame him but further enrage Dad, whose son is weak enough to cry like a girl. After his father torments him for eating one too many apples by making him eat so many apples he nearly vomits, Karl Ove thinks, "I hated Dad, but I was in his hands, I couldn't escape his power. It was impossible to exact my revenge on him." In Karl Ove's fantasies, "I could hurl him against the wall or throw him down the stairs. I could grab him by the neck and smash his face against the table. That was how I could think, but the instant I was in the same room as he was, everything crumbled, he was my father, a grown man, so much bigger than me that everything had to bend to his will. He bent my will as if it were nothing."

What makes this all the more affecting is the skill with which Knausgaard captures the boy's mixture of fear, rage, and love, the intensity with which he monitors Dad for the slightest sign of approval, the helpless joy he derives from his father's infrequent moments of contentment. A trip to the fish market and the record store, where Karl Ove's choice of music (Elvis!) pleases Dad, ends with an almost ecstatic interlude during which Dad shows his son how to "cure" the warts on his hands by rubbing them with bacon grease. All of this painfully underscores the rarity of tender or even peaceful exchanges between the child and the adult.

That we follow a multi-stop shopping trip with Dad with such rapt fascination is a tribute to Knausgaard's narrative skill, a talent that alone provides enough reason to keep reading. Our interest is sustained by the sense that we know the most essential things about everyone in the book. And each new thing we find out provides the fascination of learning some previously unknown anecdote or piece of gossip about close friends or neighbors: a family we know almost as well as we know our own.

Three quarters of the way through "Boyhood," Dad leaves for Bergen to "major in Nordic literature and become a senior teacher." Until this point he has maintained dictatorial control over everything that goes on in the house, but now Mom asks Karl Ove if he would like to bake some bread. "That might have been the year Dad lost his grip on us."

There follows an ominous sentence. "Many years later [Dad] was to say that Bergen was where he started drinking."

That is, this sentence will seem ominous—extremely so—to anyone who has read "A Death in the Family."

IT is impossible to know how Book Three of *My Struggle* would seem to a reader unfamiliar with the preceding volumes. It's like trying to imagine what it would be like to meet, for the first time, someone we imagine we know as well as we may feel we know Karl Ove after reading Books One and Two. Everything that happens is shadowed by everything that has happened, which is the result of Knausgaard's inspired decision to tell his story not chronologically but thematically, and to begin (more or less) at the end, with the death of the father whose influence he has spent his adult life trying to escape.

The first volume starts with a meditation on death, features the aftermath of what may be the most horrific (and certainly the most squalid) demise in literature, and concludes with the following sentence, the end of a thought that occurs to Karl Ove as he contemplates his father's corpse: "And death, which I have always regarded as the greatest dimension of life, dark, compelling, was no more than a pipe that springs a leak, a branch that cracks in the wind, a jacket that slips off a clothes hanger and falls to the floor."

Halfway through "A Death in the Family," Knausgaard writes, "I was almost thirty years old when I saw a dead body for the first time. It was the summer of 1998, a July afternoon, in a chapel in

Kristiansand. My father had died." Together with his brother Yngve, Karl Ove comes home for the funeral, but the ceremony—and the complex task, for the brothers, of sorting out their feelings about Dad—turns out to be the least of it. For some time, Dad had been living with his mother, Karl Ove's grandmother, drinking himself to death, while Grandma, intermittently aware of her surroundings, kept up with him, consuming massive amounts of alcohol to obliterate the pain of being feeble, incontinent, and forced to witness the spectacle of her son's slow suicide. Mother and son have constructed a sort of fortress of garbage; the rooms of Grandma's house are littered with refuse: hundreds of liquor bottles, filthy clothes, old newspapers, rotten food. The walls and floors are covered with excrement. And the brothers must clean up the mess.

Doubtless there will be readers who would rather avoid the dubious pleasure of accompanying Karl Ove and Yngve as they scour and tidy a house that makes the jam-packed dumps on *Hoarders* look like luxury spas. Once more Knausgaard spares us nothing: the smells, the sights, the prodigious quantities of cleaning products required, his own bouts of weeping and vomiting. But the point is, it *is* an experience, and a powerful one, which the reader shares with the writer, and we read "Boyhood" in a very particular way when we know (as Knausgaard did when he wrote it) the ultimate destination to which Dad was heading.

When, in "Boyhood," Karl Ove tells us how much he loves his grandma, who smells good and is the only person who is interested in him and generous with physical affection, we cannot forget the heartbreaking old woman who will wind up as Dad's housemate and drinking buddy, in whose living room Dad will die. Afterward, she will try to manipulate her visiting grandsons into having a drink, and will urinate on the floor in the midst of a conversation.

Whenever Dad even briefly disappears from "Boyhood," Karl Ove revels in the intermittent attentions of his sweet but detached and frequently absent mother. Left to his own devices, he delights in his daily life—the escapades, the freedom, the intrigues among his pals. What Knausgaard is describing is nothing less than that process so rarely captured in literature: "the conversion of a child into a person as it is happening," as John Berryman said of Anne Frank—in this case a grown man, a writer who is more or less conscious of who he is, of what he has become, and of how that transformation occurred.

Reading about young Karl Ove in "Boyhood" is a bit like watching home movies of a child—observing the gestures, the physical features, the interests, obsessions, and personality quirks that will not only persist but become even more visible in the adult. In this book, as in the first volume, Karl Ove grows obsessed with a series of local girls who, as distinct and individual as they clearly are to him, tend to merge in the reader's mind into one girl whom he cannot stop thinking about, who shows a passing interest in him—and then dumps him.

We already know about Karl Ove's propensity for erotic obsession. In "A Man in Love," that mania focuses on Linda, a poet and writer (and sufferer from bipolar disorder) who will eventually become his wife and the mother of his three children. The agonies that Karl Ove endures over his failed boyhood loves will come to seem like innocent rehearsals for a children's play when we compare them to the scene, in Book Two, in which—rejected by Linda—he returns to his room at a writers' festival and cuts his own face with a shard of glass.

In the first three books of *My Struggle*, Knausgaard mostly lets us draw our own conclusions about his parents' marriage, which in general seems to involve efforts on the part of both parents to find pressing professional reasons for living apart. By contrast, "A Man in Love" contains an unusually complete dissection of Karl Ove's own marriage to Linda, alternately passionate, resentful, joyous, tedious, grateful, and contentious, rendered in far more detail than any other marriage one can think of, in fiction or nonfiction.

His best male friend and confidant during this time (by now Karl Ove and Linda are living in Stockholm) is a man named Gerd, with whom he has soul-searching Dostoyevskian conversations about human nature and literature. In "Boyhood," we again meet Gerd, this time in an earlier incarnation as Karl Ove's childhood best friend and partner in boyish mischief.

IN the publicity surrounding *My Struggle*, there's been a surprisingly steady interest in Karl Ove's description (in Book Two) of his understandably mixed feelings about changing his children's diapers. Though perhaps it's not so surprising. We may not realize just how uncommon such passages are unless we try to think of another literary work whose author is so engaged by (and so honest about) the profound pleasures and the numbing boredom of fatherhood, and the problem—nearly always considered a women's problem, though serious women novelists don't tend to write about it, either—of how to balance the demands of being a writer with the very different demands of parenthood.

Karl Ove's anxieties are partly the result of his fear that he and Yngve might repeat Dad's failures, his uncertainty about "whether what Dad had handed down to us was in our bone marrow or whether it would be possible to break free." In "Boyhood," he reflects:

> *I have my own children, and with them I have tried to achieve only one aim: that they shouldn't be afraid of their father. They aren't. I know that. When I enter a room, they don't cringe, they don't look down at the floor, they don't dart off as soon as they glimpse an opportunity, no, if they look at me, it is not a look of indifference, and if there is anyone I am happy to be ignored by it is them. If there is anyone I am happy to be taken for granted by, it is them.*

By the time we reach this section, we understand what this happiness has cost him, especially after having read (in Book Two) about the toll taken on both Karl Ove and Linda by their bickering over housework and childcare. As he diapers and plays with his children, struggles with the shaming but undeniable fact that pushing a stroller makes him feel emasculated, and brings his children to classes and parties at which (in a series of at once funny and tragic scenes) Karl Ove feels humiliated just by having to be there, he must anticipate and fulfill his children's needs even when he desperately longs to go off somewhere and be alone and write.

> I wanted the maximum amount of time for myself with the fewest disturbances possible. I wanted Linda, who was already at home looking after Heidi, to take care of everything that concerned Vanja so that I could work. . . . All our conflicts and arguments were in some form or another about this, the dynamics. If I couldn't write because of her and her demands, I would leave her, it was as simple as that. . . . The way I took my revenge was to give her everything she wanted, that is, I took care of the children, I cleaned the floors, I washed the clothes, I did the food shopping, I cooked, and I earned all the money so that she had nothing tangible to complain about, as far as I and my role in the family were concerned. The only thing I didn't give her, and it was the only thing she wanted, was my love. That was how I took my revenge.

Once again, it is the sort of thing we may see around us, among our friends and neighbors, or even in our own homes, but rarely in a book. Unlike most novelists, who take us on the whaling voyage or the safari, as far as possible from the trivia of daily life, Karl Ove transforms that trivia into a complex, even orchestral plot, peopled by characters who happen to be his family—and himself. In his determination to cover page after page with the reality of the inner and outer life, Knausgaard seems willing to do anything to get it right: to surrender his privacy, his dignity, the impulse to seem like a good person, in the interests of explaining what it is like for him (and for all of us) to be alive on earth.

The literary voice of *My Struggle* takes up permanent residence in our consciousness, for how can we not be changed by the time and effort it takes to read thirty-five hundred pages of narrative this intense? Afterward, you may never be able to see a father pushing a stroller or a boy riding his bike, or go to a middle-class children's birthday party, or see a parent being nasty to a kid in public without thinking of Karl Ove. The emotions we may feel upon finishing "Boyhood" are akin to those that often accompany the season finale of a favorite TV series. We're sad that it is over, aware that we must wait for a new season, consoled by the fact there will be one. After reading three extremely long, detailed, and dense installments, there is still so much about Karl Ove Knausgaard's life that I can't wait to find out.

21

Elizabeth Taylor,
Complete Short Stories

TWENTY YEARS AGO, I READ *BLAMING*, ELIZABETH TAYLOR'S last novel, published soon after her death, in 1975. I immediately began to read as many of her books as I could find. I finished one and promptly started the next, one right after the other.

Recently I had a similar experience rereading one of Taylor's books and then going on to read a half dozen more, making my way, a bit gingerly, through the landscape she portrays: an enthralling but unsettling minefield of misdirected passion, marital disaffection, social embarrassment, and the bad behavior that can occur when people are being their most authentic selves. This time I started with *A Game of Hide and Seek* (1951) and finished with the *Complete Short Stories*, published by Virago, which has been heroic in keeping Taylor's work in print.

Born in Reading, England, in 1912, she worked as a librarian and governess before marrying John Taylor, a businessman. Together they settled in Buckinghamshire and raised a family. Taylor's first novel, *At Mrs. Lippincote's*, was published in 1945, when she was thirty-two. She wrote twelve novels and four volumes of stories, many of which were published in *The New Yorker*. Her literary friends and admirers of her work included Ivy Compton-Burnett, Elizabeth Jane Howard, Elizabeth Bowen, and Angus Wilson.

The best of her fiction is extremely funny, incisive, sympathetic, and beautifully written, but it can also make us squirm with uneasy recognition and tell us more than we might choose to hear about ourselves and our neighbors. Awful things happen in these narratives, not in the sense of violence and gore but of characters realizing awful truths about the lives in which they are hopelessly mired. Many of the relationships—most often between spouses but also between traveling companions, co-workers, neighbors, relatives, and friends—deliver all of the pleasures and satisfactions of the Ancient Mariner's relationship with his albatross.

One story in the collection, "The Rose, the Mauve, the White," so accurately describes being in one's early teens and not being asked to dance by any of the boys at a party that, reading it, I again felt the agony that time had mercifully dulled. After I had recovered, my dismay was supplanted by awed respect for Taylor's ability to exhume the buried but obviously undead past.

Let me suggest that readers begin with "Hester Lilly," the first story in the collection. To say that it is "about" a young woman who comes to stay at a boys' boarding school with her older cousin Robert and his wife, Muriel, and who, armed only with the weapon of youth, nearly blows apart their marriage, is to misrepresent it. For any summary runs the risk of making the story sound more familiar and less original than it is.

Here, as in Taylor's novel *Palladian*, we watch a hapless orphan girl live out her Jane Eyre fantasy. Stoked by romantic notions, determined to fall in love with the first Mr. Rochester who can fog a mirror, Hester Lilly succeeds in snagging the attention of the bored, middle-aged Robert.

As the story opens, Muriel has been fuming about Hester

Lilly's arrival at the school where Robert is headmaster. "Muriel's first sensation was one of derisive relief. The name—Hester Lilly—had suggested to her a goitrous, pre-Raphaelite frailty . . . danger to any wife." But Hester Lilly's "jaunty, defiant and absurd" wardrobe instills Muriel with "injudicious confidence." "I will take her under my wing, Muriel promised herself. The idea of an unformed personality to be moulded and highlighted invigorated her, and the desire to tamper with—as in those fashion magazines in which ugly duckling is so disastrously changed to swan before our wistful eyes—made her impulsive and welcoming."

Muriel is a glorious invention, improbably but believably combining the repressed propriety of a headmaster's wife with the self-dramatizing theatrics of the diva. She has a friend, Beatrice, with whom she has mordantly humorous and depressing conversations about how to endure the tediousness of sex and weighing the relative advantages of childlessness versus having children. Even as we're reading scenes of high comedy and following sly turns of plot that suggest art imitating life imitating soap opera, we may be surprised to find ourselves deeply moved by the dreams and disappointments of characters who are not necessarily likable, and who all want opposite things. We're tossed about by grief and anxiety for all of them at the same time.

Some of the stories in the collection are slighter, more anecdotal than others; others seem more like sketches than developed narratives. I especially liked "The Devastating Boys," "You'll Enjoy It When You Get There," "A Red-letter Day," and "The Letter-writers," but readers will have their own favorites. The informative introduction, by Taylor's daughter, Joanna Kingham, is excellent.

I've read descriptions of Taylor's work that make it sound like yet another rainy tea time among the cabbage roses. But her fiction is much more fun than that, more wicked and subversive. No one writes more honestly about the way the "wrong" emotions can surface at inconvenient times; no one has created a more appalling gallery of narcissistic, controlling mothers-in-law, nor has anyone written quite so knowingly about the ways in which married couples, thrown together on holiday or at a social event, perform for, and compete with, each other. And no one is less afraid to monitor the intensity with which our insecurities can inspire a jolt of hatred for an innocent stranger whose only crime is to have evaded the self-doubt that plagues us.

Were I new to Elizabeth Taylor's work, I'd read "Hester Lilly" and a dozen of the stories, then go on to the novels. Then I would still have the rest of the stories left to parcel out, savoring them, one by one, until enough time had passed so that I could go back and begin again, rereading one book after another.

22

Louisa May Alcott, *Little Women*

I DON'T KNOW HOW OLD I WAS WHEN I FIRST READ *LITTLE Women*. But I do remember that when I changed schools in fourth grade, I made my first friends there on the basis of our shared passion for the March sisters. It was as if my new friends and I already had old friends in common: Meg, the kindly, conventional elder sister; Beth, whose death we had wept over; the flirtatious, status-conscious Amy, about whom we harbored a range of mixed feelings; and Jo, the one we wanted to be, the one we felt we were.

By then, Louisa May Alcott had already given me a whole series of firsts: *Little Women* was the first book I compulsively re-read; Beth's the first loss I mourned; Jo the first literary character I identified with. And as I returned to my favorite sections—that is, the parts about love and death—*Little Women* was the first book that moved me in the ways in which we hope to be moved by books, and in which writers (as I now know) hope to move their readers.

When the Library of America reissued *Little Women* in 2005, together with its sequels, *Little Men* and *Jo's Boys*, it seemed to me the perfect moment to revisit this classic that I hadn't read for what, astonishingly, had been almost fifty years.

As someone who routinely blanks on my own phone number, I was stunned by how much of the book I remember, the major and minor incidents that have lodged in my mind: old Mr. Laurence's gift of the piano to Beth, the newspaper the girls publish, the way Aunt March settles the question of Meg's marriage by opposing it. Reading these sections, I have an eerie sensation, a bit like déjà vu, like getting in touch with a former, lost self. At the time—and maybe this has something to do with the way children read—I somehow never fully comprehended the fact that it was fiction; it was almost as if I imagined that these girls were real people. Now, more aware of the writer's presence, I'm surprised by how much Alcott seems to have disliked Amy, by the vanity and pretentiousness that she never fails to point out, and that suffuses the maddeningly self-involved letters Amy writes to her stay-at-home sisters from Europe.

But what surprises me most is how daring and subversive the book is in its view of the satisfactions and frustrations of being a woman, little or otherwise. If my generation claimed our right to enter the workplace and succeed there, if we believed that we were just as intelligent, ambitious, and independent as men, perhaps it's because so many of us grew up with the example of the Marches.

In the early chapters, the girls and their mother are shown living without male help or support, somewhat impoverished and understandably worried about Father in the army, but doing reasonably well on their own. Indeed, their household—headed by the endlessly understanding, tirelessly compassionate, all-knowing Marmee—seems like a nonstop pajama party. And what are her daughters doing when we first meet them? They're complaining! None of them quite seems like the model of passive, stoic nineteenth-century womanhood as they bemoan Father's absence and the privations they must endure, as Meg complains about her teaching job, Beth about the housework, Amy about school, and Jo about the trials of working for Aunt March.

From this distance, it seems clearer than ever why my friends and I so admired Jo. She's smart, brave, honest, gifted, generous, a reader and a writer, and, even more important, a born rebel and resister. If the March daughters were the Beatles, Jo would be John Lennon. A chapter is devoted to her discovery of her skills—and her integrity—as an author. She's Peter Pan without Neverland, reluctant to grow up and to see her family divided by adulthood and marriage, unwilling to submit to the pressures that the world around her exerts on young women: the pressure to conform, to submerge her identity, her desires and ideals, to trade her dreams of being a writer for a happy home life. Married and the mother of twins, Meg has already provided an example of the perils of underfunded domesticity. We shudder to imagine what might have happened to Meg's marriage had she not heeded Marmee's wise counsel, which could have come straight from any modern advice column: "You have only made the mistake that most young wives make,—forgotten your duty to your husband in your love for your children. A very natural and forgivable mistake, Meg, but one that had better be remedied before you take to different ways."

Meg's situation is hardly what Jo envisions for herself, yet neither is Jo resigned to being what she calls a "literary spinster." Like her twentieth-century counterparts, she wants it all: home and work. It's why she refuses Laurie, the handsome boy we all had crushes on and thought she should have married, the rich boy whom the more frivolous Amy not only loves but sees as the answer to her family's problems. "One of us must marry well," Amy writes to her sisters. "Meg didn't, Jo won't, Beth can't, yet,—so I shall, and make everything cosy all round." And Laurie, for his part, is quite ready to exchange Jo's high-mindedness for Amy's high style.

Ultimately, "after her many and vehement declarations of

independence," Jo accepts Professor Bhaer, who not only exhibits many of her own best qualities—modesty, intelligence, sympathy, integrity—but shares her love for Shakespeare, teaches her German, and has a similar sense of purpose and mission. When Aunt March dies and leaves Plumfield to Jo, she and the Professor turn it into "a happy, home-like place for boys who needed teaching, care, and kindness." It's an ideal marriage for Jo, though you can't help feeling that neither Meg nor Amy would have been quite so delighted with the earnest, cerebral—and considerably older— Professor.

By the time the book ends, and Marmee has bestowed her final blessing on the proceedings ("Oh, my girls, however long you may live, I can never wish you a greater happiness than this!"), we have learned a great deal about the world—and how to live in it. A world in which we get the mate we want or need—or deserve. A world in which the hard lessons and rewards may not be what we imagine. And a world in which all of us—women in particular—must insist on our right to happiness, independence, and fulfillment. While my friends and I were reading about a family of little women, Louisa May Alcott was helping us to grow up into braver and larger human beings.

23

Jane Austen

READING JANE AUSTEN'S NOVELS OR WATCHING ANY OF THE films inspired by her work may make some newly smitten Austen fans long to dress in frilly white gowns or brocade waistcoats, fall in love, arrange suitable matrimonial alliances, play the pianoforte, correct one another's manners—or indulge in any of the other forms of delicately civilized behavior that Austen makes look so attractive. Others, however, may find themselves equally overwhelmed by the desire to phone their accountants and check that their finances are in order, or place hurried calls to their lawyers and double-check that their wills are up to date.

No other writer (with the possible exceptions of Balzac and Dickens) wrote with such a clear eye so coolly focused on matters of income, real estate, and inheritance. No one had a less coy or more accurate sense of what (literally speaking) love can cost, or of the havoc wrought when a tragic or inconvenient death is rendered even more calamitous by the deceased's negligence, inability, or capricious refusal to provide for his heirs. In short, no other novelist combined such a subtle, delicate moral sensibility with such a

firm, no-nonsense grasp of the most material realities—of the fact
that money determines one's opportunity to live in the tranquil
and gracious style to which one is (or would like to be) accustomed.

Often, Austen tells us what a character is worth ("Miss Maria Ward of Huntingdon, with only seven thousand pounds . . .")
before she gets around to describing what he or she looks like; or
else the physical description is followed shortly—and with notably
greater exactitude—by the economic: "Mr. Darcy soon drew the
attention of the room by his fine, tall person, handsome features,
noble mien; and the report which was in general circulation within
five minutes after his entrance, of his having ten thousand a year."
Indeed, the plots of Austen's novels are more likely to be set in motion by financial crises and reverses than by the promptings of the
heart (as in Edith Wharton) or of the soul (as in Dostoyevsky). So
Persuasion begins when the spendthrift Sir Walter Elliot admits he
must "retrench" and, with his friend Lady Russell's able help ("She
drew up plans of economy, she made exact calculations"), agrees to
move to more modest quarters and lease Kellynch Hall to Admiral Croft—whose brother-in-law, Captain Wentworth, has already
won the heart of Sir Walter's daughter, Anne. The sufferings, dislocations, and misunderstandings that *Sense and Sensibility* documents are initially the consequence of Mr. Dashwood's leaving his
fortune to his son (and his son's shrewish wife), thus essentially dis-
inheriting his own hapless wife and three daughters.

The famously elaborate machinations of Mrs. Bennet, in *Pride
and Prejudice*, reflect her panic at having to secure the futures of
five young women. And when the serpents (disguised as Henry and
Mary Crawford) come to disturb the paradise of Mansfield Park,
Austen details, with great precision, the fiscal and moral history
behind the arrival of this shady pair of orphans:

> *They were young people of fortune. The son had a good estate
> in Norfolk, the daughter twenty thousand pounds. . . . In their*

uncle's house they had found a kind home. Admiral and Mrs.
Crawford, though agreeing in nothing else, were united in affec-
tion for these children, or, at least, were no farther adverse in
their feelings than that each had their favourite . . . The Admiral
delighted in the boy, Mrs. Crawford doated on the girl; and it
was the lady's death which now obliged her protegee, after some
months' further trial at her uncle's house, to find another home.

Given the critical role that property and income play in their
own and their loved ones' fates, it seems only fair that Austen's
characters are frequently defined (and judged) by the conscien-
tiousness with which they arrange their finances and tend to their
estates. (The sympathies of contemporary writers are more likely
to be engaged by characters who live fast, die young—and leave
only a memory behind.) In Austen's world, the morally slatternly
tumble into debt, the upright stay within their household budgets
and consider their family's future, and the truly dishonest (like
the rakish Henry Crawford) only pretend to be concerned with
their property and their dependents. ("He had introduced himself
to some tenants, whom he had never seen before; he had begun
making acquaintance with cottages whose very existence, though
on his own estate, had been hitherto unknown to him. This was
aimed, and well aimed, at Fanny. It was pleasing to hear him speak
so properly; here he had been acting as he ought to do.")

Austen examines her characters' account books with the same
meticulous care she lavishes on their romantic impulses, so that her
novels function like brief, painless—indeed, delightful—courses in
the ways that the eighteenth-century gentry put (and kept) food
on the family table, staked out their place in society, and provided
for (or impoverished) their heirs. One learns, for example, that the
"living" awarded to clergymen—of special relevance to the heroes
of *Sense and Sensibility* and *Mansfield Park*—involved a tax levied on
the parish, and that the right to bestow this living belonged to the

local landowner rather than the ecclesiastical authorities. We discover that advancement in the military could be procured by the helpful "exertions" of gentlemen like Henry Crawford, and that the purchase of an estate conferred not only financial security but social respectability—an instant pedigree that might partly compensate for having had one's fortunes acquired by "trade." ("Mr. Bingley inherited property to the amount of nearly a hundred thousand pounds from his father, who had intended to purchase an estate, but did not live to do it. Mr. Bingley intended it likewise . . . but as he was now provided with a good house and the liberty of a manor, it was doubtful to many . . . whether he might not spend the remainder of his days at Netherfield, and leave the next generation to purchase. His sisters were very anxious for his having an estate of his own.") Finally, the sad lesson of *Sense and Sensibility* is that the law of primogeniture was very much alive and well in Jane Austen's England.

For all the passionate interest she takes in the material welfare of the men and women who populate her novels, Austen disapproves of the vulgarly mercenary. Elizabeth Bennet's friend Charlotte Lucas, who marries exclusively for stability and money, is treated with irritated pity, and the adulterous elopement that ruins Maria Bertram's life is in part traceable to her decision to wed for overly calculated and insufficiently heartfelt reasons. ("Being now in her twenty-first year, Maria Bertram was beginning to think matrimony a duty; and as a marriage with Mr. Rushworth would give her the enjoyment of a larger income than her father's, as well as ensure her the house in town . . . it became, by the same rule of moral obligation, her evident duty to marry Mr. Rushworth if she could.") Nonetheless, Austen has immense sympathy for those who let their heads be turned by the lure of money, as well as for those (even the silly, grating Mrs. Bennet) who see engagement and marriage as a business transaction. For their author knew all too well that the world inhabited by her characters—especially her female characters—offered severely limited opportunities for financial self-improvement. One had better marry a man with an income or at least a respectable clerical living.

The alternatives were perfectly clear and profoundly unattractive. "Single women have a dreadful propensity for being poor," wrote Austen. Marriage rescues Emma Woodhouse's companion Miss Taylor from the cruel fate of Miss Bates, the unfortunate vicar's daughter who, after her father's death, "has sunk from the comforts she was born to; and, if she live to old age, must probably sink more." When Fanny Price rejects Henry Crawford's proposal—which, in one of the most disturbing scenes in Austen, Sir Thomas Bertram strongly suggests she accept—she's packed off to her humble family home in Portsmouth. There she will be reminded of the fate awaiting a woman misguided enough to refuse a wealthy suitor merely because he is a reprehensible human being. In fact, Fanny's resolve is sorely tested—but not, as it happens, broken—by the appalling contrast between Mansfield Park and Portsmouth:

> At Mansfield, no sounds of contention, no raised voice, no abrupt bursts, no tread of violence was ever heard; all proceeded in a regular course of cheerful orderliness; every body had their due importance; every body's feelings were consulted. . . . Here, every body was noisy, every voice was loud . . . Whatever was wanted was halloo'd for, and the servants halloo'd out their excuses from the kitchen. The doors were in constant banging, the stairs were never at rest, nothing was done without a clatter, nobody sat still, and nobody could command attention when they spoke.

What's most interesting about this passage is that the salient difference between Mansfield Park and Portsmouth is not only the gap between wealth and penury, material comfort and privation, but also the disparity between order and disorder, harmony and chaos, between rudeness and good manners. These are the two opposing futures with which Fanny is being presented. What Austen understands is how economic security greatly facilitates—though doesn't in every case guarantee—kindness, order, and civility. All the frantic concern and convoluted wrangling for incomes and investments, for real estate, livings, and property improvement, are, in essence, means of securing and preserving the higher values of "good sense and good breeding," the gentle climate in which her favorite characters (and happy couples) thrive. The goal is not the money itself so much as the pleasant life it can arrange, and the moral values that are so much easier to put into practice when one has enough food, warmth—and physical space.

Nowhere is this more obvious than in *Mansfield Park*, the last and arguably the greatest of Austen's novels. What's at stake throughout the book—what's put in jeopardy by the interloping Crawfords—is not simply the family fortune but also the traditions, values, and ideals of Mansfield Park. Though the Crawfords have incomes, they are morally flawed; they are fans of the suspect, erotically disruptive amateur theatricals; they lack respect for the established order; they redecorate and nearly wreck Sir Thomas's billiard room to construct a theater; they discuss sweeping, unnecessary "improvements" in the landscaping of the estate. In one revealing exchange, the admirable Fanny Price and the shallow Mary Crawford express opposing views on the family chapel. Says Fanny:

> *"There is something in a chapel and chaplain so much in character with a great house, with one's ideas of what such a household should be! A whole family assembling regularly for the purpose of prayer is fine!"*
>
> *"Very fine indeed!" said Miss Crawford, laughing. "It must do all the heads of the family a great deal of good to force all the poor housemaids and footmen to leave business and pleasure, and say their prayers here twice a day, while they are inventing excuses themselves for staying away."*

It's this cynical, thoughtless disregard for tradition, politesse, and (in the most elevated sense of the phrase) "family values" that endangers the future of Mansfield Park and its heirs even more than Tom Bertram's penchant for gambling away the ancestral fortune. Despite their money and facile charm, the selfish, self-indulgent, and decadent Mary and Henry Crawford prove to be highly unsuitable matches for the more innocent, naive—and nobler—Bertrams, and for Fanny. By the novel's end, even Sir Thomas has come to see that the well-being of his estate will be far better served by Edmund's marrying the poor but worthy Fanny.

Jane Austen's novels—and the array of films and television miniseries based upon her fiction—are famous for ending with seemly, neatly arranged, emotionally and artistically satisfying marriages between appealing men and women who have finally managed to remove the complex, maddening (and often self-imposed) obstacles to their union. It's this tidiness, this reassuring neatness, this lack of disquieting ambiguity and sloppy irresolution that, I think, is—in addition to the grace and wit of her sentences—partly responsible for Austen's enduring popularity. That satisfying restoration of true harmony and order (and the prudent safeguarding of the income to support it) is the happy future estate that Jane Austen has sensibly, wisely planned for her heroes and heroines, and—if we're fortunate—for us all.

24

Charles Baxter, *Believers*

IN *BELIEVERS*, A COLLECTION OF SEVEN STORIES AND A NOVELLA, Charles Baxter continues his quietly groundbreaking researches into the ways that ordinary people—midwesterners, in towns with names like Five Oaks and Eurekaville—find their lives changed forever by unpredictable, near-magical, and utterly plausible turns of fate. These give the impression of being densely plotted, though when we try to summarize them, we may find that less has happened than we'd thought. What gives the work its density is not event so much as depth: the meticulous renderings of characters' habits and longings, and of the exterior world that impinges on their private hopes and fears. Each narrative somehow manages to re-create that paradoxical process: the more we learn about anyone, the more mysterious that person seems.

Many of the stories guide their characters toward some sort of revelation, a glimpse of some intuited truth, "terrible and perplexing." In "Time Exposure," Irene Gladfelter visits a neighbor who may be a serial killer: "The room looked like a cell inside someone's head . . . someone who had never thought of a pleasantry but who sat at the bottom of the ocean, feeling the crushing pressure of the water. An ocean god had thought this room and this man up. That was an odd idea, the sort of idea she had never had before." In "Kiss Away," a woman named Jodie is offered three wishes by a fat man in a diner ("He had a rare talent . . . for inspiring revulsion. The possible images of the Family of Humankind did not somehow include him") and fails to ask for the certainty that can protect her from tormenting doubts about her lover. ("She tried to lean into the love she felt for Walton . . . but instead of solid ground and rock just underneath the soil, and rock cliffs that comprised a wall where a human being could prop herself, there was nothing: stone gave way to sand, and sand gave way to water, and the water drained away into darkness and emptiness. Into this emptiness, violence, like an ever-flowing stream, was poured.") In "Flood Show" a photographer nearly drowns at the moment of realizing that time has failed to heal the wounds of love; in "The Next Building I Plan to Bomb," a banker's life is disrupted when he finds a note that may refer to a violent conspiracy.

Nearly all the narratives concern a Manichaean battle between the power of love and the forces of violence. In "The Cures for Love," a teacher of Latin reflects on how this struggle permeates the classics: "The old guys told the truth, she believed, about love and warfare, the peculiar combination of attraction and hatred existing together. They had told the truth before Christianity put civilization into a dreamworld." And in the novella, "Believers," a lawyer speaks as if this ancient contest has already been decided: "Men like to hunt and to kill. Their aim is to dominate. They take considerable pleasure in it. . . . They enjoy the shedding of blood. Bloodshed never bores anyone, does it?"

In "Believers," the conflict between love and bloodlust reaches an apotheosis large enough to include the political and the metaphysical. Its hero is a midwestern farm boy with a "genius for rapture" and an abiding interest in "the designs of God in nature, and the designs of God in man." He becomes a Catholic priest, but loses his calling after touring Germany on the eve of World War II. There, he witnesses "evil in a relatively pure form . . . not only the infliction of suffering but its conversion into spectacle, an entertainment for others, a sideshow. That was what had enraged him and enlarged his heart's knowledge of his own proper place in the world."

Though these fictions are unrelated, each functions like one of those lenses the optometrist slips in front of our eyes, so that by the time we finish the book, we have a clear vision of the whole, of what the writer is doing. What's striking here—and what the brilliant novella brings into focus—is how religious Baxter's concerns are; he writes of reincarnation and the afterlife, of sin and redemption, faith and consolation. One feels he never doubts for a moment that his characters have souls. Yet, unlike the early theologians who proceeded by abstract speculation, sophistry, and logic, Baxter convinces us of the soul's existence by precisely representing his characters' inner lives, their imaginative sensibilities and acutely detailed perceptions. A woman is offered a job by "a man whose suit was so wrinkled that it was prideful and emblematic." Another notes that her creepy neighbor, on crutches after an accident, looks like "a bat in splints." Yet another reflects that "personality . . . is the consolation prize of middle age." A tourist in Germany remarks that no one strolls casually through the streets there; instead, "these citizens advanced powerfully toward their destinations, looking like doctors on the way to emergency surgery . . . An insomniac consciousness seemed to animate the place."

It's the beauty of the language—the quirky intelligence, the humor, the lively, rhythmic assurance of sentences and paragraphs—that (along with their surprising plots) make these stories fun to read. We're happy to eavesdrop as characters reveal themselves in speech. (When a man asks his wife what she was in a previous life, she sourly replies, "I didn't have a previous life . . . Why don't you ask Ryan over there. Maybe he had a previous life. He might know. Or else we could talk about things that really matter.") We gladly

travel with these men and women, mostly on public transportation. ("Normal people were sometimes hard to find on the bus. Frequently all you saw were people in various stages of medication.
But today no lost souls were visible on either side of the aisle.")
We're even content to watch TV in their peculiar company:

> Tonight she checked the screen now and then to see, first, a road-
> ster bursting off a cliff into a slow arc of explosive death, and then
> a teenager fitting a black shoe sensuously on a woman's foot. Ap-
> parently this movie was some sort of violent update of Cinderella.
> Now a man dressed like an unsuccessful investment banker was
> inching his way down a back alley. The walls of the alley were
> coated with sinister drippings.

More often than not, these fictions end on a note of acceptance,
with a character resolving to live bravely amid the contradictions of a
painful, frightening, deeply flawed—and ineffably beautiful—world.
On occasion, this comfort comes through the mediation of art, a descent of grace that seems like divine intercession. So an unemployed
woman staves off panic when a recording of Enrique Granados's *Goy-
escas* reassures her that "she could sit like this all morning, and no one
would punish her. It was very Spanish." In "The Cures for Love," a
Chicago woman, deserted by her boyfriend, seeks solace in a volume
of Ovid and, following its advice to avoid solitude and "go where
people are happy . . . witness the high visibility of joy," she travels to
O'Hare airport. On the bus back to the city, she has a dream in which
Ovid speaks in chatty, aphoristic blank verse so amusing and consoling that she "forgot that she was supposed to be unhappy."

Reading *Believers* reminds us that fiction can take us out of ourselves, can sharpen the outlines and colors of the visible world. It's a
book we can enjoy with admiration untainted by rancor or envy—
though writers, of course, may secretly wish that they'd written
these stories themselves.

25

Deborah Levy, *Swimming Home*

A QUESTION FOR THE WIVES: LET'S SAY YOU'VE RENTED A
holiday villa on the French Riviera, and when you arrive, along
with your philandering middle-aged poet husband, you discover
an attractive young woman, her fingernails painted green, floating naked in the pool. Mightn't it be a good idea for everyone concerned to ask the rental agent if you can still get your deposit back?

Unfortunately for the characters, and luckily for the reader, the
wife who's leased the vacation house in *Swimming Home* doesn't appear to think so. From the first brief chapters of Deborah Levy's
spare, disturbing, and frequently funny novel, which was short-
listed for the Man Booker Prize, we sense that things will turn out
badly for the nude interloper and for the villa guests. We can predict with some certainty that two marriages will be tested, possibly
ruined, and that the antique Persian gun will not stay hidden under
the bed.

But what we don't understand for a while is what sort of novel
we're reading. As we begin to settle in among the party of privileged
British vacationers—two couples, one with a teenage daughter, all

warily eyeing Kitty Finch, the girl who emerges from the pool—we may wonder: haven't we seen something like this in an early Chabrol thriller, or in that Ozon film with Charlotte Rampling? Don't the tone and the milieu suggest an improbable hybrid of Virginia Woolf, Edward St. Aubyn, *Absolutely Fabulous*, and Patricia Highsmith?

As we continue reading, we realize that *Swimming Home* is unlike anything but itself. Its originality lies in its ellipses, its patterns and repetitions, in what it discloses and reveals, and in the peculiar curio cabinet that Deborah Levy has constructed: a collection of objects and details that disclose more about these fictional men and women than they are willing, or able, to tell us about themselves.

The girl in the pool is, to say the least, unstable: anorexic, obsessive, a self-styled botanist staying (before and after a stint in a mental hospital) at the holiday property, which is owned by the luxury-real-estate investor for whom her mother cleans house. The object of her current mad obsession is a famous poet, Joe Jacobs, a complicated man with an evasive, unresolved, and perhaps unresolvable relationship to his tragic childhood. His journalist wife, Isabel, has spent more time broadcasting from war zones than at home with her husband and daughter, Nina—who, at fourteen, is just noticing the effect she has on the French guy who owns a café near the villa and prides himself on looking like Mick Jagger. Also staying at the house are Isabel's friend Laura and her husband, Mitchell, whose reckless spending has accelerated their slide from being the middle-class owners of a London shop selling "primitive Persian, Turkish, and Hindu weapons" and "expensive African jewellery" to the edge of bankruptcy and financial free fall.

Watching from the house next door is an elderly British woman doctor who knows just what kind of serpent the tourists have admitted into their garden. But no one heeds the obvious warnings, not even when Laura reports on Kitty's idiosyncratic approach to home decor: "She had seen Kitty arrange the tails of three rabbits Mitchell had shot in the orchard in a vase—as if they were flowers.

The thing was, she must have actually cut the tails off the rabbits herself. With a knife. She must have sawed through the rabbits with a carving knife."

It is suggested that Isabel has permitted Kitty to stay because she wants Kitty to serve as the missile that will finally torpedo Isabel's marriage to the unfaithful Joe. And we know, from having read the novel's opening, that Kitty and Joe will wind up returning at midnight from making love at the Hotel Negresco, hurtling at high speed along a winding mountain road.

> When Kitty Finch took her hand off the steering wheel and told him she loved him, he no longer knew if she was threatening him or having a conversation. Her silk dress was falling off her shoulders as she bent over the steering wheel. A rabbit ran across the road and the car swerved. He heard himself say, "Why don't you pack a rucksack and see the poppy fields in Pakistan like you said you wanted to?"

This passage will be repeated, with additions and variations, elsewhere in the novel. And as we learn more about the characters, we are better equipped to understand what it signifies.

We may wish that Isabel, with her experience on the front lines, had found a human time bomb less likely to inflict collateral damage on the innocent than Kitty Finch. But as we read on to discover how grisly the carnage will be, we notice that the book has taken an interesting turn. All sorts of seemingly minor details—an anecdote about a bear, an Apollinaire poem, a pebble with a hole in the middle—turn out to be connective threads in the plot.

Meanwhile, Deborah Levy is adding levels of complication that go beneath the sunny surface to get at something darker and more substantial. Among the novel's concerns are the weight of history and the past, the alarming ease with which mental illness can infect the relatively healthy, the intimacies and estrangements of marriage and family life, the insecurities of youth, and the indignities of age. Buying a scoop of caramelized nuts that she half hopes will fatally choke her, Madeleine Sheridan muses: "She had turned into a toad in old age and if anyone dared to kiss her she would not turn back into a princess because she had never been a princess in the first place."

Beneath much of what occurs is the question of what it means to be fraudulent or authentic, to lie or tell the truth. In one of the book's insightful passages, Isabel reflects on the feeling of being an inadequate actress, improvising a supporting role in the drama of her daily existence:

> She was a kind of ghost in her London home. When she returned to it from various war zones and found that in her absence the shoe polish or light bulbs had been put in a different place, somewhere similar but not quite where they were before, she learned that she too had a transient place in the family home. . . . She had attempted to be someone she didn't really understand. A powerful but fragile female character. If she knew that to be forceful was not the same as being powerful and to be gentle was not the same as being fragile, she did not know how to use this knowledge in her own life or what it added up to.

Readers will have to resist the temptation to hurry up in order to find out what happens during and after Joe and Kitty's wild ride along the coast, because *Swimming Home* should be read with care. So many of its important events occur in the spaces between chapters—between paragraphs—that it's easy to overlook how thoroughly they have been prepared for, earlier on. The reward for such forbearance is the enjoyable, if unsettling, experience of being pitched into the deep waters of Deborah Levy's wry, accomplished novel.

26

Alice Munro,
Lives of Girls and Women

READ JUST ONE OF ALICE MUNRO'S LUMINOUS, ENTHRALLING short stories and you'll want to track down all of her story collections, because to encounter her work is to remember what it was like to first fall in love with reading: to discover the joy of briefly stepping out of our familiar selves and being magically absorbed into the radiant, seductive world that an author has created. To read her is like listening to a friend tell us—in a perfectly calm, natural, confiding, and unaffected tone—the most simple and complicated, thoroughly ordinary and shockingly dramatic things that have ever happened to her and to the people she knows and loves. Her stories make us realize, with a shiver of recognition, how closely the events she's describing resemble things that have happened to us.

Originally published in 1971, *Lives of Girls and Women* seems today every bit as fresh, as groundbreaking and startlingly original, as it did when it first appeared. Few books before or since have looked more bravely or more deeply—or with more humor, forgiveness, grace, and wit—at female experience, at the harsh and reassuring, particular and universal truths that women know (but rarely reveal) about themselves, about the men they love, about their friendships and rivalries with other women. No one has a better ear for the way we tell our stories, or for the fevered tone—"ribald, scornful, fanatically curious"—in which adolescent girls talk about romance and sex. No one has a sharper (or more compassionate) perspective on the embarrassment and uneasiness we feel when we see, in our parents and older relatives, the very same quirks and traits that we ourselves have inherited. And no one manages to pack so much into a single story—birth and death, happiness and heartbreak, the history of whole generations and communities—and make it look so easy.

Officially a novel, *Lives of Girls and Women* can just as easily be read as a series of beautifully crafted, interrelated short stories, all of which concern Del Jordan, a young girl growing up in the Canadian countryside and, later, in one of the provincial, deceptively sleepy Ontario villages where most of Munro's fiction takes place. The early chapters center around Del's family and community—her brother, aunts and uncles, an eccentric neighbor known as Uncle Benny, her mother's friend Fern Dogherty, and Del's own best friend, Naomi. Del's even-tempered, well-liked father raises foxes on a farm outside the town of Jubilee. Her mother, a prickly, sympathetic presence whose powerful personality figures in—or hovers over—nearly every episode in the book, is a volatile mix of contradictions: agnostic, opinionated, fiercely individualistic, she can't help worrying about what the neighbors might think. An ardent defender of the underprivileged, she considers herself superior to the poor country folk down the road.

The thread that stitches the volume together is the steady, alternately painful and exhilarating progress of Del's education: her efforts to find out who she is and how she fits into the wider world; her struggle to fathom the mysteries of love and sex, to navigate the treacherous straits of girlhood and adolescence and to become a woman without sacrificing her individuality, her spirit, her intelligence, her bright, stubborn sense of self. Many of the chapters find Del avidly searching her surroundings for clues to the dark mysteries of adult life. In one, she watches the rocky course (and the eventual crack-up) of Uncle Benny's marriage to a half-crazed mail order bride; in another, she accompanies her mother on her rounds, selling encyclopedias—a job that embodies all of Mrs. Jordan's most intense ambitions and excruciating frustrations; in another section, Del attempts to settle "the question of God" by attending services at her town's many churches—Methodist and Presbyterian, Congregationalist and Anglican—and by testing the power of prayer during a personal crisis in Household Science class; in yet another, she monitors Fern Dogherty's romance (and initiates a perverse, furtive one of her own) with the attractive, shiftless bachelor who reads the news on the Jubilee radio station.

In later chapters, Del and her friend Naomi take their first tentative and gradually more eager steps toward the scary, enticing realm of experience they have been observing from afar. They go out drinking with older men; Naomi becomes engaged; Del ends a dutiful, cerebral relationship with her high school sweetheart ("Our bodies fell against each other not unwillingly but joylessly, like sacks of wet sand") and begins a passionate love affair with a young man who works in the local lumberyard and heads the Baptist youth group. Meanwhile, even as she is trying to reconcile romance with independence, Del is upset by a magazine article describing a young couple looking at the moon; the boy is contemplating the immensity of the universe, while the girl is thinking that she needs to wash her hair. "It was clear to me at once that I was not thinking as the girl thought; the full moon would never as long as I lived remind me to wash my hair. . . . I wanted men to love me, and I wanted to think of the universe when I looked at the moon. I felt trapped, stranded; it seemed there had to be a choice when there couldn't be a choice."

It's moments like this one—revelations of character, flashes of insight that make us stop and wonder how Alice Munro could possibly know so much about us, about precisely what we thought and felt when we were Del's age, our first friendships and first crushes—that make her fiction so unique. Reading *Lives of Girls and Women*, you can almost watch its author develop and perfect the seemingly effortless and (in fact) astonishingly masterful skills she has deployed throughout her career.

Even in this early book, she is already building her fiction by adding layers of depth, of character; already shifting gracefully and naturally between past and present; already exploring the themes of community and social class, town and country, destiny and ambition, the needs of the body and the hungers of the spirit; already allowing her plots to take surprising turns so that they almost appear to be rambling, until we realize that every word, every detail, is essential, every incident changes the way we view every small and large event, and that she is always—firmly and entirely—in control. And already she is writing beautifully, powerfully, and lyrically about familiar, seemingly everyday things. Here, for example, Del remembers falling asleep, knowing that her parents were downstairs, companionably playing cards in the kitchen:

> *Upstairs seemed miles above them, dark and full of the noise of the wind. Up there you discovered what you never remembered down in the kitchen—that we were in a house as small and shut up as any boat is on the sea, in the middle of a tide of howling weather. They seemed to be talking, playing cards, a long way away in a tiny spot of light, irrelevantly; yet this thought of them, prosaic as a hiccup, familiar as breath, was what held me, what winked at me from the bottom of the well until I fell asleep.*

In the chapter from which the book takes its name, Del's mother reflects on her daughter's future: "There is a change coming I think in the lives of girls and woman. Yes. But it is up to us to make it come. All women have had up till now has been their connection with men. All we have had. No more lives of our own, really, than domestic animals. . . . But I hope you will—use your brains. Use your brains. Don't be distracted. . . . It is self-respect I am really speaking of. Self-respect."

Typically, Del dismisses and resists her mother's advice—just as we were so frequently reluctant to listen to our own mothers' good sense. And yet we, Alice Munro's readers, know that the transformations that Mrs. Jordan predicts have already taken place. In the decades since *Lives of Girls and Women* was first published, our world has been greatly altered. But part of what's so moving and exciting about Alice Munro's work is her gift for identifying and expressing how much has stayed the same, how much will always stay the same. In her calm, unhurried, yet urgent fiction—set on farms and in small towns in Canada, in the recent or distant past—she reaches so deeply into the hearts and minds of her complex and sympathetic characters that what she is able to give us is nothing less than what is eternal and universal, unchanging and profound, not only in the lives of girls or women but in what we instinctively recognize and consciously understand as the entire human condition.

27

Jennifer Egan, *Manhattan Beach*

A THIRD OF THE WAY THROUGH JENNIFER EGAN'S NOVEL *Manhattan Beach*, a young woman named Anna Kerrigan enlists Dexter Styles, a charismatic nightclub owner and racketeer, to drive her and her severely disabled sister, Lydia, to the seashore at the edge of Brooklyn. Lydia, who cannot walk or feed herself, and who rarely leaves her family's cramped apartment, has never seen the ocean, and Anna allows herself to hope that the experience might arrest her sister's decline and jolt her out of her growing detachment from the loving domestic life around her. Dexter's palatial house abuts a private beach, and he and Anna carry Lydia, swaddled in an imported blanket from Dexter's linen closet and propped up in a specially designed chair, to the edge of the water. It's 1942, and in the distance a passenger ship sails by, presumably transporting troops to Europe.

Dexter owns several popular clubs and illegal gambling casinos, in Manhattan and the boroughs. As he and Anna chat about his profitable contribution to the war effort—"keeping the brass amused and easing the pain of rationing"—Lydia's eyes blink open and she begins to babble.

"The change in the crippled girl was extraordinary. He'd found her sprawled unconscious, as if she'd been dropped from a height, but now she sat up independently, holding her head away from the stand." Lydia's awakening is so affecting that only later do we realize what a challenge it must have been for the writer to avoid the obvious pitfalls and construct a scene that is not only dramatic but plausible and persuasive.

It couldn't have been easy, arranging for the salt air and pounding surf to work a near miracle, to make a mute girl speak, or almost speak—and not send the entire plot plummeting into bathos. Jennifer Egan succeeds partly because here, as in her other books, she combines psychological acuity with technical virtuosity: a talent for deepening what transpires on the surface of the novel with nuanced portrayals of the fictional people in its pages. We're interested not only in the eventful, elaborately orchestrated plot but also in the ways in which events—and their consequences—reveal what the characters don't know about one another and about themselves, what they are willing to admit and what they would rather keep hidden.

Wisely, Egan complicates the scene at the beach so that Lydia's remission—which, we sense, will be limited and brief—is only one of the things that hold our attention. We're equally, if not more, engaged by the motives (aside from their wish to help Lydia) and secrets that have brought Anna and Dexter to that particular stretch of sand.

Dexter is unaware that he and Anna have met before. When she was twelve, her father, Eddie, took her to play with the gangster's daughter on this same beach while the two men talked business. Anna's response to that visit, and to her own first sight of the ocean, will resonate eerily throughout the novel:

Anna watched the sea. There was a feeling she had, standing at
its edge: an electric mix of attraction and dread. What would be
exposed if all that water should suddenly vanish? A landscape of
lost objects: sunken ships, hidden treasure, gold and gems and
the charm bracelet that had fallen from her wrist into a storm
drain. Dead bodies, her father always added, with a laugh. To
him, the ocean was a wasteland.

Anna is too young to understand that her father makes his living as Dexter's "bagman"—"the sap who ferried a sack containing
something (money, of course, but it wasn't his business to know)
between men who should not rightly associate." It's Eddie's job to
deliver bribes, collect payoffs, and keep an eye on the employees at
Dexter's casinos. While her father and Dexter confer, Anna plays
out her own drama. Stubborn and appealingly proud, she rejects
the proffered gift of a doll that the gangster's daughter no longer
plays with—and that Anna desperately wants.

During the decade separating Anna's two trips to Dexter's private beach, Eddie has vanished, leaving her responsible for her
mother and Lydia. And Anna thinks that Dexter may have clues
to the mystery of who her father was, and of why he disappeared.

Helping Lydia and Anna flatters Dexter's vanity, and the good
deed allows him to see himself as a hero. He turns down an invitation to have lunch and play billiards with his patrician father-in-
law, whom he likes and admires, because he has made a promise to
Anna, whom he recently met at his nightclub. He's not ready to admit that he finds her attractive, but it's not entirely accidental that
he brings her and her sister to his house when his wife and children
are away. His tangled emotions, as well as their conversation about
the war effort, inspire a new—and ultimately unhelpful—surge of
idealism and patriotic high-mindedness that Dexter attempts to
put into practice when he meets with his boss, the ruthless gang-
land kingpin known as Mr. Q. This smart observation about the

ways in which love, even when it's unconscious, can briefly make one a more generous and noble person recalls the moment in *Anna Karenina* when Vronsky, who has just met Anna on the train, impulsively gives money to the family of the railroad guard killed on the tracks.

Typically, Jennifer Egan provides her characters with rich interior lives, rife with contradictions and complexities. In the brilliant *A Visit from the Goon Squad* (2011), a spiky, sympathetic kleptomaniac named Sasha feels such overwhelming empathy for the elderly plumber fixing a leak in her apartment that she can cope with her feelings only by stealing the old man's screwdriver. The heroine of *Look at Me* (2001) has an ability to see beneath the most meticulously groomed and cultivated exteriors, to glimpse "the nagging, flickering presence" of the "shadow selves" of those around her—"that caricature that clings to each of us, revealing itself in odd moments when we laugh or fall still, staring brazenly from certain bad photographs."

No one in *Manhattan Beach*, however, has emotional X-ray vision. Indeed, much of the plot is propelled by the characters' faulty or partial understanding of one another and of how profoundly their friends, relatives, allies, and enemies have been shaped by the social and political history of the era and the borough—Brooklyn—in which much of the novel is set.

SOME writers stake out an area of fictional territory—Flannery O'Connor's Georgia, Nathaniel Hawthorne's New England, Mavis Gallant's Paris—and find riches enough to mine for a lifetime. Jennifer Egan is of the other sort: a novelist whose work keeps taking her (and the reader) to new places. Each of her books is, at least on the surface, very different from the rest. *A Visit from the Goon Squad*, which won the Pulitzer Prize, considers, among other subjects, the mystery of time, the 1970s punk music scene in San Francisco, the

coming global water shortage, psychotherapy, and the travails of a
public relations agent hired to improve a dictator's image.

Look at Me follows three parallel, suspenseful stories until they
come together in a disastrous collision: an injured heroine's pil-
grimage as a model through the brittle milieu of haute couture; the
painful education of an intelligent, disaffected high school girl; and
the journey, from New Jersey to Illinois, of a mysterious foreigner
who may or may not be an Islamist terrorist. Set in a shadowy Eastern European castle with underground caverns and tunnels, *The
Keep* (2006) is a modern take on an old-fashioned Gothic thriller,
suffused with the pleasant creepiness of a vintage horror film.

One of the elements that joins these seemingly dissimilar
novels in a single sensibility is that they are all cinematic. In fact,
Egan's fictions usually conjure a quite specific film genre. *Manhattan Beach* combines 1940s noir—movies in which James Cagney
and George Raft played gangsters in impeccable overcoats and
snappy fedoras—with historical documentary about the New York
waterfront and the Brooklyn Navy Yard. The book's settings—
from a swanky speakeasy to a train station swarming "with soldiers carrying identical brown duffels" to a lifeboat filled with
shipwrecked, desperately thirsty sailors—feel remembered from
films seen long ago.

Yet another thread uniting Egan's novels is the unusual compression and density of her writing. The brief mini-narratives she
uses to illuminate a character are so fully developed that another
author might see, in each one, enough for an entire novel. We learn
a lot about Dexter from his response to—and his memory of—a casual affair that had begun when a woman he met on a train tapped
on the door of his first-class sleeper in the middle of the night:

> *They disembarked that afternoon in Angel, Indiana, intending—
> what? Intending to continue. They checked into a grand old hotel
> near the station as Mr. and Mrs. Jones. Immediately, Dexter felt*

*a change: now that the bleak winter landscape was all around
him, rather than sliding picturesquely past, he liked it less. Other
irritants followed: a sudden dislike of her perfume; a sudden dislike of her laugh, the dry pork chop he was served in the hotel
restaurant, a cobweb dangling from the light fixture above the
bed. After making love, she fell into a torporous sleep. But Dexter
lay awake, listening to the howling dogs, or was it wolves, wind
clattering the loose windowpanes. Everything he knew seemed
irrevocably distant: Harriet, his children, the business he'd been
charged to transact for Mr. Q.—too far gone for him ever to re-
claim them. He felt how easily a man's life could slip away, separated from him by thousands of miles of empty space.*

Other passages convey elusive sensations in an unforgettable
way. At a Manhattan nightclub, Anna enjoys her first taste of cham-
pagne: "The pale gold potion snapped and frothed in her glass.
When she took a sip, it crackled down her throat—sweet but with
a tinge of bitterness, like a barely perceptible pin inside a cushion."

Egan's gift for metaphor is evident throughout, as in this lyrical
snapshot of the nefarious Mr. Q.: "He was hulking and cavernous
at once, browned to mahogany. Time had enlarged him in an or-
ganic, mineral way, like a tree trunk, or salts accreting in a cave.
The frailty of his advanced age showed itself in the silty, tidal labors
of his breath."

Here, as in *A Visit from the Goon Squad* and *Look at Me*, Egan
opts for a panoramic and multifaceted plot divided into subplots
that dovetail at critical junctures. The architecture of the novel is
built on dramatic set pieces and deceptively minor details that will
turn out to be important. She relies on us to remember objects and
incidents—a pocket watch, a piece of jewelry, a bicycle, a street address, the name of a first love—from an earlier appearance (sometimes hundreds of pages back) in the novel. And we do recall them,
with a pleasurable pop of recognition—the sense of things having

come together that was among the rewards of *A Visit from the Goon Squad*.

Like that novel and *Look at Me*, *Manhattan Beach* aims to get the broadest possible cross section of the world—or of a certain corner of the world at a certain time—onto the printed page. Populated by characters from a range of social classes, all of them navigating by wildly divergent moral compasses, *Manhattan Beach* takes us from the exclusive Rockaways country club where Dexter's father-in-law holds court to the Kerrigans' tenement apartment, where Anna and Lydia share a room. Anna's career begins in the machine shop at the Navy Yard, where she painstakingly measures, with a micrometer, machine parts for battleships. Eventually she winds up exploring the depths of Wallabout Bay when—against the objections of almost all her male bosses and co-workers—she is promoted from her tedious measuring job to become the Navy Yard's first female diver.

Dressed in a cripplingly heavy diving suit ("The dress weighs two hundred pounds. The hat alone weighs fifty-six. The shoes together are thirty-five"), Anna sets foot on the bottom of the bay and feels "a rush of well-being whose source was not instantly clear. . . . Then she realized: the pain of the dress had vanished. The air pressure from within it was just enough to balance the pressure from outside while maintaining negative buoyancy . . . This was like flying, like magic—like being inside a dream."

On land and underwater, Anna is a rare fictional creation, in that she is a woman driven by desires—lust, altruism, competition, the impulse to do what the men around her insist she can't do—without invoking the writer's judgment. Wisely, *Manhattan Beach* doesn't spend much time exploring Anna's reasons for wanting to become a diver, but we may wonder about her unconscious motives. Eventually her expertise takes the story on a decisive turn toward a conciliatory and satisfying, if not ecstatically happy, ending.

Egan's readers may miss the sparkle of sly wit that glinted in her previous work, novels in which chic (or aspirationally chic) New Yorkers eat at a restaurant called Raw Feed, frequent a night-club named Jello, and say, "Trauma upsets the hair." In *Manhattan Beach*, one occasionally feels that Egan is so focused on getting the facts and details right that she can't allow herself (and us) to have quite as much fun.

Writers of historical fiction rightfully fear the mistake that will lose the confidence and trust of the knowledgeable reader. Recently, watching a British TV series set in the 1950s, I was distracted from a crucial conversation two characters were having by the nagging thought that the teensy, precious arrangements of food on their restaurant plates would have been more typical of restaurants in the 1990s. Nothing in *Manhattan Beach* distracts in this way.

If *Manhattan Beach* has flaws, perhaps their cause can be traced to the acknowledgments section: several pages of thanks to those who helped with the research that went into the novel. The profu-sion of vintage brand names, radio programs, comic strips, songs, and slang phrases can seem more than is strictly necessary to pro-vide a sense of authenticity. Eager to learn what happens next, we may find ourselves skimming passages like this one, which occurs as Anna prepares to make an illicit dive that may finally disclose her father's fate:

> It was a Morse Air Pump No. 1, identical to the compressors at the Naval Yard. They had anchored it to the bow, and now they cleaned its air reservoirs, oiled the piston rods, and lubricated the pump shaft handles with a mixture of oil and graphite. They'd had surprisingly little trouble removing a pair of diving crates from the Naval Yard—each containing a two-hundred-pound dress—along with six fifty-foot lengths of air hose, a loaded tool bag, two diving knives, and a spare-parts tin. It was almost too easy, they'd crowed when Anna had met them outside the Red Hook boatyard. So many divers had been commuting to the

freshwater pipeline that the marine guards barely took note when
they hauled the equipment through the Marshall Street gate onto
a small flatbed truck Marle had borrowed from his uncle.

Doubtless there are readers who enjoy obtaining information from novels, while others may be more impatient to learn
what Anna is about to discover underwater. In any case, such moments are few in this ambitious, compassionate, engrossing book.
Finishing *Manhattan Beach* is like being expelled from a world
that—despite the horrors of the war being fought in the novel's
background, despite the occasional gangster drugged and dumped
into the sea—seems more charitable, more reasonable, and less
chaotic than the one in which we live now.

28

Rebecca West

IF REBECCA WEST'S MASTERPIECE *BLACK LAMB AND GREY FALCON* is required reading for anyone wishing to understand the Balkans, *A Train of Powder* should be given to every juror in every capital case, to supplement the judge's instructions. Written between 1946 and 1954, these reportorial accounts of four controversial trials consider crime and punishment, innocence and guilt, retribution and forgiveness. As compelling as Court TV but without the frisson of voyeurism (and with the compensatory satisfactions of West's breathtakingly lucid prose style), these elegant narratives remind us of the preciousness and fragility of our right to trial by jury and of how that right depends on impartiality, intelligence, and empathy, on respect for our fellow humans and for a concept—the rule of law—that our politicians have lately labored so hard to degrade.

The book's centerpiece is "Greenhouse with Cyclamens," a lengthy three-part essay on the Nuremberg trials. Sent to Germany by *The New Yorker*, West arrived in time to cover the closing arguments and the sentencing of the Nazi leaders, to focus on a process that had dragged on for so long that the horrors of war had been reduced to the narcotizing drone of testimony. She was encouraged by a lawyer who pointed out that the shortage of newsprint during and after the war meant that few people were able to read about the trials.

The precision and clarity of West's powers of observation animate and sharpen her crisp sketches of the defendants:

> Hess was noticeable because he was so plainly mad: so plainly mad that it seemed shameful that he should be tried. His skin was ashen, and he had that odd faculty, peculiar to lunatics, of falling into strained positions which no normal person could maintain for more than a few minutes, and staying fixed in contortion for hours. He had the classless air characteristic of asylum inmates; evidently his distracted personality had torn up all clues to his past. . . .
>
> Baldur von Schirach, the Youth Leader, startled because he was like a woman in a way not common among men who looked like women. It was as if a neat and mousy governess sat there, not pretty, but never with a hair out of place, and always to be trusted never to intrude when there were visitors: as it might be Jane Eyre. And though one had read surprising news of Göring for years, he still surprised. He was so very soft. . . . Sometimes, particularly when his humor was good, he recalled the madam of a brothel. His like are to be seen in the late morning in doorways along the steep streets of Marseilles, the professional mask of geniality still hard on their faces though they stand relaxed in leisure, their fat cats rubbing against their spread skirts.

I've quoted this passage at such length because it typifies West's method: the precise metaphors and smooth turns of phrase, the thrilling attention to the shape of the paragraph and sentence. West's horror and grief over the scale and viciousness of the defendants' crimes is the given behind all this, shared by both writer and reader. But the fact that these men have committed crimes far beyond the imagination of the judicial system never diminishes West's vigilant devotion to that system, to reason and justice—thus her repugnance at the "shame" of trying a madman like Hess.

What's striking about West's descriptions of these villains is the waves of surface particulars that sweep us toward the most private recesses of the defendants' souls. That is the destination to which she sets out by calling Nuremberg a "citadel of boredom" from which, in the trial's eleventh month, everyone longs to escape—everyone but the accused. To make us see the Nazis as eager to prolong the trial (just as we would be in their situation, if we could imagine being in their situation) is to forge a daring, imaginative link between our humanity and that of men we consider morally subhuman. Similar leaps are made in the book's other essays: reports on a lynching case in Greenville, South Carolina, and on two British trials, one for murder, another for espionage.

Though the structures of the essays often suggest the cagey withholdings and revelations of the murder mystery, the real source of narrative tension is their author's determination to get under the skins and into the psyches of everyone in the courtroom, from the French judges at Nuremberg to the South Carolina jurors:

> *What was to be marveled at about this jury was its constitution. As Greenville is a town with, it is said, twenty-five millionaires and a large number of prosperous and well-educated people, it may have seemed peculiar that the jury should consist of two salesmen, a farmer, a mechanic, a truck driver, and seven textile workers. . . . The unpopular task of deciding a lynching case therefore fell to an unfavored group who had not the money to hire a bodyguard or to leave the town. They would, let us remember, have been in a most difficult position if they had returned a verdict of guilty.*

Characteristically, West seems to be looking everywhere at once, gazing past the quotidian rituals of the trials to observe the larger communities from which the participants come. But always her attention keeps tracking back to the accused. Her obsession with criminals is partly metaphysical, for she is one of those writers who believe that concrete details can be piled up like a ladder to bring us closer to some higher mystery, or truth. Here, the mystery is that of evil; early in her Nuremberg essay, West tells a story that encapsulates what most confounds us about the Nazis' inner lives. A French doctor in charge of the exhibits that document Nazi atrocities says, "These people . . . send me in my breakfast tray strewn with pansies, beautiful pansies. I have never seen more beautiful pansies, arranged with exquisite taste. I have to remind myself that they belong to the same race that tortured me month after month, year after year, at Mauthausen."

Ultimately, West's fascination with those on trial has less to do with philosophy than with morality and compassion. Always her effort is to see (and make us see) that these demons are men, and that whatever we might learn from them and their crimes will be lost to us if we insist on assigning them to some other species. Frequently she reminds us that "if a trial for murder last too long, more than the murder will out. The man in the murderer will out; it becomes horrible to think of destroying him." And she describes the Nazi war criminals as they are about to be sentenced:

Their pale and lined faces all looked alike; their bodies sagged inside their clothes, which seemed more alive than they were. They were gone. They were finished. It seemed strange that they could ever have excited loyalty; it was plainly impossible that they should ever attract it again. . . . They were not abject. These ghosts gathered about them the rags of what had been good in them during their lives.

West is present when the men are told they are going be hanged. "No wise person," she asserts, "will write an unnecessary word about hanging, for fear of straying into the field of pornography." Yet she concludes the first part of "Greenhouse with Cyclamens" with a bloodcurdling disquisition on the history of this form of execution, a description of the eleven condemned men slowly choking to death, and of Ribbentrop struggling in the air for twenty minutes.

Ultimately, West's faith in justice transcends the individual criminal and the seriousness of his crime. She is less concerned with the pathology of the condemned than with the collective health of whole communities, countries, civilizations—entities that, in her view, are also on trial in these proceedings. It's not the cruelty of hanging that alarms her so much as what that cruelty can trigger in human nature: "For when society has to hurt a man it must hurt him as little as possible and must preserve what it can of his pride, lest there should spread in that society those feelings which make men do the things for which they get hanged."

This astonishing book makes us long to know what Rebecca West would have made of the grisly mass entertainments—these gory cockfights staged on a colossal scale—that we have come to accept as legal proceedings on which men and women's lives depend. *A Train of Powder* makes us look harder to see what she might have seen: her flashes of insight into the minds of criminals and victims, her long gaze into the future to discern the distant shock waves, the social repercussions of trials and of the ways in which justice is served or betrayed. It makes us pay a different sort of attention to the sensational legal battles that periodically turn our living rooms, our offices, our neighborhood barbershops and bars into annexes of the courtrooms on which all the rest depends.

29

Mohsin Hamid, *Exit West*

EARLY IN MOHSIN HAMID'S REMARKABLE NOVEL *EXIT WEST*, A young couple fall in love in an unnamed city where—as we learn in the opening sentences—war is about to break out. The streets and parks are crowded with stunned and dying refugees, but so far the local unrest has been limited to "some shootings and the odd car bombing, felt in one's chest cavity as a subsonic vibration like those emitted by large loudspeakers at music concerts." Despite the distant crackling of automatic gunfire and the unnerving indications that the life they know is soon to end, Saeed and Nadia, who meet in an evening class on corporate branding and product identity, do what humans so often—and so instinctively—do in similar circumstances: they act as if they have all the time in the world. "That is the way of things, with cities as with life, for one moment we are pottering about our errands as usual and the next we are dying, and our eternally impending ending does not put a stop to our transient beginnings and middles until the instant when it does."

Employed by a firm that sells outdoor advertising, Saeed has been trying to design a billboard campaign for a soap company.

Having liberated herself, at great cost, from her traditional family, Nadia lives alone in a rented apartment, works for an insurance company, drives a motorbike, and wears a full-length black robe—not as a sign of religious devotion but for protection, as a way of dealing with "aggressive men and with the police, and with aggressive men who were the police." The couple's first after-class conversation touches on the subject of prayer (Saeed prays, Nadia doesn't, a difference between them that will grow more divisive as the novel progresses).

Saeed and Nadia flirt, have dinner, smoke weed, take psychedelic mushrooms. Saeed suggests they abstain from sex until they are married. Nadia is intrigued by her attractive classmate but determined to preserve her hard-won independence. The tentative advances and inevitable stalls of their courtship might seem more familiar and less urgent if we weren't so regularly reminded of how fragile and doomed their world is.

Reading this part of the novel feels a bit like looking at before-and-after photos of a bombed-out city. Hamid gives us a sort of binocular vision of the apartment where Saeed lives with his mother, a retired teacher, and his father, a semi-retired university professor; it's at once a pleasant family home—and the ruin it will soon become. The view from their windows "might command a slight premium during gentler, more prosperous times, but would be most undesirable in times of conflict, when it would be squarely in the path of heavy machine-gun and rocket fire as fighters advanced into this part of town: a view like staring down the barrel of a rifle. Location, location, location, the realtors say. Geography is destiny, respond the historians."

Unsurprisingly, the historians prove to be more prescient than the realtors. As the worsening conflict between the government and the fundamentalist rebels—and a strictly enforced new curfew—makes it increasingly dangerous to meet, Saeed invites Nadia to move in (and live chastely) with him and his parents. Nadia hesitates, until history decides for her; the risks she faces living alone have become too great, and she worries about Saeed traveling back and forth to see her.

No matter how often Hamid has warned us about what is about to occur, it still comes as a shock to the reader—as it does to Saeed and Nadia—when the city in which they have been so happy turns into a war zone. Or perhaps what's startling is how quickly and dramatically a modern society can be dismantled and reduced to rubble and chaos.

Firefights erupt in disputed neighborhoods. Nadia's cousin is blown "literally to bits" by a truck bomb. The ponytailed entrepreneur who sold Nadia the hallucinogenic mushrooms is beheaded, "with a serrated knife to enhance discomfort." The militants occupy strategic territory; people vanish, leaving their loved ones with no idea if they are alive or dead; drones and helicopters hover overhead; Saeed's father sees some boys playing soccer with a human head; an upstairs neighbor is killed at home by militants hunting down a particular sect, and his blood seeps through the ceiling. One by one, the ordinary comforts and conveniences—cell phone signals, plumbing, running water—disappear. There are nonstop public and private executions, bodies hang "from streetlamps and billboards like a form of festive seasonal decoration. The executions moved in waves, and once a neighborhood had been purged it could then expect a measure of respite, until someone committed an infraction of some kind, because infractions, although often alleged with a degree of randomness, were inevitably punished without mercy."

Windows become borders "through which death [is] possibly most likely to come," and doors take on an entirely new meaning: "Rumors had begun to circulate of doors that could take you elsewhere, often to places far away, well removed from this death trap of a country. Some people claimed to know people who knew people who had been through such doors. A normal door, they said, could become a special door, and it could happen without warning, to any door at all." When Saeed and Nadia realize that they can't survive much longer in their embattled homeland and decide to leave, we learn that these mysterious doors are portals through which refugees can pass—and find themselves somewhere else.

The existence of these magical doors is a clever literary device that allows Hamid to skip over linking passages and bypass strict chronology, thus sparing the writer and his reader from having to follow, in detail, the hardships of embarkation and disembarkation, perilous sea voyages and heroic rescues, horrors that we may feel we already know quite a bit about from reading the news. Oddly, or not so oddly, these transitional sections turn out to be unnecessary in advancing the plot. After all, fiction, unlike life, can skip around in time and compress a long and difficult journey into the space of a chapter break.

After the couple pay an agent to guide them through one such door, they wind up on the Greek island of Mykonos, living at the edges of vast camps crowded with people like themselves. Exiting through yet another door, they reach London, where households of squatters occupy palatial homes left vacant by wealthy absentee owners. Meanwhile, the refugee crisis has destabilized society and set off yet more violence—riots and attacks sparked by nativist rage at the city's swelling migrant population, conflicts that remind Nadia of the brutality she thought she'd left behind.

"The fury of those nativists advocating wholesale slaughter was what struck Nadia most, and it struck her because it seemed so familiar, so much like the fury of the militants in her own city. She wondered whether she and Saeed had done anything by moving, whether the faces and buildings had changed but the basic reality of their predicament had not."

Gracefully, almost without our noticing, the novel's setting has fast-forwarded into the near future, a time in which the tide of refugees has grown larger, stronger, impossible to stem or control—and, consequently, necessary to reckon with. The assaults on migrants—now restricted to workers' camps, fenced off from the larger society and given strict rules about what they must do in order to begin the process of assimilation—taper off, and an uneasy accord is reached.

The influx of the desperate and homeless transforms whole areas—for example, Marin County, California—from bucolic exurbs into sprawls of squatters' shacks that cover hillsides and are flimsy enough to tumble down ravines. Amid the international community of migrants in London, and again in the relative safety of California, Nadia and Saeed's love is tested to—and ultimately pushed past—the breaking point by the cumulative stress and weight of everything they've endured together, and by the divergent ways in which they have come to understand and define their separate religious, cultural, and sexual identities.

By now it should be clear that Hamid, who was born in Lahore, Pakistan, and has lived in London, New York, and California, has done something astonishing. He has written a novel, a real novel, about the daunting subject of the global refugee crisis—a novel with a nervy original structure, with complex, plausible characters, a fast-moving plot, and, perhaps most important, beautiful sentences. The depth of characterization and the force of the language have a lot to do with the fact that we never feel we are being educated or lectured to about a real event, an "important" sociopolitical phenomenon. Nothing here resembles those novels (and films) that are little more than dramatized newspaper articles or fictionalized journalism, as if all one had to do was give a character a name, a smattering of background, and a few lines of dialogue in order to turn a story "ripped from the headlines" into literature.

What's striking is how rapidly Hamid makes us care about his characters; not only do we sympathize with these people, but we come to feel attached to them, so that we find their losses and dislocations wrenching. When Saeed's mother is killed by a stray

bullet, her death seems almost unendurable, and it's startling to realize that her murder has taken place within a few succinct phrases,
in the midst of a complex sentence, at the end of a chapter, only
seventy pages into the novel. A horrifying scene in which Nadia is
groped—assaulted, really—by a stranger while waiting in a panicked mob of people trying to withdraw money from a bank should
put to rest forever the question of whether a male author is capable
of writing convincingly from a female character's point of view.

The novel moves deftly back and forth between the particular
and the general, between concrete detail and abstract generaliza-
tions about history and human nature. Even as Hamid describes a
series of worsening crises, he never lets us forget that we are reading a love story, and that these events are happening to individuals
we have come to know, and whose fates move us deeply. As Saeed
and Nadia enjoy a brief moment of respite—the "battle of London"
has briefly abated, and they are watching rain fall on their balcony—
we are reminded of their profound feelings for each other:

> Nadia watched Saeed and not for the first time wondered if she
> had led him astray. She thought maybe he had in the end been wa-
> vering about leaving their city, and she thought maybe she could
> have tipped him either way, and she thought he was basically a
> good and decent man, and she was filled with compassion for
> him in that instant, as she observed his face with its gaze upon
> the rain, and she realized she had not in her life felt so strongly for
> anyone in the world as she had for Saeed in the moments of those
> first months when she had felt most strongly for him.
>
> Saeed for his part wished he could do something for Nadia,
> could protect her from what would come, even if he understood,
> at some level, that to love is to enter into the inevitability of one
> day not being able to protect what is most valuable to you. He
> thought she deserved better than this, but he could see no way
> out, for they had decided not to run, not to play roulette with yet

another departure. To flee forever is beyond the capacity of most: at some point even a hunted animal will stop, exhausted, and await its fate, if only for a while.

Hamid's language is surer and more eloquent than in any of his previous novels: *Moth Smoke, How to Get Filthy Rich in Rising Asia*, and *The Reluctant Fundamentalist*, the book for which he is perhaps best known here. Throughout *Exit West* there are long (in some cases, extremely long) sentences that never feel excessive or muddled, overwritten or strained, and that make us realize how much depth and information can be packed into the space between the capital letter that begins a sentence and the period that concludes it. Phrase follows phrase with perfect clarity and creates a breathless urgency and an incantatory rhythm that would have been diminished if these passages had been broken up into smaller units. The assault that Nadia endures in the "unruly crowd" at the bank occurs within the confines of a sentence that covers more than a page, describing the growing terror and sense of helplessness that necessity compels her to suppress until she gets her money from the teller and finds a money changer and a jeweler to convert her cash into viable currencies, and into gold.

Here, to take just one example, is a single sentence in which Saeed, Nadia, and Saeed's father attempt to navigate their way around the apartment that Saeed's mother's death has transformed into a minefield in which her survivors can, at any moment, be wounded by a memory or a souvenir:

> *Saeed's father encountered each day objects that had belonged to his wife and so would sweep his consciousness out of the current others referred to as the present, a photograph or an earring or a particular shawl worn on a particular occasion, and Nadia encountered each day objects that took her into Saeed's past, a book or a music collection or a sticker on the inside of a drawer, and*

evoked emotions from her own childhood, and jagged musings
on the fate of her parents and her sister, and Saeed, for his part,
was inhabiting a chamber that had been his only briefly, years
ago, when relatives from afar or abroad used to come to visit, and
being billeted here again conjured up for him echoes of a better
era, and so in these several ways these three people sharing this
one apartment splashed and intersected with each other across
varied and multiple streams of time.

One of the longest and most complex sentences in the book is
a self-contained set piece, a story within a story, set in Vienna. In-
terpolated throughout the narrative are brief, unrelated narratives
so cinematic that they seem almost like treatments for short noir
films. All of them work to increase the steadily building intimations of menace—and, more tellingly, to ramp up our awareness
that the growing threat is not local but global.

In the first of these, which takes place in Sydney, Australia, a
woman is asleep at home; her husband is away, her house alarm de-
activated, her window slightly ajar. A stranger enters the bedroom,
looks around, thinks about how little it takes to kill someone, then
slips through the window, "dropping silkily to the street below." In
the next of these sections, set in Tokyo, a sinister man who speaks
Tagalog, dislikes Filipinos, and has a gun in his pocket follows two
Filipina girls leaving a bar. In yet another, an old man in San Di-
ego finds his house surrounded by men in uniform. "The old man
asked the officer whether it was Mexicans that had been coming
through, or was it Muslims, because he couldn't be sure, and the
officer said he couldn't answer, sir."

The most sustained and dazzling of these apparent digressions
from Saeed and Nadia's story begins when militants from Saeed
and Nadia's country, hoping perhaps "to provoke a reaction against
migrants from their own part of the world," stage a series of bloody
attacks, massacring innocent Viennese in the street. The next week,

a young woman who works in an art gallery hears that her coun-
trymen are planning to attack an encampment of immigrants lo-
cated near the zoo. Heading across town, wearing a peace badge, a
rainbow pride badge, and a migrant compassion badge, she is terrified to find herself in the midst of a bloodthirsty, vengeful mob of
men "who looked like her brother and her cousins and her father
and her uncles, except that they were angry, they were furious, and
they were staring at her and at her badges with undisguised hostil-
ity, and the rancor of perceived betrayal, and they started to shout
at her, and push her." Escaping unharmed, the young woman continues on toward the zoo, to join "the human cordon to separate
the two sides . . . and all this happened as the sun dipped lower
in the sky, as it was doing above Mykonos as well, which though
south and east of Vienna, was after all in planetary terms not far
away, and there in Mykonos Saeed and Nadia were reading about
the riot, which was starting in Vienna, and which panicked people
originally from their country were discussing online how best to
endure or flee."

As we read *Exit West*, it's difficult not to imagine that any of
us—attending our evening classes, enjoying our street drugs and
our quotidian domesticity, meeting and falling in love—might be
standing on the brink of an abyss much like the one that threatens
to swallow Saeed and Nadia. If there's any consolation at all to be
had for the reminder that some humans seem to enjoy killing and
mistreating other humans, perhaps it can be found in the fact that
a writer like Mohsin Hamid has the compassion, the talent, and the
skill to describe both individual and "planetary" experience—to
take our indifference and panic, the failure of our humanity and
our collective historical nightmare, and to alchemize the raw material of catastrophe into art.

30

On Clarity

IF WE ARE HOPING TO COMMUNICATE SOMETHING—anything—nothing is more important than clarity. The dangers of not being clear are obvious. Is that driver approaching the intersection signaling right or left? Is the brain surgeon asking for a scalpel or a clamp? One could argue that the consequences of writing an unintelligible sentence are not nearly so drastic as a car wreck or a botched operation. But it's a slippery slope. Which one of the rungs in the ladder were we warned to watch out for? Was it the basement or the bathtub that Auntie Em told us to take shelter in when the tornado hit Kansas?

Explaining what it means to be clear should, in theory, be easy. But in fact it's surprisingly difficult to define this deceptively obvious concept. The simplest definition may be best: To write clearly means writing so that another person can understand what we mean. Someone (not us) can figure out what we are trying to say.

Of course, an intelligent seven-year-old could point out the problems with this. Maybe some people will understand what we mean, but some people never will, and inevitably someone will think we meant something entirely different from whatever we had in mind. Endless variables can affect what, and how, and how much we understand: age, class, language, culture, gender, history, and so forth. And perfect communication can occur without one word being spoken.

But let's say that you *have* written something, and it turns out that *no one* has the faintest idea what in the world you could possibly mean—no one but you, the writer. And in the absence of clarity, even the writer may forget the formerly obvious purpose that has somehow managed to burrow and hide beneath a fuzzy blanket of language. On the other end of the spectrum is the sentence or paragraph that the reader can not only comprehend instantly but see straight through to the writer's intention, so that reader and writer are communicating directly, brain to brain, like aliens in science fiction.

Obviously, it is easier to write a short clear sentence than a long clear one. One sentence that I think most people would agree is clear is the opening of Albert Camus's novel *The Stranger*: "Mother died today."

A more recent translation by Matthew Ward begins "Maman died today." In a preface, Ward argues that *Maman*, more affectionate than *Mother*, better expresses the narrator's feelings. "No sentence in French literature in English translation is better known than the opening sentence of *The Stranger*. It has become a sacred cow of sorts, and I have changed it. In his notebooks Camus recorded the observation that 'the curious feeling the son has for his mother constitutes *all* his sensibility.' And Sartre . . . goes out of his way to point out Meursault's use of the child's word 'Maman' when speaking of his mother."

Maybe we should venture deeper into colloquial English and say, "Mom died today." Not according to the *New Yorker* blog post in which Ryan Bloom argues that Ward's use of the French word may be helpful to younger readers unaware that *The Stranger* is set in French colonial Algeria. *Maman*, Bloom claims, somewhat contradictorily, is also preferable because the American reader will "understand it with ease, but it will carry no baggage." So it won't affect our opinion about Meursault's response to the death of his mother. But, Bloom goes on, the translation of *"Aujourd'hui, maman est morte"* really should be "Today, *Maman* died." Beginning the sentence with "Today" signals that "Meursault is a character who, first and foremost, lives for the moment."

Mother died today. Maman died today. Today, Maman died. My mother died today. Today, my mother died. What all these versions have in common is that they are clear. Each suggests a slightly different shade of meaning, a refinement of our understanding of the complex responses elicited by the word *mother* in any language, along with a slightly different emphasis on *when* her death occurred. But for the moment, let's forget subtext and focus on basic clarity: what can be understood.

Regardless of how the narrator feels about his mother, regardless of how critical the exact day of her death was, regardless of our knowledge of the colony in which the novel takes place, it's hard to imagine a reader who doesn't understand what is being communicated: the narrator's mother died today. Later we can look back on this line as a key to who the narrator is, to the mystery of why he does what he does, and to the consequences of his actions. But no matter what we conclude, the fact remains that we have understood the first thing he has told us.

Camus's sentence contains three words. Most of the three-word sentences that come to mind—*She likes chocolate. The sun shone. I love you*—are clear, even if we interpret their meaning in different ways. It is hard, but not impossible, to put three words together in ways that don't make sense. *The elephant and. Down tree dog. Big along also.* Lacking either a subject or a verb, or both, none of these are proper sentences.

Three random words in isolation can sound like surrealist

poetry. But they are less amusing when we actually want or need to understand them. Few readers would have the patience for a long novel featuring page after page of nonsense. And what if the directions for assembling the children's bunk bed were written like that—and made even less sense than they ordinarily do?

I've heard the writer Jo Ann Beard say that an exercise she does with her students is to tell them to open the book or story they are studying, turn to a page at random, put their finger on a sentence, and read the sentence aloud. Is it true? Is it clear? Is it beautiful?

You can pick up a volume of Chekhov's stories and open it anywhere and, no matter how well or poorly the Russian has been translated, you will probably have a hard time finding a sentence you can't understand. This is because, as much as any other writer and more than most, Chekhov put such a premium on writing comprehensibly, without flowery language or unnecessary adornment.

In his critical but tactful letter to Maxim Gorky written in January 1899, Chekhov delicately approaches the problem of the younger author's overwriting:

> Your nature descriptions are artistic; you are a true landscape painter. But your frequent personifications (anthropomorphism), when the sea breathes, the sky looks on, the steppe basks, nature whispers, talks, grieves, etc.—these personifications make your descriptions a bit monotonous, sometimes cloying, and sometimes unclear. Color and expressivity in nature descriptions are achieved through simplicity alone, through simple phrases like "the sun set," "it grew dark," "it began to rain," etc.

Ten months later, he again writes to Gorky, who seems not to have followed the advice Chekhov gave him in the earlier letter. Either forgetting or politely pretending that he is saying something entirely new, Chekhov more or less repeats the substance of his earlier letter. But he puts it in a different way, focusing on description in general rather than descriptions of nature in particular:

> *Another piece of advice: when you read proof, cross out as many modifiers of nouns and verbs as you can. You have so many modifiers that the reader has a hard time figuring out what deserves his attention, and it tires him out. If I write, "A man sat down on the grass," it is understandable because it is clear and doesn't require a second reading. But it would be hard to follow and brain-taxing were I to write, "A tall, narrow-chested, red-bearded man of medium height sat down noiselessly, looking around timidly and in fright, on a patch of green grass that had been trampled by pedestrians." The brain can't grasp all of this at once, and the art of fiction ought to be immediately, instantaneously graspable.*

After Chekhov has finished writing about Gorky's work, the gloves come off. Like many of his letters, this one contradicts the contemporary image of Chekhov as a sort of literary Dalai Lama, or, as Janet Malcolm has written, "When someone speaks Chekhov's name, it's as if a baby deer has come into the room." In his letter, Chekhov rips into *Life*, a Communist journal that Gorky wrote for, and in the process he shreds two of its contributors: "Chirikov's story is naive and dishonest. Veresayev's story is a crude imitation of something or other, possibly of the husband in your 'Orlov and His Wife.' It is crude and naive as well."

The letter ends with a paragraph as melancholy and *Chekhovian* as the speeches the characters in his plays give when, like Uncle Vanya and Sonya at the end of *Uncle Vanya*, they are renouncing love and passion and dedicating their entire lives to hard work and self-sacrifice. Earlier, Chekhov has suggested that Gorky move to a major city, that it would be better for his work, and the younger writer has replied that, for now, he'd rather remain on the move, bumming around, seeing things and having experiences.

"Vagabondage," writes Chekhov, "is all well and good and quite alluring, but as the years go by, you lose mobility and become attached to one spot. And the literary profession has a way of sucking you in. Failures and disappointments make time go by so fast that you fail to notice your real life, and the past when I was so free seems to belong to someone else, not myself." When Chekhov wrote this, he was thirty-nine. He would be dead in five years.

THOUGH Chekhov's adjective-heavy, "unclear" sentence—the tall, narrow-chested, red-bearded man sitting down timidly and so forth—is in fact not all that hard to follow, we know what he is saying. And he has put his finger on a problem that often affects writers and just as frequently stands in the way of clarity: the belief that every noun needs an adjective, that every sentence must be elaborate, that every turn of phrase must be lyrical, poetic, and above all *original*, and that it represents some sort of shameful *failure of the imagination* to use language in a way that can be readily understood by all.

In part, this problem may have something to do with the ease and frequency with which students misinterpret the well-meaning advice of teachers who suggest they use *strong* adjectives and *forceful* verbs (why should a character walk when he can stride, why should he speak when he can expostulate?), and avoid the passive tense.

Everything we write is, in a sense, translated from another language: from the chatter we hear inside our head, translated from that interior babble (more or less comprehensible to us) into (what we hope will be) the clearer, more articulate language on the page. But during the process of that translation, basic clarity often suffers—sometimes fatally!—when, for whatever reason, we feel that we are translating our natural speech into a foreign language: in other words, when we are writing.

For many students, this foreign language is one that I have

come to think of as paper-ese: the language of the classroom es-say, peppered with awkward transitions ("Thus we see," "Further-more"), clumsy locutions ("it can be observed that," "we are made to have"), and words that only the most eccentric twenty-first-century person would employ in everyday speech. I have never heard a student use, in conversation, the words *attire*, *surmise*, or, especially, *deem* ("the story can be *deemed* as being ironic," "her face could be *deemed* as kindly"), but these words recur, almost every year, in the first papers they write for my classes. This prob-lem is aggravated when they have been exposed to academic jar-gon and feel compelled to use the terminology of a particular field of study.

In an effort to counteract this, I ask students to write the fol-lowing sentence in their notebooks, in capital letters: "WOULD I SAY THIS?" And I tell them not to write anything that they wouldn't say. This does not mean that they should write exactly as they speak, but rather that they avoid, in their writing, anything they would not say out loud to another human being. *Hi, Mom and Dad. I surmise you won't be too mad if I deem it necessary to go to my boyfriend's house for Thanksgiving.*

It's remarkable how rapidly students' writing improves—how much clearer it becomes—when they feel liberated from the bur-den of forcing their ideas through the narrow channel of "thus we see," the constricted passageway of "furthermore, the man's attire could be deemed characteristic of his gender and social status." I also require them to bring in a passage of especially thick, im-penetrable jargon, together with their own translation into plain speech. In class, they read aloud both versions, and it's always in-teresting, and often very funny, to note how quickly the bombast of the jargon collapses; this exercise often seems to inspire another dramatic improvement, a quantum leap in my students' writing.

Perhaps I should also ask my students to copy out "A man sat down on the grass" on the same page as "Would I say this?"

Chekhov's sentence is a model of what it means to be clear. But like "Mother died today," it is short and compact.

Obviously, it's easier to be clear when one is using fewer words—in Chekhov's case, only seven. As a sentence gets longer, lucidity becomes more of a challenge. How can we be sure of being clear when we are constructing a sentence that needs to be long because, were it shorter, were it broken up into more easily manageable components, it would be less graceful, less informative, and less beautiful? Watching a writer spin out an extremely long but nonetheless clear sentence is like watching a tightrope walker cross from one end of the wire to the other. You want to cheer when the sentence makes it all the way to the period without a false step, so that the reader is still easily following along.

Here are some long sentences I continue to admire for their grace, their clarity, and the bravado with which they add one word to another without fear of confusing us or of losing our attention.

The first is the well-known final sentence of Abraham Lincoln's Gettysburg address: "It is rather for us to be here dedicated to the great task remaining before us—that from these honored dead we take increased devotion to that cause for which they here gave the last full measure of devotion—that we here highly resolve that these dead shall not have died in vain—that this nation, under God, shall have a new birth of freedom, and that government of the people, by the people, for the people, shall not perish from the earth."

The second is from the U.S. Constitution: "We the people of the United States, in order to form a more perfect union, establish justice, insure domestic tranquility, provide for the common defence, promote the general welfare, and secure the blessings of liberty to ourselves and our posterity, do ordain and establish this Constitution for the United States of America."

Reading the sentences above makes one want to know how and where Abraham Lincoln and Thomas Jefferson learned to

write. It will come as no surprise that they were both avid readers. Lincoln, a partial autodidact, was particularly fond of the Bible,
Aesop's Fables, and *The Pilgrim's Progress*; later he read Lord Byron
and *Macbeth*. As a privileged Virginia boy, with tutors, Thomas Jefferson learned Latin, read the Greeks, and studied mathematics and
British philosophy at the College of William and Mary. You can
hear echoes of what both men read in the sentences they wrote.

Another eloquent long sentence appears near the beginning of
the majority opinion authored by Justice Harry Blackmun in the
landmark 1973 Supreme Court case *Roe v. Wade*: "One's philosophy, one's experiences, one's exposure to the raw edges of human
existence, one's religious training, one's attitudes toward life and
family and their values, and the moral standards one establishes
and seeks to observe, are all likely to influence and to color one's
thinking and conclusions about abortion."

No matter how we ourselves feel about the complicated and
emotionally fraught issue of abortion, it's difficult not to admire
the thoughtful and cautious precision of Justice Blackmun's writing, impossible not to imagine how long it took him to write this,
to come up with a phrase as delicate and compassionate as "the
raw edges of human existence." Blackmun himself grew up in a
working-class neighborhood in St. Paul, Minnesota, where his father sold fruits and vegetables. He received a scholarship to Harvard, attended Harvard Law School, and, decades later, due partly
to the intercession of his childhood friend Chief Justice Warren
Burger, was appointed to the Supreme Court by President Rich-
ard Nixon. Among his other distinctions were his great talent as
a writer and his gift for clear thought and clear expression. Other
examples of his way with words and with ideas are the following
well-known quotations: "In order to get beyond racism, we must
first take account of race," and, "No longer is the female destined
solely for the home and the rearing of the family, and only the male
for the marketplace and the world of ideas."

Considering how many of Chekhov's characters live on the raw edges to which Justice Blackmun referred, we can assume that, despite the obvious divisions in culture and background, despite the dissimilar times in which they lived, the Russian writer would have known what the American jurist meant in his ruling on *Roe v. Wade*—regardless of the fact that Blackmun's sentence, like the ones from the Gettysburg Address and the U.S. Constitution, is considerably longer and more complicated than "A man sat down on the grass" or "Mother died today."

Obviously, these very short and very long sentences take different amounts of time to read, different amounts of time to process and understand. What they have in common is that they are clear. We can understand them.

THE first step toward being clear is like the first step in an addiction recovery program: admit that there is a problem. Or if clarity is not a problem, at least it is a concern. Human beings assume that something that is clear to them will be clear to other people, but, sadly, that is not the case. At every stage of writing—for the student and the teacher, for the authors of grocery lists, conference notes, e-mails, text messages, poems, and novels—it is shocking to be misunderstood. It's like the insult of finding out that someone doesn't like us.

It might help to know what we're being when we're *not* being clear. But once again, it's hard to define: the opposite of clarity. Obscurity, I suppose. But something can be obscure (an obscure film, an obscure reference) and still be clear. *Unintelligible*, *murky*, and *confusing* come closer, but these are adjectives whose noun forms (unintelligibility, murkiness, confusion) are awkward, and something can be extremely unclear and only mildly confusing. And at what point does the reader decide that something is simply too much trouble to bother to untangle and understand?

It would be too easy to pick one of the thousands of unclear sentences I've read in student papers. It would seem like a violation of a privileged communication, and besides, it would be unfair to hold up examples of what this or that person did wrong before he or she learned to do better. So to illustrate what I mean by an unclear sentence, I will quote from the work of a well-known writer, from *No Time Like the Present*, a novel by Nadine Gordimer: "This young comrade parent or that was in detention, who knew when she, he, would be released, this one had fathered only in the biological sense, he was somewhere in another country learning the tactics of guerilla war or in the strange covert use of that elegantly conventional department of relations between countries, diplomacy to gain support for the overthrow of the regime by means of sanctions if not arms."

Another unclear sentence, less convoluted but possibly more obscure, occurs in *Slow Man*, a novel by Gordimer's fellow South African and fellow Nobel Prize winner J. M. Coetzee: "That was why, later on, he began to lose interest in photography: first when colour took over, then when it became plain that the old magic of light-sensitive emulsions was waning, that to the rising generation the enchantment lay in a *techne* of images without substance, images that could flash through the ether without residing anywhere, that could be sucked into a machine and emerge from it doctored, untrue."

I can't imagine that Gordimer and Coetzee meant their sentences to be so awkward, so needlessly bothersome to read. Perhaps they hoped we'd get more than we do once we'd sorted everything out, or perhaps one danger of the Nobel Prize is a silencing of the voice that nags the writer to be clear, a voice that haunts my students, laboring so hard to improve.

In order to be clear, it is necessary to at least consider the possibility that we actually may *not* be. It requires stepping outside of oneself, reading a sentence as if we were another person (not us)

who didn't understand and even sort of admire the newly minted
gold on the screen or the page. It requires a kind of humility, an
ability not to take everything personally and to separate ourselves
from our work. Clarity is not only a literary quality but a spiritual
one, involving, as it does, compassion for the reader.

One can't blame people for not wanting to subject their work to
the real or preemptively imagined scrutiny of a reader who wants
to understand, who tries to understand, but finally just can't. How
much care and effort we've put into choosing words and putting
them together, into *making something* out of nothing: printer ink and
paper. How disappointing to discover that we may have failed, that
we may have to fix what's wrong or start over from the beginning.

The most helpful editors—professionals and friends—are the
ones who will talk for ten minutes (or exchange a chain of e-mails)
about a single word. Let's say about the difference between *convince*
and *persuade*. The ones who make me realize how many words and
sentences can be taken out without anyone (including me) being
aware that anything is missing. The ones who have the courage to
say, "This isn't clear. It doesn't make sense." Eventually, their voices
take up residence in one's head, like friendly editor earworms.

Suppose we've admitted a problem exists. Something is not
clear. What is the second step?

It's old-fashioned but helpful to have a basic command of
grammar, of the rules and conventions that help make language
clear. It has always seemed amazing to me that so few people learn
grammar and so many learn to drive, which is so much harder,
scarier, and more demanding! Grammar—parts of speech, subject-
verb agreement, what follows a comma—makes life easier for the
reader; words fall into a kind of order so that there is no need to go
scrambling back through the sentence to figure out what everything means and what describes what.

Unlike most other subjects, grammar is one of those things you can study and forget about and still know. Many middle schoolers of my generation learned to diagram sentences, to break a sentence up into words we arranged on an odd little armature of lines, arrows, hooks, and chutes. I no longer need to do that to read a sentence and make the first of the decisions (subject? verb?) that would have directed where I wrote the words on the diagram. A minimal knowledge of grammar lets you understand the most complex sentence, or to write your own and be reasonably certain that it is clear.

No one wrote more clearly than Virginia Woolf did, in her essays, which, if we read them slowly enough, make perfect sense. But in case we find ourselves tripping over the long and lushly forested paths that her sentences lead us down, grammar gives us something—a sort of guide rail—to hold on to as we confront the product of a mind readily able to skip around and keep several subjects and verbs (to say nothing of ideas) in play at once.

Here, for example, is a sentence from Woolf's perceptive, beautiful, and comically ambivalent tribute to the invalid poet Elizabeth Barrett Browning, in a passage from an essay entitled "Poets' Letters": "The vigour with which she threw herself into the only life that was free to her and lived so steadily and strongly in her books that her days were full of purpose and character would be pathetic did it not impress us as with the strength that underlay her ardent and sometimes febrile temperament." It takes each of us a varying amount of time to figure out that it's the *vigour* that would be pathetic, with a lifetime in between. The sooner we figure that out, the sooner we get the sentence. The rapid switching back and forth between admiring and critical adjectives and adverbs (*steadily, strongly, pathetic, ardent, febrile*) is itself a key to the range of Woolf's responses, now generous, now judgmental. Her views alternate through these two paragraphs on Browning, which are not only clear but exhilarating, thanks to Woolf's elegant mix of the skeptical and the respectful.

Not only was she a very shrewd critic of others, but, pliant as she was in most matters, she could be almost obstinate when her literary independence was attacked. The many critics who objected to faults of obscurity or technique in her writing she answered indeed, but answered authoritatively, as a person stating a fact, and not pleading a case. "My poetry," she writes to Ruskin, "which you once called 'sickly' . . . has been called by much harder names, 'affected,' for instance, a charge I have never deserved, if I may say it of myself, that the desire or speaking or spluttering the real truth out broadly, may be a cause of a good deal of what is called in me careless or awkward expression."

The desire was so honest and valiant that the "splutterer" may be condoned, although there seems to be no reason to agree with Mrs. Browning in her tacit assertion that the cause of truth would be demeaned by a more scrupulous regard for literary form.

Attentive readers will notice that, while we know what Woolf is saying, sentence by sentence, her opinion of Elizabeth Barrett Browning is mixed; she thinks several things at once. She considers her at once admirable and irritating, heroic and at best a minor poet. Also we may notice that Woolf, employing all of those adjectives, is doing precisely what Chekhov told Gorky not to do. But so what? The result is the same. You can open a volume of Woolf's essays, like one of Chekhov's stories, and not only follow what she is saying but find the sort of marvels produced when clarity of expression is combined with the intelligence, imagination, and ability to look at the world and tell us what she observes, which is always just a little more than we do.

Here is another passage from Woolf, one that I particularly like, in which—in a 1908 essay entitled "Château and Country Life"—she offers us a new way to view the familiar pleasures of train travel:

Their comfort, to begin with, sets the mind free, and their speed is the speed of lyric poetry, inarticulate as yet, sweeping rhythm through the brain, regularly, like the wash of great waves. Little fragments of print, picked up by an effort from the book you read, become gigantic, enfolding the earth and disclosing the truth of the scene. The towns you see then are tragic, like the faces of people turned toward you in deep emotion, and the fields with their cottages have profound significance; you imagine the rooms astir and hear the cinders falling on the hearth and the little animals rustling and pausing in the woods.

FOR those who don't want to learn grammar, who don't want to apply its rules, and who don't feel they have the time to read the Latin and Greek classics in the original like the Founding Fathers did, an alternate route to clarity, which initially may seem like a shortcut but ultimately demands more practice and effort than learning grammar, is to somehow develop an ear for the clear sentence. There are people who can read a sentence, or hear it in their heads, and more or less instantly know that it is, or isn't, clear. When it isn't, something seems wrong; an off note has been sounded. Everyone who speaks has felt this. What you said wasn't what you meant to say. Your meaning wasn't clear. Like an ear for music, an ear for clarity is a mysterious talent.

If I knew more about music, or the neurology of music, I would probably know better than to suggest that clarity of language stimulates the same cerebral pleasure points as the charming and beautiful piano pieces that Bach wrote for his second wife, Anna Magdalena, compositions that many beginning music students learn on their way to something requiring more technical skill. Clarity of language is not the *St. Matthew Passion*. It is the fact that the singers can say all the words and hit all the notes. It is not an end in itself but a means to an end. Which is not to say that clarity is not a beautiful thing.

Here are the clear and beautiful first lines of four of Charles Dickens's novels:

David Copperfield: "Whether I shall turn out to be the hero of my own life, or whether that station will be held by anybody else, these pages must show."

Dombey and Son: "Dombey sat in the corner of the darkened room in the great arm-chair by the bedside, and Son lay tucked up warm in a little basket bedstead, carefully disposed on a low settee immediately in front of the fire and close to it, as if his constitution were analogue to that of a muffin, and it was essential to toast him brown while he was very new."

Nicholas Nickleby: "There once lived, in a sequestered part of the county of Devonshire, one Mr. Godfrey Nickleby: a worthy gentleman, who, taking it into his head rather late in life that he must get married, and not being young enough or rich enough to aspire to the hand of a lady of fortune, had wedded an old flame out of mere attachment, who in her turn had taken him for the same reason."

Our Mutual Friend: "In these times of ours, though concerning the exact year there is no need to be precise, a boat of dirty and disreputable appearance, with two figures in it, floated on the Thames, between Southwark Bridge which is of iron, and London Bridge which is of stone, as an autumn evening was closing in."

Here are four opening sentences from the (certainly compared with Dickens) lesser-known British novelist Barbara Comyns, most of whose books were first published during the 1950s:

The Vet's Daughter: "A man with small eyes and a ginger moustache came and spoke to me when I was thinking of something else."

Sisters by a River: "It was in the middle of a snowstorm I was born, Palmer's brother's wedding night, Palmer went to the wedding and got snowbound, and when he arrived very late in the morning he had to bury my packing under the walnut tree, he always had to do this when we were born—six times in all, and none of us died, Mary said Granny used to give us manna to eat and that's why we didn't, but manna is stuff in the bible, perhaps they have it in Fortnum & Mason, but I've never seen it, or maybe Jews' shops."

Who Was Changed and Who Was Dead: "The ducks swam through the drawing room windows."

Our Spoons Came from Woolworths: "I told Helen my story and she went home and cried."

And here, occupying a sort of middle ground of complexity and length, are three sentences each of which appears at the start of one of Mark Twain's short stories. There is also the wry, seemingly rambling, but in fact controlled and modulated sentence that follows the last of the three beginnings:

"Fenimore Cooper's Literary Offenses": "It seems to me that it was far from right for the Professor of English Literature in Yale, the Professor of English Literature in Columbia, and Wilkie Collins to deliver opinions on Cooper's literature without having read some of it." (It's the "some of," the "some of it" that makes the sentence great.)

"Extracts from Adam's Diary": "Monday.—This new creature with the long hair is a good deal in the way." You have to know who Adam and Eve are, but many people still do.

"A Petition to the Queen of England": "Madam: You will remember that last May Mr. Edward Bright, the clerk of the Inland Revenue office, wrote me about a tax which he said was due from me to the Government on books of mine published in London— that is to say, an income tax on the royalties. I do not know Mr. Bright, and it is embarrassing to me to correspond with strangers; for I was raised in the country and have always lived there, the early part in Marion County, Missouri, before the war, and this part in Hartford County, Connecticut, near Bloomfield and about eight miles this side of Farmington, though some call it nine, which it is impossible to be, for I have walked it many and many a time in considerably under three hours, and General Hawley says he has done it in two and a quarter, which is not likely; so it has seemed best that I write your Majesty."

Does anything need to be said about the feet-shuffling country-boy ramble with which we intuit Twain will be asking not to be taxed on the royalties for his books?

What all these sentences have in common is that they are carefully put together, transparent, and deep, complete in themselves yet suggestive of a promise: new information is still to come in the sentences that will follow.

WHETHER you run a passage of writing through the checklist of grammar or put it to the test of the ear, clarity requires attentiveness to each sentence. It demands the time, the energy, and the patience needed to ask if the sentence is clear. Then fiddling with it until it is. Is it clear now? What about now? Unless you are one of those magical beings who gets it right the first time so that language fountains out of you: burbling, transparent music.

It is actually very hard to write an unintelligible sentence on purpose—as Chekhov has already demonstrated—and no one plans to do that. At least very few people do once they are out of their teens, when they half hope that every communication could be coded in a language that only a select few (or sometimes just the author) can decipher. Writers want to be understood, even if the writer is Faulkner, pouring phrase after phrase into the Southern Gothic rants that go on for pages of *Absalom, Absalom!*; even if the writer is James Joyce, composing the soliloquy at the end of *Ulysses*, which also rattles on for pages, ranging through time and geography, through experience and fantasy, opinion, sex, rumination, delivering specific information about what Molly Bloom is saying and also more general observations (embedded in the text) about the ways in which memory and consciousness function.

Just to complicate things further, I'll mention one of my favorite sentences, one that takes the kind of sentence Chekhov advised Gorky to write ("The sun shone") and adds a few carefully chosen words so that it stays completely clear and at the same time goes completely crazy.

That is the famous first sentence of Samuel Beckett's first novel, *Murphy*: "The sun shone, having no alternative, on the nothing new."

We get the sunshine, and at the same time the fact that the voice that is speaking to us is hilariously sour and possibly quite far out on the raw edges of human existence.

In one sentence, Beckett gives us Chekhov, Camus, and a dope slap. For Beckett, adding those few words shows the reader the same scene (sunshine) and sharpens the focus, like the lens on an old-fashioned camera, reaching beyond the sunshine to Murphy, who has tied himself to a rocking chair and is rocking and rocking and rocking to ward off the anxiety of being dispossessed from a home where he isn't any more or less happy than he was in his last home, or will be in the next.

Beckett isn't the easiest writer to understand. Nor did he mean to be. One feels that it would have enraged him to be told to slow down and make sure we are keeping up. But there are moments like this one, instances when he is dazzlingly lucid, giving us the weather report and, with just a few words, shining a high-intensity beam on a universal but understandably underexplored corner of the human psyche.

Having no alternative. On the nothing new. Nothing could be clearer, more mysterious, or more thrilling. If a sentence is a tight-rope from one pole to another, Beckett's sentences are test-dummy rides, slamming his readers into the wall of a perpetual three o'clock in the morning. Though Beckett might be surprised to hear it, the amount and the quality of the information communicated in *Murphy*'s opening sentence recall something that Virginia Woolf—one of the publishers of the press that Beckett called the Hogarth Private Lunatic Asylum—wrote at the conclusion of the essay "Château and Country Life," the piece that begins with her description of the pleasures of train travel: "There is a reason to be grateful when anyone writes very simply, both for the sake of the things that are said, and because the writer reveals so much of her own character in her words."

Like Beckett's sentence, Woolf's presupposes that there is such a thing as character, and that we might be interested in it, and that, if we are talking about such complicated subjects as character, it is important to be clear.

31

Reiner Stach,
Is That Kafka? 99 Finds

ALMOST A CENTURY AFTER HIS DEATH, IN 1924, FRANZ
Kafka has become a sort of modern-day saint, one of those artist-
martyrs revered, like Vincent van Gogh and Frida Kahlo, partly
for their work and partly for the suffering they endured in order to
create it. The process of Kafka's "canonization" is thought to have
begun with his literary executor, Max Brod, who preserved the letters, diaries, and manuscripts from the flames to which the ailing
Kafka instructed Brod to consign them.

In his 1937 biography of Kafka, Brod described the aura of be-
atitude that he believed he had observed brightening around his
friend:

> The category of sacredness (and not really that of literature) is
> the only right category under which Kafka's life and work can
> be viewed. By this I do not wish to suggest that he was a per-
> fect saint. . . . [But] one may pose the thesis that Franz Kafka
> was on the road to becoming one. The explanation of his
> charming shyness and reserve, which seemed nothing less than

supernatural—and yet so natural—and of his dismayingly se-
vere self-criticism, lies in the fact that he measured himself by no
ordinary standard, but . . . against the ultimate goal of human
existence.

Among the things one learns from Reiner Stach's informative
and charming *Is That Kafka? 99 Finds* is that Brod was not the first
person to portray Kafka as a species of holy man. Stach's book—a
compilation of anecdotes, letters, documents, gossip, little-known
facts, and texts culled from the research he did for his three-volume
biography of Kafka—includes an obituary that appeared in a
Czech newspaper a few days after Kafka's death, written by Milena
Jesenska, Kafka's Czech translator and lover and, most famously,
the recipient of his *Letters to Milena*. In her brief tribute, Milena describes him as having had a "sensitivity bordering on the miraculous," as someone who could "clairvoyantly comprehend an entire
person on the basis of a single facial expression. His knowledge of
the world was extraordinary and deep. He himself was an extraordinary and deep world."

It's telling that this testament to Kafka's superhuman qualities
should be the last of Stach's *99 Finds*, since, as Stach explains in a
preface, his principal intention was to humanize Kafka, to provide
evidence suggesting that the writer was, at least in some ways, a
regular guy, fond of beer, of gambling and slapstick humor, an im-
perfect creature who cheated on his school exams, who could be
petty about money, and who was given to spitting from the balcony even after his tuberculosis was diagnosed. Arguing against
the clichés and images ("a cobblestone alley damp with rain in
nighttime Prague, backlit by gas lanterns . . . piles of papers, dusty
in the candlelight . . . the nightmare of an enormous vermin") that
have contributed to the stereotypical view of Kafka as an "alien:
unworldly, neurotic, introverted, sick—an uncanny man bringing
forth uncanny things," Stach provides a series of "counter-images"

and seems to have had a great deal of fun chipping away at the myth of Kafka's pure asceticism, his moral and spiritual perfection.

> *These 99 Finds from Kafka's life and work display him in unexpected contexts, in unexpected lights, and they allow us to hear rarely detected undertones and overtones. . . . Taken together—and this is the chief criterion for their selection—they quietly divorce us from the clichés, and allow us to see that it might be useful after all to try other approaches to Kafka, approaches that were always there, but—plastered over with "Kafkaesque" images and associations—largely forgotten.*

LUCIDLY and elegantly translated from the German by Kurt Beals, ingeniously designed, illustrated with photographs of Kafka and the people he knew, of places he visited and paintings he admired, and with facsimiles of newspaper articles, manuscripts, notes, and letters, *Is That Kafka?* is a handsome object. Its cover—on which a fragment of Kafka's face is visible beneath a small circle cut from the black-and-white book jacket—captures and conveys the essence of the pages inside: a game of peekaboo in which the author beguiles the reader with fleeting glimpses of his elusive subject. Two sections entitled "Is That Kafka?" reproduce photographs of crowds—the audience at an air show near Brescia; fifteen thousand German-speaking residents of South Tyrol assembled in 1920 to protest the Italian occupation of the region—and playfully suggest that Kafka can be spotted among them.

> *In the lower middle of the photograph . . . two distinctive men can be seen . . . observing the passing musicians up close. In contrast to the rural demonstrators, who are almost all dressed in dark colors, these two men are wearing light-colored summer suits, much like one that Kafka owned. The figure on the left has*

Kafka's strikingly slim, unusually tall build and—to the extent
that this can be seen in the picture—his characteristically youth-
ful features. While we can't be certain, there is a high probability:
That's him.

Stach's "finds" are numbered one through ninety-nine and divided thematically into groups: idiosyncrasies, emotions, reading
and writing, slapstick, illusions, and so forth. Each text and image
is followed by a passage in which Stach explains or comments on
what we have just seen or read. The first find begins with a quote
from one of Kafka's letters to Milena, an account of the confusion
he experienced as a small boy, uncertain about the best way to give
money to a beggar; Stach suggests that the story was Kafka's way
of defending his behavior after he'd appalled Milena by offering
a beggar woman a two-crown coin—and then asking her to give
him one crown back. The ninety-ninth find—Milena's obituary—
precedes a section containing helpful biographical sketches of the
people who appear in the book.

Some of Stach's finds will surprise even those familiar with the
details of Kafka's life. I was particularly interested in the discarded
first draft of the opening chapter of *The Castle*, and in the fact that
Kafka at one point planned to write the novel in the first person. I'd
had no idea that Kafka wrote a scheme for a social utopia, a "work-
force without property" that was much admired by André Breton.
Kafka's ideal society was to provide housing for the sick and elderly,
mandate a six-hour workday ("for physical labor four to five"), insist that individual possessions be turned over to the state, exclude
independently wealthy, married men and women, and be governed
by strict regulations and "duties": "To earn one's livelihood only by
working. Not to shy away from any work that one has the strength
to perform without damaging one's health. Either select the work
oneself or, if this is not possible, to follow the orders of the workers'
council, which is subject to the government."

Another find informs us that Kafka composed two earlier versions of his impassioned, novella-length letter to his father, the first of which was far more conciliatory and timid than the one with which we are familiar. "I am beginning this letter without self-confidence, and only in the hope that you, Father, will still love me in spite of it all, and that you will read the letter better than I write it." We learn, too, that Kafka and Brod concocted a scheme ("to make us millionaires") for a series of guides advising travelers on how to visit Italy, Switzerland, Paris, Prague, and the Bohemian spas "on the cheap." Though their plan was never realized, it was (like so much that Kafka imagined) prescient; half a century later, guides of this sort would make a great deal of money indeed. It's satisfying to discover that a well-known story about Kafka's 1916 public reading, in Munich, of "In the Penal Colony"—several distressed listeners allegedly fainted during the performance, and Kafka went on reading—is, as one might have suspected, apocryphal. Other aspects of Kafka that Stach brings to light—that he distrusted conventional medicine and was a fan of faddish health regimes, that he frequented brothels, that he was not unknown and isolated in Prague but enjoyed a measure of literary success, that he liked reading his work aloud to friends—are more widely known.

A sequence of finds portrays Kafka, in contrast to the mournful, melancholic image we may have of him, as having had a robust sense of humor. In one of his letters to his fiancée Felice Bauer, he describes, at considerable length, a fit of nearly uncontrollable laughter that seized him during a formal speech by the president of the Workmen's Accident Insurance Institute, where Kafka worked. But it's hard to imagine the idea of Kafka's humor coming as a shock to the majority of his readers, who will doubtless have noticed that, despite its frequently grotesque and disturbing subject matter, his fiction can be delightfully (if horribly) funny.

Some of Stach's finds are amusing but slight. Why do we need to know that another man named Franz Kafka lived in Berlin at the same time as the writer? Or that Karl Kraus declined to read a letter from Kafka concerning a literary dispute between Kraus and Max Brod, or that Kafka received a note from a reader named Siegfried Wolff, asking him to explain *The Metamorphosis*—a request that Kafka, unsurprisingly, seems to have ignored?

We finish Stach's book having learned quite a number of new (that is, to us) fun facts about Kafka. But has our picture of him been fundamentally altered—or subverted? What keeps Stach's admirable efforts to present Kafka in "unexpected contexts" and "unexpected lights" from being entirely successful is that, nearly every time he quotes from Kafka and allows us to hear his literary voice, we find ourselves seeing Kafka in the expected light, the old context: self-lacerating, paralyzed by uncertainty and doubt, alienated, painfully sensitive, and pathologically worried about his place in the world and his effect on others. On the page, Kafka sounds like Kafka.

Consider, for example, this 1920 diary entry that Stach includes, about a painting that Kafka admired—*Boulter's Lock, Sunday Afternoon,* by Edward John Gregory—and that he reflected on, writing about himself in the third person:

> Now he imagined that he himself was standing on the grassy bank. . . . He observed the festivities, they weren't festivities exactly, but you could still call them that. Of course he would have loved to take part, he was practically yearning to, but he had to tell himself in all honesty that he was closed off from their festivities—it was impossible for him to insinuate himself there, it would have required so much preparation that not only this one Sunday, but many years, and he himself would have passed on, even if the time had been willing to stand still here, no other outcome would have been possible, his whole genealogy, his upbringing, his physical training would have had to go so differently.
>
> So that was how far he was from these holiday-makers, but

at the same time he was very close, and that was even harder to
grasp. After all, they were people like him, nothing human could
be fully alien to them, and if you were to search their minds you
would have to find that the same feeling that dominated him and
excluded him from their boating trip was present in them as well,
except that it did not come close to dominating them, but only
lurked in some dark corners.

In Stach's thirty-fourth find, we watch Kafka trying and fail-
ing to write a book review with an even minimal relation to *The*
Powder-Puff: A Ladies' Breviary, the collection of sketches by Franz
Blei that he has been tasked with reviewing:

He who casts himself into the world with a great exhalation,
like a swimmer plunging from the high platform into the river,
disoriented at first and sometimes later as well by the currents,
like a sweet child, but always drifting into the distant air with
the beautiful waves at his side, may gaze across the water as one
does in this book, aimlessly but with a secret aim, this water that
bears him up and that he can drink and that has grown bound-
less for the head resting on its surface.

A short, lovely meditation by Kafka begins: "Now I've taken
a closer look at my desk and realized that nothing good can be
produced on it." This text, Stach tells us, breaks off, followed by a
note: "Wretched, wretched, and yet well intended. It's midnight . . .
The burning lightbulb, the quiet apartment, the darkness outside,
the last waking moments entitle me to write, even if it's the most
wretched stuff. And I hastily make use of this right. This is just who
I am." A fragmentary piece entitled "In the Management Offices"
features an employer interviewing—and humiliating—a prospective employee in a manner that evokes the tone in which Josef K.
is accused and berated throughout *The Trial.* In an early letter to

Milena Jesenska, Kafka refers to her translation of his "abysmally bad story" "The Stoker." Eventually, one may feel that Kafka is resisting Stach's attempts to portray him as a beer-drinking, slapstick-loving fellow, that he is insisting on representing himself as a solitary insomniac, awake while the rest of the world sleeps, struggling to write his "wretched" and "abysmally bad" stories.

REINER Stach is not the first writer to have challenged Max Brod's hagiographical (and consequently one-dimensional) reading of Kafka. Walter Benjamin and Milan Kundera disagreed with Brod, and Nabokov's brilliant lecture on *The Metamorphosis* (which appears in his *Lectures on Literature*) includes his sharp, clever critique of Kafka's biographer: "I want to dismiss completely Max Brod's opinion that the category of sainthood, not that of literature, is the only one that can be applied to the understanding of Kafka's writings. Kafka was first of all an artist, and although it may be maintained that every artist is a manner of saint (I feel that very clearly myself), I do not think that any religious implications can be read into Kafka's genius."

But Brod's view seems to have prevailed, at least in the popular imagination. Throughout Prague's historic center, souvenir shops sell Kafka coffee mugs, Kafka cell phone cases, Kafka T-shirts and memo pads. The author's haunted and haunting black-and-white portrait is everywhere, and one can watch tourists deliberating over the Kafka refrigerator magnets with the rapt attention of pilgrims deciding which image of Saint Bernadette to carry home from Lourdes.

So perhaps the interesting question, and one that *Is That Kafka?* addresses only tangentially in its preface, is the matter of why this little book seems necessary, of why it has been intended as a necessary corrective—of why Kafka has proven to be such a natural candidate for literary beatification, and why it is so difficult to change our minds about him. Why does his image offer us such consolation? Why does he so stir our imagination and excite our compassion? Why do we continue to venerate him as the exemplar of the suffering artist—even now, in an era when, it often seems, we no longer want our artists to suffer in isolation, but would prefer them to be successful, famous, visible: celebrities who somehow find the time to write, or paint, or compose music.

Perhaps one reason that Kafka has assumed the role of the contemporary saint is that the instruments of his martyrdom were not the arrows and spiked wheels that dispatched the early Christians, but rather the quotidian psychic torments—isolation, self-doubt, boredom, and neurosis—of ordinary modern life. A German Jew living among Czech-speaking Catholics, he was, from birth, an outsider. He worked, as many of his readers do, at an unrewarding, time-consuming office job. His relationship with his father was a source of profound unhappiness, as were his affairs with the women to whom he wrote letters of such nakedness, panic, and shame that Karl Ove Knausgaard's *My Struggle* seems, by comparison, reticent and self-protective. The aphorisms that have come down to us ("A book must be the ax for the frozen sea within us," "There is infinite hope, but not for us") reinforce our notions of his pessimism and melancholia, and of the obsessive inner struggles so thoroughly documented in his diaries.

Even more to the point is the way in which Kafka's readers so frequently conflate him with his characters. It seems paradoxical—and somehow unfair—that such an imaginative and fantastical writer should so often be assumed to be a more narrowly autobiographical one. Asked to picture the face of Gregor Samsa (before his transformation into an insect) or of Josef K. or of Georg Bendemann in "The Judgment," many readers would likely admit that they imagine these unfortunate men (whom of course Kafka *invented*) as looking very much like their creator. And though these works contain, undeniably, certain autobiographical elements, they are not self-portraits. Apparently, this confusion between Kafka and his characters started early—during Kafka's lifetime. In Gustav Janouch's *Conversations with Kafka* (1968), Janouch, whose father was a business associate of Kafka's, describes his first meeting with the older writer, whose work he knew and esteemed. The two men consider the advantages of writing when it is dark outside, without the distractions of daylight. "If it were not for these horrible sleepless nights," says Kafka, "I would never write at all. But they always recall me again to my own dark solitude." And Janouch thinks, "Is he not himself the unfortunate bug in *The Metamorphosis?*"

The answer is no: he wasn't. Not so much because, as Stach tells us, Kafka flirted with country girls and was kind to children, but because—unlike his hapless traveling salesman turned insect—Kafka was able to transmute his fears, his grief and discomfort, into magnificently inventive and compressed narratives, into simple, beautifully crafted sentences, into the judicious, indeed perfect deployment of metaphor, dialogue, and description. And ultimately it is the genius, rather than the suffering or the myths about the suffering, that has Reiner Stach and his readers poring over a photo of a massive demonstration in the South Tyrol and hoping—despite our better judgment—that the fuzzy image of the tall man in the light-colored summer suit might actually be Kafka. Yes, that's him.

Regardless of how often we tell ourselves that Kafka was not Gregor Samsa, regardless of how convincingly Stach persuades us that Kafka was a tormented soul but also more complicated than a tormented soul, we will continue to see him that way. Perhaps something in the human psyche requires us to revere that sort of saint: the holy man who lives alone in the wilderness, who mortifies his body, has visions, and fights off demons. These days, the religious figures most likely to be canonized are those who have had glorious careers as missionaries or as the founders of convents and charities known for their work among the poor and dying.

And hermits are everywhere regarded with suspicion and mistrust. In any case, the saint I found myself thinking of as I read *Is That Kafka?* was Saint Francis of Cupertino, who insisted on levitating and swooping around the church, high above the congregants, despite the well-intentioned efforts of his brother monks to keep his feet safely on the ground.

32

What Makes a Short Story?

THERE MUST BE MORE DIFFICULT QUESTIONS THAN "WHAT makes a short story?"

What is man, that thou art mindful of him? What does a woman want? What is love? What walks on four legs at dawn, two legs at noon, and three legs in the evening? Where is fancy bred: in the heart or in the head?

Yet all of these seemingly impossible questions are, in fact, far easier to address than the deceptively straightforward matter of what constitutes the short story. For all of these classic puzzlers—except for the Sphinx's riddle—suggest variant solutions and multiple possibilities, invite expansion and rumination. Whereas any attempt to establish the identifying characteristics of the short story seems to require a narrowing, a winnowing, a definition by exclusion. A short story is probably this—but definitely not that.

The real problem is that the most obvious answer is the most correct. We *know* what a short story is: a work of fiction of a certain length, a length with apparently no minimum. An increasing number of anthologies feature stories of no more than a page, or a single flashy paragraph, and one of the most powerful stories in all of literature, Isaac Babel's "Crossing into Poland," at less than three pages long, is capacious enough to include a massive and chaotic military campaign, a soldier's night of troubled dreams, and the report of a brutal murder.

But after a certain point (to be on the safe side, let's say seventy or eighty pages, though one short story theoretician has argued that Conrad's *Heart of Darkness*—not one word more or less—defines the outer limits of the form) the extended short story begins to infringe on novella territory.

Lacking anything clearer or more definitive than these vague mumblings about size, we imagine that we can begin to define the short story by distinguishing it from other forms of fiction, by explaining why it is not a sketch, a fairy tale, or a myth.

And yet some of our favorite stories seem a lot like the sort of casual anecdote we might hear a friend tell at a dinner party. Somerset Maugham claimed that many of Chekhov's stories *were* anecdotes and not proper stories at all. ("If you try to tell one of his stories you will find that there is nothing to tell. The anecdote, stripped of its trimmings, is insignificant and often inane. It was grand for people who wanted to write a story and couldn't think of a plot to discover that you could very well manage without one.") And just to confuse things further, many fairy tales—the best of Hans Christian Andersen and the Brothers Grimm—are as carefully constructed, as densely layered, as elaborately crafted as the stories (or are they tales?) of Hawthorne and Poe.

Why do we feel so certain that a masterpiece such as Tolstoy's "The Three Hermits" is a short story, though it so clearly bears the stamp of its origins in "an old legend current in the Volga district," and though its structure has more in common with the shaggy-dog story than with the artful, nuanced studies of Henry James? In fact,

James insisted, a short story "must be an idea—it can't be a 'story' in the vulgar sense of the word. It must be a picture; it must illustrate something . . . something of the real essence of the subject."

Just to take on James, let's look at "The Three Hermits," which could hardly be more of a "story," in the most unashamedly "vulgar sense of the word." The protagonist, if we can call him that—we know nothing about his background or the subtler depths of his character, absolutely nothing, in short, except that he is a bishop of the Orthodox Church—is traveling on a ship that passes near an island on which, he hears, live three monks who spend their lives in prayer. The bishop insists on being ferried to the island, where he meets the hermits, again described with a minimum of the sort of physical and psychological description that, we have been taught, is essential for fiction in general and for the short story in particular. One of the monks is tall, "with a piece of matting tied around his waist"; the second is shorter, in a "tattered peasant coat"; and the third is very old and "bent with age and wearing an old cassock." To his horror, the bishop discovers that the hermits have their own way of praying ("Three are ye, three are we, have mercy upon us") and have never heard of the Lord's Prayer.

The bulk of the story, the shaggy-dog part, concerns the bishop's efforts to teach these comically slow learners how to pray correctly—a task that consumes the entire day and is completed, more or less, to the visitor's satisfaction. That night, as the bishop is sailing away from the island, he sees a light skimming toward him across the water. "Was it a seagull, or the little gleaming sail of some small boat?" No, in fact, the radiance is an aura surrounding the hermits, flying hand in hand over the water, desperately chasing the bishop's boat because they have forgotten what they learned from the church official, who—educated at last—tells them, "It is not for me to teach you. Pray for us sinners."

Even in summary, this story retains some of its power to astonish and move us, and yet the full effect of reading the work in its entirety is all but lost. Which brings us to one of the few things that *can* be said about the short story: Like all great works of art, it cannot be summarized or reduced without sacrificing the qualities that distinguish an amusing dinner party anecdote from a great work of art—depth, resonance, harmony, plus all the less quantifiable marks of artistic creation. This is especially true of stories in which the plotline is not so clear, so succinct, so distilled to its folkloric essentials, and of writers who achieve their effects almost entirely by the use of tone, by the accretion of minute detail, and by the precise use of language.

What can we conclude about Turgenev's "Bezhin Meadow" when we hear that it concerns a few hours that the narrator spent among a group of peasant boys who scare themselves and one another by telling ghost stories? At the end of the story, we learn—in a sort of brief epilogue—that one of the boys was killed a short time after that evening on the meadow. When we hear it summarized, the plot seems sketchy and indistinct. Why is this not a vignette or a "mood piece"? But when we read the story itself—a work of art that feels utterly complete and in which every sentence and phrase contributes to the whole—we are certain that it is indeed a story. We cannot imagine anything that needs to be added or omitted.

What remains of the humor and breathtaking originality of Katherine Mansfield's "The Daughters of the Late Colonel" when we describe it as a story about two childlike (but in fact adult) sisters attempting to get through the days following the death of their father? What survives of the many small gestures and lines of deceptively whimsical dialogue that lead us to understand that the distribution of power between the more "grown-up," sensible Josephine and the fanciful, impulsive, skittish Constantia is the same as it must have been in early childhood? In summary, what remains of Josephine's certainty that their dead father is hiding in his chest of drawers, or of his former nurse's—Nurse Andrew's—upsetting, "simply fearful" greed for butter, or of the "white, terrified" blancmange that the cook sets on the table, or of the final, elliptical moment in which we observe the sisters' forgetfulness—an ending that makes us understand the tragic cost of remembering?

It is hard to *recognize* Chekhov's "The Lady with the Dog" from the following description: A jaded womanizer falls deeply in love, despite himself and for the first time, and in the course of that love affair discovers that his whole world—that he himself—has changed. How sentimental and obvious it sounds, how romantic and unconvincing. Yet when we read the story, we feel that it is of enormous, immeasurable consequence and resonance, and that it tells us all we need to know about Gurov and Anna's whole lives. We feel that the story's details—the slice of watermelon in the hotel room, the description of Gurov's wife's eyebrows—are as important as its "action," and that if we left out these details, the perfect but somehow fragile architecture of the story would crumble.

Not much remains of the short story retold in summary—but not *nothing*. For this also can be said of the short story: if we find a way to describe what the story is *really* about, not its plot but its essence, what small or large part of life that has managed to translate onto the page, there is always *something* there—enough to engage us and pique our interest.

But isn't the same true of novels? What do we lose when we try to explain what *Mrs. Dalloway* is *about*? Or when we become hopelessly mired in the tangles—of lovers, generations, narrators, stories within stories, frames within frames—in *Wuthering Heights*? Or when we say that we just read the most harrowing novel about a provincial French housewife whose life is ruined by her impractical fantasies of love and romance? The answer's the same: nearly everything, though some "germ" (to quote James again) stays ineradicably present.

One distinction often made between the short story and the novel is that the short story more often works by implication, by indirection, that it more frequently achieves its results by what has *not* been said or what has been left out. But while certain stories do function this way—the situation that has come between the lovers in Ernest Hemingway's "Hills Like White Elephants" is never directly mentioned in the course of their painful conversation—it is also true that in the greatest works of fiction, regardless of their length, every line tells us *more* than it appears to communicate on the surface. So, even in Proust's *In Search of Lost Time*, each seemingly insignificant phrase and incident assumes additional meaning and resonance as the book progresses; every incident and minor exchange takes on a significance that we cannot apprehend until we go back and reread the whole. In fact, the best way to read—the way that teaches us most about what a great writer does, and what we should be doing—is to take a story apart (line by line, word by word) the way a mechanic takes apart an automobile engine, and to ask ourselves how each word, each phrase, and each sentence contributes to the entirety.

In their efforts to define the formal qualities of the short story form, critics are often driven to invoke basic Aristotelian principles (short stories have a beginning, a middle, and an end) and to quote the early masters of the genre, writers who must have had a more sharply focused view of the new frontier toward which they were heading. This is why introductions to anthologies, textbook chapters, and surveys of the latest developments in the academic field of "short story theory" are all fond of invoking Edgar Allan Poe's notion of the "single effect":

> *A skilful literary artist has constructed a tale. If wise, he has not fashioned his thoughts to accommodate his incidents; but having conceived, with deliberate care, a certain unique or single effect to be wrought out, he then invents such incidents—he then combines such events as may best aid him in establishing this preconceived effect. . . . In the whole composition, there should be no word written, of which the tendency, direct or indirect, is not to the one pre-established design. And by such means, with such*

care and skill, a picture is at length painted which leaves in the
mind of him who contemplates it with a kindred art, a sense of
the fullest satisfaction. The idea of the tale has been presented
unblemished, because undisturbed; and this is an end unattain-
able to the novel.

More recent—and also frequently quoted—is V. S. Pritchett's
characteristically elegant and incisive formulation: "The novel
tends to tell us everything whereas the short story tells us only
one thing, and that, intensely. . . . It is, as some have said, a 'glimpse
through,' resembling a painting or even a song which we can take
in at once, yet bring the recesses and contours of larger experience
to the mind."

No sensible reader could argue with Pritchett or Poe. But then
again, few readers could explain exactly what "a single effect" is,
or what, precisely, is the "one thing" that our favorite short story
is telling us. Indeed, the minute one tries to make any sweeping
declarations about the limitations or boundaries of the short story,
one thinks of an example—a masterpiece!—that embodies the very
opposite of the rule that one has just proposed. So let's take just a
few of the many assumptions that the casual reader—or the student hungry for some definitive parameters—might make about
the short story.

One might assume that for reasons of economy or artistic
harmony, the short story should limit itself to depicting the situation of a main protagonist, or at least a somewhat restricted—
manageable—cast of characters. And many stories do. There are
only three major characters—the narrator, his wife, and the blind
man—in Raymond Carver's "Cathedral." And only one character,
really, in Poe's "The Pit and the Pendulum." In Flannery O'Connor's "Everything That Rises Must Converge," we have the over-
bearing, heartbreaking mother and her snobbish, long-suffering
son, Julian. And in James Baldwin's "Sonny's Blues," the narrator

and Sonny are the big moon around whom the others—Isabel, the mother and father, the other musicians—revolve.

But who, one might ask, is the "big moon" in Tim O'Brien's "The Things They Carried," or in Chekhov's own "In the Ravine," a story that focuses not on any central character but on the life of an entire community, Ukleevo, a village that "was never free from fever, and there was boggy mud there even in the summer, especially under the fences over which hung old willow-trees that gave deep shade. Here there was always a smell from the factory refuse and the acetic acid which was used in the finishing of the cotton print." In this polluted and horrifically corrupt little hamlet, the most powerful family—a clan of shopkeepers—devote themselves to lying and cheating their neighbors; their dishonesty and general depravity are repaid, eventually, by heartbreak and ruin.

The story does have a villain, Aksinya, and a heroine, the peasant girl Lipa, who does not appear until quite a few pages into the story. Nonetheless, we feel that Chekhov is less interested in depicting particular destinies than in painting a broader picture. The story is the literary equivalent of a monumental canvas, crowded with figures: Rembrandt's *The Night Watch*, for example.

But even the story that lacks a central character should, presumably, limit itself to a single point of view, a controlling intelligence that guides us through the narrative. Or should it? Once more the answer seems to be: not necessarily. Baldwin's "Sonny's Blues," Carver's "Cathedral," and John Updike's "A & P" are examples of short fictions that stay fixedly within the consciousness of their narrators. Kafka's "The Judgment" adheres more or less faithfully to the close-third-person viewpoint through which we observe the tormented last hours of Georg Bendemann.

Yet another of Kafka's stories—*The Metamorphosis*—also begins in the close third person, with the understandable astonishment of Gregor Samsa, who has just woken in his bed to find that he has been transformed, overnight, into a giant insect. And there the story remains until the narrative must leave the room in which Gregor is imprisoned in order to follow the action in the other parts of the apartment and chart the effects that his transformation has had on his family. Finally, after Gregor's death, the story can—for obvious reasons—no longer be told from his point of view, and a more detached omniscience describes the process by which his parents and his sister recover and go on with their lives after the demise of the unfortunate Gregor.

Still other stories pay even less heed to the somewhat schoolmarmish admonition that they color neatly within the lines of a single perspective. Alice Munro's "Friend of My Youth" begins with a dream that the first-person narrator has about her mother, and then tells the rest of the story from the point of view of "my mother," with occasional swings back to that initial "I." Katherine Mansfield's "Prelude" moves seamlessly from one family member to another, exposing the innermost thoughts of an extended family: a mother and father, their children, and the mother's unmarried sister. Tatyana Tolstaya's "Heavenly Flame" behaves as if it has never heard of point of view, skipping around from character to character and alighting from time to time on a sort of group perspective, a "we" representing the mini-society vacationing at a country house near a convalescent home.

But even if the short story refuses to fall in line with any of our notions about the number and range of its characters, and the importance of a single perspective, shouldn't it observe the most (one would think) easy to follow of the Aristotelian conventions: the prescriptions concerning the length of time that the action may comfortably span? It's true that "Hills Like White Elephants" restricts itself to a single conversation, and that Tillie Olsen's "I Stand Here Ironing" takes place entirely during a session at the ironing board.

On the other hand, "Sonny's Blues" moves back and forth through decades of the two main characters' histories, covering the most significant parts of the lifetimes of two men; at the same time, it fits a huge wedge of social history into the confines of a short story. And Lars Gustafsson's "Greatness Strikes Where It Pleases" takes as its subject the existence—and the inner life—of an unnamed man who grows up in the country and spends his later years in a home for the disabled. In the space breaks, the blank space between sections, months, days, or years elapse—gaps that matter far less than we might have supposed, since our hero has been liberated by consciousness from the narrow strictures of time. As much as we might like the short story to keep its borders modest, crisp, and neat, the form keeps defying our best efforts to wrap it up and present it in a tidy package.

Pick up those helpful, instructional books—"Anyone Can Write a Short Story"—and you're bound to find one of those diagrams, those EKGs of the "typical plotline," its slow ascent, its peak and valley (or peaks and valleys) meant to indicate the tensing or slackening of dramatic interest. But any attempt to draw such a chart for a story such as Bruno Schulz's "Sanitarium under the Sign of the Hourglass"—with its labyrinthine plot turns and disorienting switchbacks—will look less like that chart than like one of the webs spun by those poor spiders whom scientists used to torment with doses of mind-altering drugs. How does one chart "The Things They Carried," which is structured like an obsessive, repetitive list of stuff—the objects and equipment that a group of soldiers are humping through a jungle in Vietnam—and contains, hidden inside, a story of life and death.

Some stories have huge amounts of plot—it has been said that Heinrich von Kleist's *The Marquise of O.* was used, unedited, as a shooting script for Eric Rohmer's full-length film of the same name. And some stories—"A & P," "Cathedral"—have almost no plot at all.

The understandable longing to keep things tidy and nice and neat also leads many critics and teachers to put the "epiphany"—the burst of understanding, self-knowledge, or knowledge about the world that may occur to a character at some crucial point in the story—at the highest peak of that EKG graph. Some even insist that this sort of mini-enlightenment is necessary for the short story—is, in fact, a hallmark and sine qua non of the form.

It's my understanding that the word *epiphany* first came into common currency—in the literary rather than the religious sense—in connection with the fiction of James Joyce, many of whose characters do seem to "get something" by the end of his brilliant stories. And sometimes, characters in stories do learn something. By the end of "Sonny's Blues," the narrator has had a vision of what music means to his brother, and of what sort of musician his brother is. The recognition that her precious new hat is the very same one worn by the black woman on the bus has overwhelming—and tragic—consequences for the mother in "Everything That Rises Must Converge."

But one could spend pages listing fictions in which characters come out the other end of the story every bit as benighted as they were in the first sentence. By the end of "Everything That Rises Must Converge," Julian could hardly not know that something has happened to change his life. But the story concludes before he—or the reader—has had a chance to intuit what that change is, or what it will mean. It's hard to say what the unnamed narrator learns in Samuel Beckett's thrilling and upsetting story "First Love." To insist that every short story should include a moment of epiphany is like insisting that every talented, marvelous dog jump through the same narrow hoop.

A story creates its own world, often—though not always—with clear or mysterious correspondences to our own. While reading the story, we enter that world. We feel that everything in it belongs there, and has not been forced on it by its creator. In fact, we tend to forget the creator, who has wound the watch of the story and vanished from creation.

Unlike most novels, great short stories make us marvel at their integrity, their economy. If we went at them with our blue pencils, we might find we had nothing to do. We would discover that there was nothing the story could afford to lose without the whole delicate structure collapsing like a soufflé. And yet we are left with a feeling of completeness, a conviction that we know exactly as much as we need to know, that all of our questions have been answered— even if we are unable to formulate what exactly those questions and answers are.

This sense of the artistic whole, this assurance that nothing has been left out and that nothing extraneous has been included, is part of what distinguishes the short story from other pieces of writing with which it shares certain outward characteristics—what separates it, for example, from the newspaper account, which, like the short story, most often features characters and at least some vestige of a plot. But the newspaper version of "The Lady with the Dog"— MAN'S AFFAIR TURNS SERIOUS—manages to leave out every single thing that makes the story so beautiful, significant, and moving.

To communicate the entirety of what a short story has given us, of what it has done for us, of what it has helped us understand or see in a new way, would involve repeating the whole story. It would mean quoting every one of our favorite stories, sentence by sentence, line by line, word by word—and thus providing the only useful answer to the question *What makes a short story?*

33

In Praise of Stanley Elkin

IN THE SUMMER OF 1995, I WAS ASKED TO READ A PASSAGE from Stanley Elkin's work at a memorial service for him, to be held during the Sewanee Writers' Conference, at the University of the South, in Sewanee, Tennessee. Stanley had died that May.

I was honored to have been asked, because I was a huge fan of Stanley's fiction and because he had been a dear friend.

In fact, I was such an ardent fan that it often struck me as astonishing and highly unlikely that we had become friends. To me, spending time with Stanley seemed like the equivalent of being invited to hang out with the Dalai Lama on a beautiful porch—on a succession of beautiful porches—at the various writers' conferences (first Breadloaf, then Sewanee) at which Stanley and I taught. Actually, it seemed *better* than hanging out with the Dalai Lama: Stanley was funnier and louder, told dirtier jokes, and had a bigger personality. Certainly Stanley was a more eloquent complainer than I imagined the Dalai Lama being, even (or especially) at the spiritual leader's lowest moments. There was something about crankiness, Stanley's own crankiness and the crankiness of others—the performative aspect of crankiness, let's say—that delighted him. I always felt he liked me best when I was most irritated, or irritable, and when I was able to transform that irritability (and he did, so well) into humor.

For more than a decade before his death, Stanley and I had spent weeks in the summer on those porches, most often with our families—with my husband, Howie, and Stanley's wife, Joan, and sometimes with our children, for whom those conferences provided an excuse to enact their version of some Lost Boys or (worst case) *Lord of the Flies* scenarios, running wild across the scenic campuses with the other writers' kids. Stanley and Joan's daughter, Molly, older than my own kids, was already great fun to talk to, as she has remained.

When we weren't sitting on the porches, we were eating (mostly awful) conference food, attending readings, giving readings, teaching classes, reading student manuscripts, and having manuscript conferences. Those last three elements of our job description were the main focus of Stanley's complaints, which would rise to a fever pitch of annoyance, of grievance, of righteous fury—and then subside. And then he would go off to meet his lucky, grateful, and understandably anxious students. Stanley was known to be a fierce critic of student work; to say that he didn't suffer fools gladly doesn't begin to describe the intensity of his disapproval, of his response to anything he found careless, false, or second rate.

AS I've said, I was honored to have been asked by the conference director and poet Wyatt Prunty to speak at Stanley's memorial. But I was also nervous about it, for several reasons.

One of those reasons was that, unlike many writers, Stanley was a terrific reader of his own work. He managed to get it all across: the cadence, the force and sheer exuberance of his language, the nervy plots, his frequently pathetic, repulsive, and profoundly sympathetic characters, the grossness and obscenity, the poetry, the all-too-rare gift for writing "serious" fiction that could make its readers laugh out loud. The off-the-charts energy of his sentences, his ability to reanimate and reconstruct the written word, his talent for using a particular word in a way in which (as far as you knew) it had never been used before, and which made you stop and think until you figured out how and why it was precisely the right word, that no other word would have done.

And his *maximalism*: the continual testing, testing, to see how much weight a sentence could sustain, how long it could go on without losing its clarity, its logic. In an interview, Stanley said that there were writers who took things out and writers who put things in, and that he was one of the latter. One of the things I remember saying at the memorial service was that I kept several of Stanley's novels near my desk, and that whenever I felt I'd written a lazy sentence, a cliché, or a sloppy or inexact passage of description, I'd open one of Stanley's books at random, and every sentence I read would inspire me to go back to my own writing and work harder. I still have his books near my desk, and his sentences still function that way for me.

I'd heard Stanley read many times, and every one of those readings had been a stellar and unforgettable performance. He usually claimed to be reading from a work in progress, but how could something so perfect and polished be *in progress*? In progress *toward what*? Each performance outdid the previous one in its brilliance, its poetry, its humor, its honesty, its pure cringe-inducing ballsiness.

I heard him read the early pages of *The Magic Kingdom*, in which a grieving father named Eddy Bale manages to convince the Queen of England to kick-start his obsessive, well-meaning, but ultimately disastrous program to bring dying children to Disneyland; a description of heaven and hell (some of it in the voice of God) from *The Living End*; the beginning of *The Rabbi of Lud*, one of the darkest and funniest meditations on Judaism (and New Jersey) ever written. It's telling that both Howie and I remember Stanley standing up when he read, though by the time we met him, his multiple sclerosis had advanced to the point at which that would have been unlikely, or impossible. He was sitting—it only *seemed* as if he were standing.

One thing I knew for certain was that I didn't want to read, at Stanley's memorial service, anything I'd heard him read. I didn't want to hear his voice in my head, reminding me—as he would never have done in life, because, for such a notorious curmudgeon, he was unfailingly polite and kind to me—of what a lousy job I was doing.

And also, because he'd died just a few months before, and because I was still extremely sad about his death, I was afraid I might find it hard to keep my composure throughout the reading. I have strong feelings about speakers at memorial services not compelling the assembled mourners to witness their emotional breakdowns. It always seems somehow . . . unhelpful. I'd spoken at several memorial services in the months leading up to that summer (it was one of those times when, as sometimes happens, a number of loved ones die in dizzyingly quick succession) and somehow I'd managed to keep it together when I'd been asked to say something.

I found it consoling to recall an evening, several summers before, en route to dinner in Vermont, when we'd passed a lovely rural cemetery and Stanley had greeted the tombstones—the dead—with a hearty, expansive wave. "See you soon, guys!" he'd called out.

Stanley loved to be right.

so the question was: What to read?

The one thing I knew was that it needed to be outrageous. Stanley once said that he didn't realize his work was funny until someone else told him that it was, but really, he *had* to have known that it was shocking—to most people, if not to everyone. Why else would he have begun the Elizabeth and Stewart Credence Memorial Lecture, which he delivered at Brown University in 1987, a talk that, in theory, was about the significance of names, with a passage that—to the distinguished audience in attendance—would have made *Lolita* sound like *Mary Poppins in the Park*?

Could you be mugged by a Stanley? Could a Stanley rape you? Tops, I might molest your kid, but you'd never know it, and neither would she. What, a little suntan lotion rubbed along the bottom of her swimsuit like a piping of frosting around a birthday cake? What, a spot of spilled tea on the sunsuit, my finger in the bespittled handkerchief moist from what it wouldn't even occur to you was drool before it was saliva, and vigorously brushing across what won't be breasts for another half dozen years yet, my grunt the two- or three-tone guttural hum of deflection, nervous and oddly dapper as the tugs, pats, and twitches of a stand-up comic, distracting as the shot cuffs of magicians and cardsharps, all random melody's tangential rove? Because how could you ever guess at my intentions and interiors, my inner landscapes and incisor lusts, the thickening at my throat like hidden shim, the ponderous stirrings of my ice-floe blood, deep as resource, buried as oil in my gnarled and knotty groin, my clotted sexual circuits?

Incisor lusts. Ice-floe blood. Those two phrases illustrate what I mean by Stanley's use of words in ways that have never been used before, locutions that stop us and make us pause until we're struck by their perfect correctness.

I felt that Stanley would have wanted the passage I read at his service to be extreme, delighting (even wallowing) in the demands and the aspirations, the exaltations and humiliations, the protuberances and excrescences of the flesh, as only Stanley—and I am not exaggerating here—as only Stanley could.

But if that was the criterion, I certainly had a range to choose from. I could have picked a section from *The Dick Gibson Show*, one of the passages in which a pharmacist named Bernie Perk becomes infatuated with, stalks, and finally falls deeply in love with a female customer, entirely because of the size (super-large) and quantity of the sanitary napkins and female hygiene products that she purchases in his shop each month. I could have chosen the raunchy sexual encounter with his wife that Eddy Bale recalls while waiting to make his sales pitch to the Queen of England.

Stanley could be as funny and unrelentingly forthright about death and disease as he was about sex. I could have read the scene in which Ellerbee is killed in *The Living End*, or opened *The Franchiser* at random and read about the onset and inexorable progress of its hero's multiple sclerosis. If all I'd wanted was to offend my audience, I could have gone for the always reliably upsetting subject of race and quoted the opening of *The Bailbondsman*.

But somehow the choice seemed . . . preordained. The only passage I could read, the only passage I *wanted* to read, was from *The Making of Ashenden*, a novella that is among my favorite of Stanley's works.

Specifically, I wanted to read the scene in which the hero, Brewster Ashenden, fucks a bear.

I know one dirty joke about a sexual relationship between a man and a bear (punch line: the bear says, "You don't come here for the hunting, do you?") and I've been told that there is actually a whole category of jokes about that species (as it were) of bestiality. It seems unlikely that, in his long career as a joke teller and joke listener, Stanley didn't hear one such joke.

But one of the reasons that I admire the novella so much, and why it seems to me so characteristic of Stanley's work, is that it takes something that could be a joke, and that in fact *is* sort of a joke, and turns it into something profound, something beautiful and mysterious—that is, into art. By the novella's conclusion, the apparent joke has become something as transcendent and primal as the cave paintings at Altamira—as mystical and vibrant as one of those Northwest Coast bear masks that seem to come alive, to jitter and wink as you look into their abalone-shell eyes.

At least at the beginning, *The Making of Ashenden* is not a joke about a bear—but a joke about the rich. Brewster Ashenden is an old-school rich guy, not one of those thuggish modern rich guys, like the Trump boys, but an American aristocrat. In a 1930s or '40s movie, he would have been played by Cary Grant or David Niven.

His inherited family money is not only historical but elemental, having come from land (real estate), air (Brewster's grandmother, a chemical engineer, discovered how to store oxygen in tanks), fire (Brewster's father promoted and sold the first matchbooks), and water (a branch of the family pioneered the sale of bottled mineral water). He lives a life of leisure and perpetual motion, insinuating himself into heroic human rights interventions, running with the bulls at Pamplona, hanging out with mafiosi, diving with Cousteau. He is the Most Interesting Man in the World without the beard or the cockiness. He is also the perfect houseguest:

> All my adult life I have been a guest in other people's houses, fol-
> lowing the sun and seasons like a migratory bird, an instinct in
> me, a rich man's cunning feel for ripeness, some oyster-in-an-r-
> month notion working there which knows without reference to
> anything outside itself when to pack the tennis racket, when to
> bring along the German field glasses to look at a friend's birds,
> the telescope to stare at his stars, the wet suit to swim in beneath
> his waters when the exotic fish are running. It's not in the Times
> when the black dinner jacket comes off and the white one goes on;
> it's something surer, subtler, the delicate guidance system of the
> privileged, my playboy astronomy.

Near the start of the novella, Ashenden's parents die, and death hangs over the book, reappearing, as death is accustomed to do, at unexpected moments and in new and unusual guises. As usual, love and death go hand in hand—propelling Ashenden out of the shallows and into waters deeper than any he could have prepared for or anticipated.

Among his hosts is a wealthy Briton named Freddy Plympton, who has, on the grounds of his castle, a private zoo—housing only animals that appear on the family crest and coat of arms. "Lions, bears, elephants, unicorns ('a pure white rhinoceros actually') leopards, jackals . . . pandas, camels, sheep and apes. The family is an old one, the list long."

And the bear? The bear is at once domesticated (after all, she lives in a zoo) and totally wild: libidinous, uninhibited, impassioned.

PROBABLY Stanley would have preferred me to read the entire novella, and I wished that I could have. Then I could have included more of the passages that I most love—for example, Ashenden's description of the funerary customs (and the haberdashery) of the rich attending his mother's and father's funerals, weeks apart.

> *Couturiers of Paris and London and New York . . . taxed to the breaking point to come up with dresses in death's delicious high fashion, the rich taking big casualties that season, two new mourning originals in less than two weeks and the fitter in fits. The men splendid in their decent dark. Suits cunningly not black, off black, proper, the longitudes of their decency in their wiry pinstripes, a gent's torso bound up in vest and crisscrossed by watch chains and Phi Beta Kappa keys in the innocent para-militarism of the civilian respectable, men somehow more vital at the graveside in the burdensome clothes than in Bermudas on beaches or dinner jackets in hotel suites with cocktails in their hands, the band playing on the beach below and the telephone ringing.*

Or the moment when Ashenden, out for a walk on Freddy's land, catches a smell in the air that makes him realize he is not strolling in a lovely, verdant park, but in a zoo without cages:

The odor of beasts is itself a kind of meat—a dream avatar of alien sirloin, strange chops and necks, oblique joints and hidden livers and secret roasts. There are nude juices in it, and licy furs, and all the flesh's vegetation. . . . Separated as we are from animals in zoos by glass cages and fenced-off moats, and by the counter odors of human crowds, melting ice cream, peanut shells crushed underfoot, snow cones, mustard, butts of bun—all the detritus of a Sunday outing—we rarely smell it. What gets through is dissipated, for a beast in civilization does not even smell like a beast in the wild.

And yet I continued to believe that if Stanley had been obliged to choose a selection for me to read, he would have chosen the scene with the bear.

I can't imagine or exactly recall what I actually read. I am not a prudish person; at least I don't think of myself that way. But some of the passages describing Ashenden's romance with the bear are so (not to put too fine a point on it) filthy that I honestly couldn't see myself reading them to a roomful of strangers. I just don't think I would have had the nerve to do that—to say those words. I don't have a marked-up copy, so I can't be sure, but I assume that I must have read a bowdlerized (sorry, Stanley!) condensation that would have included relatively mild paragraphs such as these:

It was a Kamchatkan Brown from the northeastern peninsula of the U.S.S.R. between the Bering and Okhotsk seas, and though it was not yet full grown it weighed perhaps seven hundred pounds and was already taller than Ashenden. It was female, and what he had been smelling was its estrus, not shit but lust, not bowel but love's gassy chemistry, the atoms and hormones and molecules of passion, vapors of impulse and the endocrinous spray of desire. What he had been smelling was secret, underground rivers flowing from hidden sources of intimate gland, and what the bear smelled on Brewster was the same. . . .

The bear snorted and swiped with the broad edge of her forepaw against each side of Ashenden's peter. Her fur, lanolized by estrus, was incredibly soft, the two swift strokes gestures of forbidden brunette possibility . . .

And of all the things he'd said and thought and felt that night, this was the most reasonable, the most elegantly strategic: that he would have to satisfy the bear, make love to the bear, fuck the bear. And this was the challenge which had at last defined itself, the test he'd longed for and was now to have. *Here was the problem:* Not whether it was possible for a mere man of something less than one hundred and eighty pounds to make love to an enormous monster of almost half a ton; not whether a normal man like himself could negotiate the barbarous terrains of the beast or bring the bear off before it killed him; but how he, Brewster Ashenden of the air, water, fire and earth Ashendens, one of the most fastidious men alive, could bring himself to do it—how, in short, he could get it up for a bear!

But he had forgotten, and now remembered: it was already up.

Surely, that would be enough, perhaps more than enough, for the audience to get a sense of what this section was about—and to be properly outraged and (I hoped) amused and moved. Enough for them to leave the service with some sense of how unique Stanley was and how far—into some entirely new literary domain, some unexplored region of our psyches—he was willing to take us, his grateful readers.

———

I don't know how I somehow missed the part about the memorial service not being only for Stanley. Either no one told me or (more likely) I wasn't paying attention. Or maybe they told me and I chose not to listen or believe it; maybe it occurred to me how much Stanley would have hated sharing the bill with someone else, even another brilliant and singular writer.

In fact, two writers were being memorialized, both of whom— their presence, their spirit, their work—had exerted a significant and lasting influence at Sewanee. The other honoree, who had also died that year, was the great Peter Taylor, whose work—including his marvelous novel *A Summons to Memphis*, with its restrained, mannerly, yet devastating portrait of a southern family—could not have been, at least on the surface, more unlike Stanley's.

Peter Taylor had close connections in the area. He had roots in Tennessee. He had been married to the sister of Jean Justice, who was married to the poet Donald Justice, who also taught at the conference. His connections were southern folk with soft voices and impeccable manners.

I suppose I was just so preoccupied with what I had to do that afternoon that I failed to notice that the people filing into the room were not your usual writers' conference crowd—not just the students and faculty members and staff I'd grown to know. Gradually it occurred to me: all of these strangers were white, nearly all were old, most of them had white hair. Or blue hair. They were proper southern men and women, to whom old money and position, like Brewster Ashenden's, were by no means a joke.

I had a moment of hesitation (actually, more like terror) when the truth finally dawned on me and I saw who would be listening to me read Stanley's graphic description of Brewster Ashenden—a younger and perhaps more cosmopolitan version of some of the gentlemen in the audience—and his tryst with a bear.

In my memory, Stanley's part of the service came second. And I was far too distracted by the daunting task ahead of me to listen to what was being said about Peter Taylor, though under other, less stressful circumstances, I would have been eager—fascinated—to listen to the eulogies of, and the readings from, this extraordinary American writer.

Finally it was my turn. I looked out at the innocent, polite, genteel fans, the readers—and mourners—who had no idea that they were about to hear a raunchy ursine love scene. I'd believed that it was my mission to be outrageous—but *this* outrageous, with *these* people? I felt almost sick—on the edge of panic. Over the edge of panic.

Then I saw, in the audience, Joan and Molly Elkin and my husband, and any number of writers I loved and admired, writers and friends who had also loved and admired Stanley. And again I felt that certainty: this was what Stanley would have wanted. Go out there and shock the hell out of these decent, upstanding citizens of the South.

I read the scene between Ashenden and the bear, and I tried not to look at anyone but Joan and Molly and Howie. I read the final paragraph, in which it ultimately becomes clear that Ashenden's attachment to his new animal friend has progressed from the purely carnal to something more spiritual—something closer to love.

> He started back through art to the house, but first he looked over his shoulder for a last glimpse of the sleeping bear. And he thought again of how grand it had been, and wondered if it was possible that something might come of it. And seeing ahead, speculating about the generations that would follow his own, he thought, Air. Water, he thought. Fire, Earth, he thought . . . And honey.

Then I went outside and, as soon as I got to a sheltered place where I hoped no one could see me, I burst into tears.

A year or so before, I had been one of the judges on the panel when Stanley's *Van Gogh's Room at Arles*, a collection of novellas, was chosen as a finalist for the PEN/Faulkner Award. After a long and heated discussion among the panelists, a process—having to decide between Stanley Elkin and Philip Roth—that illustrates the basic folly of literary contests and prizes, it was decided that the prize would go to Roth, for *Operation Shylock*. The winner and the finalists were all invited to attend the ceremony and accept their prizes for winning and for almost winning.

Molly Elkin accepted the award for her father, conveying his regrets for not attending, for having been prevented from doing so by a disease. That illness wasn't the multiple sclerosis, Molly explained, but a writer's ego.

The audience laughed. I remember thinking that while Stanley could hardly be said to hold his talent in low regard, he was, in his work, among the least egomaniacal and vain of writers. A more self-conscious, more self-protective novelist would never have revealed what Stanley revealed: things that no one—the writer included—was supposed to think about, let alone put on paper. I can think of many writers who seem always to be peeking at us from around the edges of their work, as if to remind us: *This isn't me. I don't really think like this. I don't know how I even* know *about these things, or these words*. But Stanley wasn't one of them.

Stanley was not only a maximalist of language, but also one of truth. That was one of the most astonishing and special qualities of his work: that piling on more and more—more metaphors, more words, more sentences, more humor, *more energy*—as a way of delving into, bringing to light, and forcing us to look directly into the heart of the simultaneously dark and scintillating mystery of what makes us human. He should be read widely, praised endlessly, admired by everyone. Well, maybe not *everyone*, but certainly by all those who care about language, about literature, about life.

PERMISSIONS

ABOUT THE AUTHOR

FRANCINE PROSE is the author of twenty-one works of fiction, including *Mister Monkey*; the *New York Times* bestseller *Lovers at the Chameleon Club, Paris 1932*; *A Changed Man*, which won the Dayton Literary Peace Prize; and *Blue Angel*, a finalist for the National Book Award. Her works of nonfiction include *Anne Frank: The Book, The Life, The Afterlife*, and the *New York Times* bestseller *Reading Like a Writer*. The recipient of numerous grants and honors, including a Guggenheim, a Fulbright, and a Director's Fellow at the Center for Scholars and Writers at the New York Public Library, she is a former president of PEN American Center and a member of the American Academy of Arts and Letters and the American Academy of Arts and Sciences. She lives in New York City.

ALSO BY FRANCINE PROSE

READING LIKE A WRITER
A Guide for People Who Love Books and for Those Who Want to Write Them

New York Times Bestseller

"Prose's little guide will motivate 'people who love books'…Like the great works of fiction, it's a wise and voluble companion."

—*New York Times Book Review*

MISTER MONKEY
A Novel

"An indelible cast of characters… In this strong, humane, and funny novel, Prose has treated us to an enthralling entertainment both on and off stage."

—*Boston Globe*

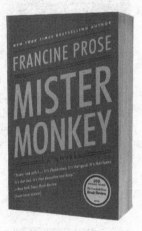

LOVERS AT THE CHAMELEON CLUB, PARIS 1932
A Novel

New York Times Bestseller

"Walk through the door of the Chameleon Club, and you'll be entranced by the way Prose plumbs the enigma of evil, the puzzle of history, and the mystery of valor."

—*Washington Post*

HarperCollins*Publishers*
DISCOVER GREAT AUTHORS, EXCLUSIVE OFFERS, AND MORE AT HC.COM.

ALSO BY FRANCINE PROSE

MY NEW AMERICAN LIFE
A Novel

"Utterly charming. Savvy about the shady practices of both US immigration authorities and immigrants themselves, *My New American Life* is powered by a beguiling Albanian heroine and her hapless American employers. Entertaining, light yet not trivial, a joy to read."

—Lionel Shriver

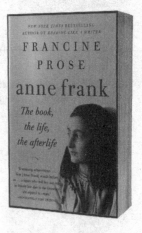

ANNE FRANK
The Book, The Life, The Afterlife

"A definitive, deeply moving inquiry into the life of the young, imperiled artist, and a masterful exegesis of *Diary of a Young Girl*…Extraordinary testimony to the power of literature and compassion"

—*Booklist* (starred review)

GOLDENGROVE
A Novel

"With perfect pitch and no trace of sentimentality, Prose…lands on the precise emotional key for this novel… *Goldengrove* explores the intoxication and heartache of female adolescence…allowing humor and compassion to seep through the cracks of an otherwise dark tale."

—*San Francisco Chronicle*

ALSO BY FRANCINE PROSE

THE GLORIOUS ONES
A Novel

"[Prose] navigates serenely between the real and the fantastic, between the rational and the supernatural."

—*The New York Times*

A CHANGED MAN
A Novel

"Francine Prose has a knack for getting to the heart of human nature . . . *A Changed Man* moves ahead at a swift and entertaining pace . . . We enter the moral dilemmas of fascinating characters whose emotional lives are strung out by the same human frailties, secrets and insecurities we all share. Most telling is the way Prose cleverly draws a fine line between fanatics and idealists."

—*USA Today*

BLUE ANGEL
A Novel

National Book Award Finalist
New York Times Notable Book

"Screamingly funny... *Blue Angel* culminates in a sexual harassment hearing that rivals the Salem witch trials."

—*USA Today*

🔲HarperCollins*Publishers*
DISCOVER GREAT AUTHORS, EXCLUSIVE OFFERS, AND MORE AT HC.COM.

ALSO BY FRANCINE PROSE

GUIDED TOURS OF HELL
Novellas

"Irresistibly readable...Wit, knowingness, and an intimate familiarity with guilt and anxiety—Francine Prose has these qualities in abundance."

—David Lodge, *The New York Times Book Review*

CARAVAGGIO
Painter of Miracles

"Racy, intensely imagined, and highly readable. . . Prose brings to Caravaggio a fresh and unflinching eye."

—*New York Times Book Review*

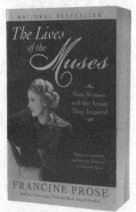

THE LIVES OF THE MUSES
Nine Women & the Artists They Inspired

"In Francine Prose's exhilarating study of nine women who have inspired artists, you get to enjoy something rare: a book fo serious ideas that is also addictively juicy."

—*Boston Globe*

HarperCollins*Publishers*

DISCOVER GREAT AUTHORS, EXCLUSIVE OFFERS, AND MORE AT HC.COM.